# Psychotherapy with Women

## Feminist Perspectives

## Also by Marilyn Lawrence

*The Anorexic Experience*
*Fed up and Hungry*
*Women's Secret Disorder* (with Mira Dana)
*Fighting Food: Coping with Eating Disorders* (with Mira Dana)


## Also by Marie Maguire

*Living with the Sphinx: Papers from the Women's Therapy Centre*
(with Sheila Ernst)
*Men, Women, Passion and Power: Gender Issues in Psychotherapy*

# Psychotherapy with Women

## Feminist Perspectives

Edited by
Marilyn Lawrence and Marie Maguire

Consultant Editor
Jo Campling

MACMILLAN

First published 1997 by
MACMILLAN PRESS LTD
Houndmills, Basingstoke, Hampshire RG21 6XS
and London
Companies and representatives
throughout the world

ISBN 0–333–60973–5 hardcover
ISBN 0–333–60974–3 paperback

A catalogue record for this book is available
from the British Library.

10   9   8   7   6   5   4   3   2   1
06  05  04  03  02  01  00  99  98  97

Typeset by T&A Typesetting Services
Rochdale, England

Printed in Hong Kong

# Contents

# Foreword

It is very exciting that this book should be published at a time in which feminism and psychotherapy are being discussed with such energy, controversy and passion. The discussions that preoccupy both are translated into regular press columns on the one hand while clinical understanding reflects the extent to which many domestic relationships hide much suffering. This book, like the work at the Women's Therapy Centre, inevitably links the two as it seeks to explore women's psychology from a woman's point of view.

In the past five years, while I have been developing the course that originally inspired this book, I have been delighted and impressed by the numbers of women, from many different cultures and many different professions, who wish to use the ideas to develop themselves personally and professionally. How does the social context influence us in our personal worlds as mothers, daughters and lovers?

There are many different feminist perspectives but modern feminism encourages both women and men to understand that what takes place at home is influenced by the social context; we develop psychologically through our relationship to those experiences. Psychoanalysis describes how we internalise the external world and then reproduce and develop it through our personal relationships. We are all interested in what makes us the way we are and these areas of thought challenge us to think again. This book is part of that challenge and invites us to concentrate on certain themes that apply to all of us as women and therefore must be useful to men as well.

SUE EINHORN, 1996

# *Acknowledgements*

The editors would like to thank Tricia Bickerton for her help with the Introduction; Ruth Porter for generously sharing her knowledge and experience; Sue Einhorn, Course Tutor on the Women's Therapy Centre one-year course, and Sally Berry, Clinical Director of the Women's Therapy Centre, for their comments; Geoffrey Pearson and Barbara Taylor for their constructive and practical help.

Thanks to Jo Campling for her enthusiasm and support throughout the project and to Susan Littlechild for coming to our rescue at the end.

# Notes on the Contributors

**Barbara Daniel**, a clinical psychologist in an NHS hospital, is currently training as a psychotherapist. She has taught on Women's Therapy Centre Courses.

**Sheila Ernst** is a group analyst who was on the staff of the Women's Therapy Centre for many years. She teaches psychodynamic counselling at Birkbeck College and teaches for the Institute of Group Analysis. She is in private practice with the Group Analytic Network. She is the co-author of *In Our Own Hands* and the co-editor of *Living with the Sphinx*.

**Sue Krzowski** was formerly a staff member at the Women's Therapy Centre and for several years was Course Tutor of the course 'Working Psychodynamically with Women'. She was involved in setting up and continues to supervise on the group work project for incest survivors at the Centre. She runs training courses on working with adult survivors of sexual abuse for the NHS, social services and voluntary sector agencies. She is a member of the Guild of Psychotherapists and has a private psychotherapy practice. She is co-editor of *In Our Experience*.

**Patricia Land** is a psychoanalytic psychotherapist in private practice. She is co-editor of *In Our Experience*.

**Carol Mohamed** is a psychoanalytic psychotherapist. She has a background in psychology and social work, and presently works as a psychotherapist in private practice and at the Women's Therapy Centre, and as a university student counsellor. Her particular interests are in intercultural psychotherapy and brief work. She offers training in a range of areas and supervises counselling and social work students.

**Susie Orbach**, co-founder of the Women's Therapy Centre, is a psychotherapist and author of many books, including *Fat is a Feminist Issue* and *Understanding Women*.

**Joanna Ryan** works as a psychoanalytic psychotherapist. She trained at the Philadelphia Association, London, and has a Ph.D. in psychology from Cambridge University. Her publications include

*The Politics of Mental Handicap, Sex and Love* (with S. Cartledge), and *Wild Desires and Mistaken Identities: Lesbianism and Psychoanalysis* (with N. O'Connor).

**Valerie Sinason** is a poet, writer and psychoanalytic psychotherapist. She is a research psychotherapist in the Department of the Psychiatry of Disability, St George's Hospital Medical School, and a consultant child psychotherapist at the Tavistock Clinic and Anna Freud Centre. She specialises in work with learning disabled and abused and abusing patients. Her books include *Mental Handicap and the Human Condition, Understanding Your Handicapped Child, Treating Satanist Abuse Survivors*, a full length poetry collection *Night Shift*, and a book on the false memory syndrome *Memory in Dispute*. She is training at the Institute of Psycho-Analysis.

**Ruthie Smith** is a UKCP registered psychotherapist working at the Women's Therapy Centre and in private practice. She is a tutor on the Women's Therapy Centre one-year course, 'Working Psychodynamically with Women', and teaches on other therapy and counselling modules at North London University.

**Tara Weeramanthri** is a consultant child and adolescent psychiatrist in the Bethlem and Maudsley NHS Trust. She is also a family therapist. She is interested in using both psychoanalytic and family systems perspectives to develop clinical practice with children and families. She trained at the Tavistock Clinic and also has an interest in the dynamics of groups and institutions and has worked as a staff member on several group relations conferences.

# Introduction

This book arises from a course entitled 'Working Psychodynamically with Women' which was set up at the Women's Therapy Centre in London. The course organisers were aware that gender issues were increasingly seen as central within helping professions, and that women's psychology was a topic on many counselling and psychotherapy courses. Some of the chapters of this book originate in lectures which shared the clinical experience of psychotherapists at the Centre. Others draw together information about psychotherapeutic work with women in the public sector.

Questions about sexuality and gender have always been central to the psychoanalytic endeavour. Not surprisingly, psychoanalytic theory and clinical practice have always attracted both interest and opposition from feminists – women who are concerned with sexual equality – and their male supporters. Psychoanalysis was one of the first professions to welcome women and promote them to prominent positions, but psychoanalytic theories about female psychology have proved fiercely controversial amongst feminists from the 1920s to the present day.

By the 1970s, psychoanalysis had gained a reputation, particularly in North America, as an ideology which encouraged women to adapt to the situations which had created their unhappiness. Despite this initial mistrust, some feminists gradually began to reassess the usefulness of psychoanalytic theory and practice. They wanted to understand how unconscious feelings and fantasies might be preventing them from making the kinds of personal changes which they consciously desired. Realising that they could not simply will themselves to be 'new women', they sought psychotherapy for themselves, and looked for ways to use these insights and skills in political and professional work. The work of Susie Orbach and Luise Eichenbaum (1983) and Nancy Chodorow (1978) exemplifies this tradition.

At the same time, psychoanalytic theory itself has continued to develop, and contemporary perspectives on gender provide a rich, controversial and thought-provoking account of femininity. Examples of this from France, Britain and the USA are the groundbreaking work of Janine Chasseguet-Smirgel (1964) and Juliet Mitchell (1974), and the more recent contributions of Jessica Benjamin (1988), Dinora Pines (1993) and Dana Breen (1993).

The Women's Therapy Centre was set up in 1976 as part of that tradition of thinking about how psychotherapy can help women to change. The all-female staff offer individual and group psychotherapy to all women, regardless of their ability to pay. Special services are offered to certain groups, including those with eating problems, survivors of childhood sexual abuse and victims of domestic violence. As well as a training and education programme for professionals, the Centre offers a public advice and information service about psychotherapy and workshops for women in a variety of languages used in the local community.

These chapters are based on the first year of lectures on a course, the content of which is constantly changing and developing. Reading the book is, of course, no substitute for attending the course, which students have consistently experienced as an exciting opportunity for personal change and professional renewal. Some of the chapters share the experience of psychotherapists at the Women's Therapy Centre. For instance, Chapter 2 by Susie Orbach, who co-founded the Centre with Luise Eichenbaum, gives an insight into the political and clinical philosophies behind the organisation. Sheila Ernst offers another perspective on the all-female therapeutic dyad, while Ruthie Smith and Carol Mohamed give an account of current thinking at the Centre on brief psychotherapy and cross-cultural issues. Other chapters, especially Chapters 3, 5 and 9–11, describe work done in quite different settings, including National Health Service hospitals and clinics and private psychotherapy practice.

The orientation of the Centre is primarily that of psychoanalytic psychotherapy, which differs from other forms of therapy in its emphasis on elucidating how the client's unconscious processes are re-enacted in the 'here and now' of the therapeutic transference relationship. The psychoanalytic psychotherapist also uses her own counter-transference – her emotional reactions to the patient, and particularly to the transference – to further the therapeutic work. This is a book about clinical practice rather than theory, and a series of technical questions are raised in the chapters, more or less explicitly. For instance, does psychotherapy with women require particular theoretical perspectives or knowledge, or even differences in technique? Is it necessary to work in different ways with different groups of women?

Interestingly, the contributors generally argue for a classical technique, in which the therapist remains as neutral as possible in order to elicit a transference which then becomes the focus of the work. Valerie Sinason's account of work with a young woman with a learning disability is particularly interesting in this respect. In her initial consultation, Sinason is careful to avoid the premature use of her client's first name, since this could, she believes, immediately create a dynamic of inequality, suggesting a relationship between an adult woman and a child or person of lesser social status. In the event, the therapist does have to take certain actions, such as making phone calls, which would not usually be part of a therapist's role. Sinason's chapter poignantly demonstrates the necessity for therapists to understand and explore issues of femininity and sexuality with this client group. It is clear that within the therapeutic relationship the client felt free to explore her competitive feelings towards another woman in a way that would certainly have enriched her own female identity.

Similarly, in Chapter 8 Sue Krzowski shows that the traditional reserve and attention to boundaries which is the hallmark of psychoanalytic psychotherapy is crucial to women who have experienced an incestuous relationship.

Some contributors do, however, suggest that innovations of technique are sometimes essential. For instance, Ruthie Smith and Carol Mohamed argue that in brief psychotherapy the clinician should draw up an explicit contract, giving a clear explanation of the nature and aims of the therapeutic work. They describe how they use the transference relationship in different ways, depending on the needs of particular clients.

Drawing on a wide spectrum of theoretical perspectives, ranging from the work of Freud and Jung to more contemporary British and North American psychoanalytic theories, the contributors address a series of questions about how women's unequal social status might be reflected in their psyches. How, for instance, do physiology, culture and unconscious processes interact to create psychological womanhood as we know it? And what happens to women's capacity to assert their own needs and desires and to use their aggression constructively? These are the themes which have always preoccupied feminists and analysts interested in gender. But the book also bears testimony to the ways in which feminist views on psychotherapy have altered since the 1970s. During the 1970s, there was a tendency for feminists to emphasise the psychological similarities between women. This led many writers to argue that the same dynamics exist in all mother–daughter relationships because of our shared experience of inequality. Now the focus has shifted (see Chodorow, 1978, 1989, 1994). The 'second sex' in this book is not a homogenous group and it is recognised that there are radical divergences in women's experience. The contributors explore the impact of differences in race, culture and class on female psychology and sexuality. They also look at the ways in which disability affects the internal world, and at women's differing needs at each stage of the physiological life cycle.

In Chapter 7, Ruthie Smith and Carol Mohamed focus on the psychological meaning of cross-cultural issues in the therapeutic dyad between female therapists and clients. For instance, they look at the complex constellation of positive and negative psychic and cultural meanings which can accrue to categories such as black and white within the transference and counter-transference.

Patricia Land explores women's different psychological experiences at each stage of the physiological life cycle. She looks at how culture and bodily experience affect the psyche during adolescence, the reproductive years, and the menopause. Tara Weeramanthri's chapter focuses mainly on psychotherapy with children and adolescents.

At the other end of the spectrum, Barbara Daniel describes the particular counter-transference issues for female psychotherapists working with elderly women clients. She argues that clinicians must have worked through their ambivalence about their own (perhaps elderly) mothers if they are to avoid idealising or denigrating their clients. Daniel suggests that in societies where traditional structures of family life are disintegrating, ageing presents a quite unique set of dilemmas and opportunities for each new generation of women. This means that the therapist needs an acute awareness of how prevailing gender expectations may be affecting the way women clients face ageing and death.

The fundamental issue for those wishing to eliminate gender inequality in society is whether the child can come to terms with difference, most importantly those between the sexes and the generations, without judging one sex to be inferior. In feminist psychoanalytic theorising this is associated with a crucial question: how can girls develop a stronger sense of their own psychic autonomy and a greater confidence in their own worth?

Changes in power relations between the sexes have led to great controversy amongst feminists and psychotherapists about the psychic and cultural significances of each parent. Freud's theory revolves around paternal power, and Jacques Lacan retained this emphasis. For them, the major psychological task of children of both sexes is to come to terms with the power of the father. They argue that at the moment the girl recognises sexual difference she is forced to acknowledge her unenviable lack of potency within a male-dominated social structure. In contrast, many British and North American psychoanalysts have focused on the psychological power of the mother and the therapist's use of the maternal transference.

All psychoanalytic clinicians share a belief in the importance of Freud's theory of the Oedipus complex, although they understand it in different ways. Freud described a process whereby every child has to construct its own identity, its own sense of what it means to be psychologically male or female, through piecing together fragments of fantasy and experience in relation to its parents and the society in which it lives. It is essentially a triangular configuration.

In her chapter on working with lesbian clients, Joanna Ryan problematises the notion of identity within psychoanalytic and feminist theories. She argues for a more complex and multi-levelled understanding of the way cultural and theoretical constructs impact on the transference and counter-transference between the lesbian client and her female therapist. Drawing on clinical material, Ryan explores the way that dilemmas about sexual orientation can mask deeper anxieties about intimacy, including fears about loss of the other and destruction of the self.

Some feminists have argued that because we live in a patriarchal society it is crucial that we understand how the power of the father and of men is reproduced in the mind of the child (Mitchell, 1974, 1984). The founders of the Women's Therapy Centre, however, took a very different position. Susie Orbach's chapter illustrates the way in which many feminists have drawn on contemporary mother-centred psychoanalytic theory to create a new understanding of the experience of mothers and daughters. She describes how a shared sense of cultural oppression leads to an ambivalence between mother and daughter and profound difficulties in forming a separate identity. She argues that if the status of women and mothering is to gradually change, men must play an equal part in early childcare. A less ambivalent experience of early mothering (by a male or female parent) will lead to changes in female psychology.

Since the 1980s, however, in Britain and the United States, there has been a growing questioning of the recent psychoanalytic preoccupation with the mothering function. Lacanians have always argued that neglect of the paternal transference can lead to a therapeutic impasse where the therapist colludes with the patient's illusion that she can remain forever within an exclusive relationship with the mother, rather than coming to terms with the existence of the father, the third party who represents external reality. Jungian as well as Kleinian and object relations psychoanalysts have recently begun to re-examine the role of the father, and to elaborate on the crucial significance of our feelings and fantasies about the parents as a sexual couple (Samuels, 1985; Britton, 1989; Limentani, 1991).

How do feelings and fantasies about fathers manifest themselves in the transference between female therapist and client? Sue Krzowski discusses how fathers who commit incest with their daughters inevitably subvert the girl's process of psychic differentiation from the mother. She explores how the ensuing confusions of identity emerge in the therapeutic relationship. Ruthie Smith and Carol Mohamed suggest that the time limit set within the brief psychotherapy contract can act symbolically as a paternal boundary, thus helping the woman to work through Oedipal processes of individuation.

The topic of fathering raises controversial political and psychological questions. Are we talking here about the biological father and the functions associated with him, or his cultural and symbolic position? Can a woman fulfil the fathering function? In Chapter 4, Marie Maguire points out that what is significant for the single mother is her unconscious relationship with her own internal father and the conventionally 'masculine' elements of her personality.

From the very beginning, psychoanalysis has been preoccupied with such questions. Although Freud did not focus specifically on the relationship between mothers and daughters, in one sense he set the ball rolling with his discovery of a particular kind of object relationship. Writing in 1914, in his paper 'On narcissism: an introduction' (1984), he described a type of object relationship which he termed 'narcissistic'. The term is derived from the classical myth of Narcissus, who fell in love with his own reflection in a pool, the pool in which he finally drowned.

The contributors to this volume would not agree with Freud's implication that women are more psychologically narcissistic than men. But many of us would agree that prevailing gender stereotypes foster different forms of narcissistic defences against intimacy in each sex. There is as much psychological difference within the sexes as between them. Yet women in therapy can often recognise in themselves a tendency to live vicariously through others with whom unconsciously we believe ourselves to be psychically fused. In contrast, boys growing up in Western societies are encouraged to defend themselves against emotional vulnerability through fantasies of absolute psychological independence.

During the 1980s, feminists influenced by British psychoanalytic theories often focused on the mother–daughter relationship with the distinctive merged, unseparated, blissful but also stultifying quality which Freud described. The theme is vividly taken up by Susie Orbach in her chapter on women's development, in which she describes the mother–daughter relationship as inherently problematic. Sharing the same gender identity, daughters have difficulty in achieving a sense of separateness and autonomy in relation to a mother who often still feels herself to be unconsciously merged with her own mother.

Sheila Ernst explores the theme of separateness and difference in the therapy relationship and is alert to the danger that therapists, as well as patients, may feel anxious and uncertain about difference, especially where this entails conflict. Drawing on her experience as a psychotherapist and supervisor, Ernst examines the special nature of the clinical relationship between a woman therapist and her female client. She focuses on particular gender-mediated hopes and anxieties which may shape the transference and counter-transference and the difficulties these can create.

A common objection to feminism is that it tends to idealise relationships between women, stressing sisterhood, minimising difference, fostering among women a longing for that undifferentiated state of blissful union with another, where conflict, envy, destructiveness were unknown. Conflict and difficulty, so the objection goes, is all located in relation to men, to the other, the different one. Many of the contributors address this issue. They recognise the value of sharing certain experiences with other women, but they do not assume, as many feminists did in the early 1970s, that a woman would inevitably benefit more, politically or therapeutically, from being treated by a woman therapist.

What, then, does it mean when a woman seeking help for her emotional difficulties asks for a woman therapist? How are we to understand this request? It may be that she has, for reasons connected with her own past history, an intense distrust of men or, alternatively, it may come from a particular wish to explore her feelings towards her mother. On the other hand, she may be expressing a wish to form a particular kind of relationship, one in which separateness and difference no longer exist. For some women, the very idea of 'therapy' involves a fantasy in which there is a relationship of no conflict, no difference, a relationship which is a blissful replication (in their minds) of the earliest sense a baby has of its mother: two, cocooned together as one. What has to be denied at all costs is that the therapist can have a life or a mind of her own and is able to interact creatively and freely with her patient.

How do these fantasies of idealised merger affect the female therapist? Tara Weeramanthri argues that women in the caring professions and organisations staffed predominantly by female workers are often unconsciously dominated by a fantasy of an all-knowing, all-powerful maternal figure. This idea of maternal omnipotence can, she argues, generate profoundly unrealistic expectations in female practitioners as well as in clients and colleagues. Bearing in mind this dynamic, Weeramanthri draws on her own experience as a clinician and supervisor to explore the particular anxieties that children and adolescents can generate in mothers and female clinicians.

In her chapter on envy, Marie Maguire focuses on conflict between women, particularly mothers and daughters, and suggests that merging, feeling at one with, being 'best friends', may serve as a defence against envy, this most destructive of psychic forces. She argues that in so far as women disown their aggression, seeing it as an attribute that exists mainly in men, they lose access to their own fighting spirit and cannot then use feelings such as envy to make creative changes in their own lives.

The theme of separateness is also paramount in Patricia Land's chapter on the body. Again, this discussion was in a way pre-empted

by Freud in the 'Narcissism' paper when he talked about certain
women who are really more interested in themselves than in their
objects, concerned rather with being loved than loving. Land
discusses this in terms of a woman's relationship to her body as
something other, something which she herself observes and judges as
if she were outside it. A woman, in effect, may take her own body as
her object.

Within the all-female clinical setting each participant must, then,
negotiate anew what they share and how they differ psychologically
from their own sex. As the client struggles to define herself through
identification with real or imagined similarity, she must at the same
time fight to assert her distinctive separateness. For herself and her
therapist this reworking of the individuation process involves a
recognition that each woman possesses capacities and qualities
associated in her culture with men and fathering as well as with
'femininity' and mothering.

There are no easy answers or comfortable certainties in these
accounts of the interface between feminism and psychoanalysis in
everyday clinical practice. A series of unresolved questions resonate
through the chapters. The contributors cast a fascinating new light on
enduring political and clinical controversies whilst simultaneously
acknowledging how much we still have to learn about the
therapeutic relationship between women.

## References

Benjamin, J. (1988) *The Bonds of Love: Psychoanalysis, Feminism and the
    Problem of Domination*, Random House, New York.
Breen, D. (1993) *The Gender Conundrum*, Routledge, London.
Britton, R. (1989) *The Oedipus Complex Today*, Karnac, London.
Chasseguet-Smirgel, J. (1964) *Female Sexuality*, Maresfield, London 1985.
Chodorow, N. (1978) *The Reproduction of Mothering: Psychoanalysis and the
    Sociology of Gender*, University of California Press, Berkeley CA.
—— (1989) *Feminism and Psychoanalytic Theory*, Polity Press, London.
—— (1994) *Femininities, Masculinities, Sexualities*, Free Association Books,
    London.
Freud, S. (1984) 'On narcissism: an introduction' (1914), *Penguin Freud
    Library 11*, Penguin, Harmondsworth.
Limentani, A. (1991) 'Neglected fathers in the aetiology and treatment of
    sexual deviations', *International Journal of Psycho-Analysis*, 72, 4:573–84.

Mitchell, J. (1974) *Psychoanalysis and Feminism*, Allen Lane, London.
—— (1984) *Women: The Longest Revolution*, Virago Press, London.
Orbach, S. & Eichenbaum, L. (1983) *Understanding Women*, Penguin, Harmondsworth.
Pines, D. (1993) *A Woman's Unconscious Use of her Body*, Virago Press, London.
Samuels A. (1985) *The Father, Contemporary Jungian Perspectives*, Free Association Books, London.

# Chapter 1

# The therapy relationship

*Sheila Ernst*

## Introduction

When feminists started the process of pinpointing aspects of traditional psychoanalysis and psychotherapy that had been detrimental to women, the question of what might constitute a therapy relationship which would be helpful to women was also carefully considered. The very establishment of the Women's Therapy Centre was based, in part, on the idea that there was a particular value for a woman in having a therapy relationship with another woman, someone like herself. At the Centre this discussion has continued as thought is given to whether particular groups of women, such as Black women or lesbians or disabled women, may need to see women who are 'like' them, whether the structure of the actual therapy relationship may have to be modified or whether what is needed is awareness of and sensitivity to the effects of a particular social experience on the therapy relationship.

Since, as we shall see in this chapter, current psychoanalytic thinking has placed an increasing emphasis on the use of the therapist's own internal experience in relation to her client, this poses some crucial questions for feminists who are approaching psychoanalytic counselling or psychotherapy. How will the therapist address social power and social difference so that she does not mistake personal responses for objectivity and potentially abuse her power? How will the therapist ensure that she maintains an appropriate balance between the reality of the client's current and past experience in the outside world and the importance of what transpires between therapist and client within their relationship?

There are no simple or straightforward answers to these questions. First of all we need to understand the development of the ideas of transference and counter-transference within psychoanalysis. Then we have to add to this tradition an awareness of social issues, so that the therapist is always asking herself questions about such issues as gender or race or class and how they may be impacting upon her experience and that of her client. Lastly we must understand how reality and fantasy interact within ourselves and our clients so that both become a part of the therapy relationship.

I will not be making generalisations about how gender affects the therapy relationship, but rather will try to show how incorporating gender, and other social terms, into our thinking can affect and improve the therapy we give and receive.

## The special relationship

A woman seeks therapy because she is in distress. She feels desperate; perhaps she cannot function in her daily life or perhaps she can function but gets no satisfaction from doing so. She may abuse drugs or food; she may be phobic about travelling; she may be desperate because a relationship has come to an end. She comes wanting to 'do something' about her problem(s) and what she is offered is someone to talk to, or a group of other sufferers to talk to, with whom she can make a relationship. She is not offered advice, though she may be offered some understanding. The help she will receive will come from her relationship with the psychotherapist and, in a group setting, with the other group members too.

The idea that it is helpful to talk to an empathic professional or even a group of other people with their own difficulties has become a commonplace in our culture. Magazines and newspapers have their 'agony aunts', the radio has a telephone counsellor, and even in 'soaps' characters go for counselling. This is often seen in common-sense terms as 'A trouble shared is a trouble halved'. It helps to know that others have the same kinds of thoughts, feelings and experiences as you do; that you are not alone in your distress.

However, in the plethora of common-sense approaches to counselling and psychotherapy, it is easy to ignore what is special and even strange about the relationship that is established within psychoanalytically oriented counselling or psychotherapy between psychotherapist/counsellor and patient/client.[1]

The client brings to the therapy relationship all that is closest to her heart, both consciously and unconsciously, although this will not often be expressed in any kind of straightforward way. She comes with concerns about herself and her relationships in the present and in the past, affected as she has been both by the most intimate personal experiences and by the surrounding culture and history within which these experiences have taken place.

The therapy relationship is structured in such a way that it facilitates the client and therapist's joint discovery of much that was initially hidden both from and about the client, much that may never have reached thought let alone articulation – what the psychoanalyst Bollas (1987) has termed the 'unthought known'. It is in the very process of this voyage of discovery (the discovery of the relationship), rather than the simple talking about the client's problems, that the working through takes place. Similarly, in an analytic therapy group it is relationships between group members and the group analyst and the communication which takes place within the group which is therapeutic rather than any simple recounting or interpretation as such. Thus, in the current practice of object relations psychoanalytic psychotherapy at the Women's Therapy Centre (this is the most commonly practised orientation within Britain, many European countries and the USA), it is the understanding of what transpires within the therapy relationship which is the core of the therapy.

For many people the basic structure of the psychoanalytic therapy session is familiar and taken for granted. For others it may be seen as part of a meaningless ritual which makes them suspicious of this form of psychotherapy. The structure of the therapy session places a clear boundary of time, place and contact around the relationship between psychotherapist and client. The session traditionally lasts for 50 minutes, or an hour and a half for a group. In contrast, for instance, to a consultation with a general practitioner, nothing is allowed to interrupt the session and if, inadvertently, there are interruptions, the effects on psychotherapist and client would be carefully explored. Similarly, anything which affects the boundary of the session is seen as significant material; the psychotherapist's holiday break or a group member's lateness are seen as having ripples which will have a meaning within the 'pool'. Once an agreement to begin psychotherapy is established the psychotherapist will make every effort to offer continuity, and when she cannot do so she will again see the reactions to this as important material within the process. Perhaps the most unusual part of the relationship lies in the apparent discrepancy between the intimate nature of what the client divulges and the fact that there is no physical contact and usually no contact outside sessions and that the psychotherapist does not talk about herself. These structures go back to Freud's own practice; for Freud this was a way of hiding himself so as to facilitate the emergence of the analysand's feelings about significant past figures in the patient's life which are then projected onto the analyst and thus become available for interpretation. This is what Freud termed the 'transference'. As we shall see, the understanding of the interaction between client and psychotherapist has changed considerably since then, with far more emphasis being based on the therapy relationship as a two-way process in which, firstly, the therapist can of course be 'seen' and, secondly, the therapist's own response to the client's material is itself considered a vital part of the process (the 'counter-transference'). Nevertheless it is still felt that this basic structure (with certain modifications which will be looked at) is crucial for the development of the therapy relationship.

## The transference

It is difficult to begin to discuss how the ideas of transference and counter-transference are used without clarifying the ways in which they have developed and changed since Freud first used them. Freud remarked that the analytic process does not create transference but reveals it (Freud, 1912).

It was one thing, however, to recognise the existence of transference, and another to realise its therapeutic potential and devise a method of therapy which involved drawing out the transference rather than seeing it as a block to treatment. Freud's colleague Breuer had found that his treatment, through hypnosis, of his patient Anna O. had led Anna to develop an erotic response to him which he found too powerful to handle, and as a respectable married physician, he fled. Freud described having a similar experience, again with a woman patient whom he was treating with hypnosis, but he realised that the woman's flinging her arms around him was not to do with his 'irresistible personal attraction' (Freud, 1925) and began instead to ask himself what the meaning was of the emergence of these erotic feelings.

Gradually Freud came to see that this very process of transferring hidden unconscious feelings from a figure in the past onto the analyst could be a way of giving both analysand and analyst access to previously unconscious material through what appeared to be happening in their relationship. Initially Freud saw this entirely in terms of the analysand's repressed erotic desires for forbidden people (e.g. the daughter's desire for her father), but later he broadened this view to encompass painful repressed feelings towards another person which needed to be worked through. This meant that the analyst had to be able to accept the analysand's transference, and to enable the analysand to explore its meaning rather than explaining to him or her that it was a delusion or misperception. Thus, in the case of the woman who flung her arms around Freud's neck, Freud saw the validity of her erotic feelings towards him, explored what this meant for her, but, as he later said, did not take them as real in the sense of seeing himself as a highly desirable man. In fact, nowadays we might even be asking whether Freud's awareness of the transference nature of his analysand's erotic response to him could not be taken even further, wondering whether she was in fantasy not flinging her arms around a male figure from the past but perhaps enacting an erotic transference to the mother. Such thoughts will be followed through later in this chapter.

It can help us to understand the significance of Freud's break-through in recognising the therapeutic potential of the transference if we look a little more closely at how difficult it can be to sustain the transference. In this example I show how an apparently straight-forward interchange between my client and myself became highly emotionally charged because of the transference between us. Moreover the particular nature of the transference caught me in a vulnerable area (rather like Anna O.'s transference to Breuer did for him) and I had to think clearly in order to stay working with my client in the transference, keeping in mind that what she was expressing were her fantasies about me based on her past experience.

It is nearing a holiday break and my client and I have been talking about her friends and which of them she will see and be able to talk to while I am away. We are in the process of acknowledging a significant change in her relationships with people outside the therapy, in that she can now express more of her feelings, particularly when she is depressed or feels irrationally incapable of doing things.

I have in mind that it is important for her to acknowledge this change with me – to allow me to see that she now has some good objects inside her, but that this does not mean that she can let me go off for my break without any anger, sadness or envy. I begin to feel my way towards expressing these ideas when she cuts across what I am saying with considerable spite in her voice and says that she doesn't know why we are talking about a relationship when, after all these years, she feels completely cold towards me and knows I have no feelings for her.

I find this accusation rather painful. I start to feel resentful, then contend with wanting to tell her off rather defensively and fall prey to the fear that she is actually right – that she doesn't care for me and I have no feelings for her. There is something familiar here and my sense is that it connects with my own personal experience of many years of being both a mother and stepmother; my gendered sense of self is relevant. I feel I am being accused of being a bad mother and I have particular difficulties with this accusation. All this goes through my mind in a flash, to be reflected upon as I begin to struggle with the recognition that this spoiling, spiteful response is very real at this moment to my client and that we will have to understand what it is about. Then we may both be able to learn something important about this impending separation through the transference. Being aware of the gendered aspect of myself tied up with difficulties in accepting maternal ambivalence has helped me to stay on course with my client. This is not to say that all women therapists would have felt this way, nor that no male therapists would have a similar response.

Freud's version of the transference referred to the analysand's feelings and attitudes expressed towards him, which did not correspond to current reality and could be hypothesised to be disguised forms of the analysand's earlier relationships. Thus, with the example above, I might wonder whether the impending break in the therapy was leading my client to transfer onto me the very same feelings as perhaps she had when she was a child and felt, for example, that her mother left her to be with her father.

As psychoanalytic practice and theory have developed, so the ideas about transference – its meaning, its function within psycho-analysis and its relationship to counter-transference – have changed. The concept of transference has been extended to refer not just to the kind of occurrence described above, in a sense 'provoked' by the therapy relationship, but to any reaction which a person has to another in the present which is inappropriate to the situation and person and seems to be derived from the person's past experience. However, perhaps even more importantly for our task in understanding the therapy relationship, the major change which has taken place has been the move from seeing the transference as being an enactment of an old relationship to seeing it as an experience which takes place within the therapy setting between the client and psychotherapist, and which can be interpreted, making its content conscious, including the way in which the patient's past history may be affecting present perceptions.

Thus the focus on the interpretation of the transference relationship as being central to the task of psychoanalytic work has subtly changed so that everything which happens within the session is transference material. The changing perception of the transference relationship can be understood when it is connected to the Kleinian development within psychoanalysis. As Spillius (1988), a Kleinian analyst, points out in her introduction to a volume of Kleinian papers on psychoanalytic practice:

> The emphasis of Klein and her successors on the pervasiveness of transference is derived from Klein's use of the concept of unconscious phantasy, which is conceived as underlying all thought, rational as well as irrational, rather than there being a special category of thought and feeling which is rational and appropriate and therefore does not need analysing and a second kind of thought and feeling which is irrational and inappropriate and therefore expresses transference and needs analysing.

The process of transference was also seen in terms of a Kleinian concept, that of projective identification. The analysand externalises the internal object relationships, projecting them into the analyst who perceives the transference through her own experience and interprets this back to the analysand.

Another way of looking at the transference in this more global sense is to take up Winnicott's (1986) metaphor for interaction between two people in terms of object usage, as Bollas does (1987). I find this a more difficult but also less mechanistic way of thinking about the process. For Winnicott, using an object refers to the attempt by the 'user' to behave towards the object in such a way as to eventually elicit from the object a response which clarifies the distinction between the objects existing in the internal world of the 'user' and the object which has its own existence (i.e. is a subject). In a sense, the exploration of the transference relationship can be seen to involve exactly the same process. Initially the experience of the 'user' must be fully addressed so that she can gradually come to face the emotional implications of her own psychic separateness from the object. Wherever a psychotherapist's sympathies may lie in this complex debate, in accepting a broader definition of the transference she must inevitably involve herself with her own responses to the transference, her counter-transference. Before going on to look at this concept in more detail some issues are raised by the discussion of the transference which need to be addressed.

Initially the idea of the transference was that it developed as the psychoanalysis progressed. Thus there was a notion of a real relationship between analyst and analysand within which a 'treatment alliance' was formed. This allowed the analysand to stay with her analysis even when, in the transference, she might see the analyst at times as, for instance, a very threatening figure. One of the problems with the Kleinian concept of transference is that it appears to do away with the idea that the client can see anything real about the psychotherapist. As Pines (1993) argues cogently:

> I do not adhere to this broadened view myself, for it may place the person of the analyst beyond the reality-testing of the patient, and obstruct the analyst's need for self-scrutiny and observation . . . . In my view, however, if the patient has accurately perceived that the analyst is in a subdued or painful state of mind, it is important for the analyst carefully to acknowledge the reality of this, since otherwise it may reinforce the patient's infantile situation of not trusting her own feelings and perceptions of her parents.

This is a particularly crucial point for feminists who are concerned that the therapist should be prepared to look at herself and see the ways in which she might be allowing sexist or racist attitudes to pervade her interpretation of the transference.

Another change from the Freudian concept of transference concerns Freud's idea that most transference relates to the Oedipal period. Klein's work with children had led her to place an increasing importance on the pre-Oedipal period and particularly on what happens in the first year of life. Thus all transference could be assumed to be related to early infancy. This raises the question of whether later stages of development cannot also be significant in the formation of the client's internal world and can appear in the transference.

As a psychotherapist who is concerned with the early psychological development of women clients, I accept the importance of the early pre-Oedipal development of the infant and the relationship between the infant and her carers. However, I concur with the view of Pines (1993) who, through many years of working with women patients as a dermatologist and then a psychoanalyst, found that women used the changes in their bodies and in their reproductive life cycles as opportunities to rework early psychic conflict, suggesting that important psychic change does not only take place in early infancy. While fully accepting the importance of early infantile experience, she writes:

> during an analytic session the patient, in the relationship with the analyst, may relive infantile feelings and affects which are linked with the object relationships of childhood. In the same session she may switch to a later stage of development and re-experience feelings, affects and object relationships from adolescence, and the analyst must carefully monitor the changes that invariably occur during the course of the hour.

As well as having implications in particular for women, this viewpoint has a wider impact, for it implies that we must be able to make interpretations based on the transference of other social, political or historical material. This point is made by writers such as Samuels (1993), postulating a political aspect of the psyche, and Hopper (1985). Hopper gives an example from an analytic group where members seem to be expressing envy towards him. Noting the references to Jews, Arabs and Nazi Germany, he interprets the group's envious feelings in terms of their unconscious anti-Semitism rather than, as he puts it to them, 'explaining everything away in terms of your mothers and fathers when you were babies'. The point he is making is that sometimes the conventional psychoanalytic interpretations might be a cover for the more deeply unconscious thoughts and feelings about painful social issues.

My later examples and those offered in the following chapters in the book will show how clinical work with women from different backgrounds and of lesbian and heterosexual orientation leads to an understanding of the transference which is not limited to interpretation in terms of infantile experience.

In extending the transference to include the here-and-now experience of the therapy relationship within the session, the psychotherapist faces a technical problem of how and when she makes the link for the client between what she thinks is happening in the present and how that might relate to the past. Within psycho-analysis there has been much debate about this, with some analysts arguing that links with past experience should not be brought in straight away since this cools down the immediacy of the emotional situation (e.g. Joseph, 1988). Others (e.g. Rosenfeld, 1987) argue that interpretations about the past are not necessarily less immediate and emotive, should always be part of the transference and in some cases may be essential, since the constant referring to the relationship in the room can repeat the behaviour of a self-centred parent demanding to be the child's primary concern.

My own experience leads me to think that all of these positions can be right at different times and that what is crucial is, as Spillius herself says, not to apply any model mechanistically in order to confirm an already held theory. I have found myself making a connection with a client's past experience only to have her shout at me for avoiding the issue in the here and now. She may well have been right in feeling that we had engaged in something which I was finding 'too hot'. Likewise I have found, as Rosenfeld and others have said, particularly with traumatised clients (e.g. incest survivors or those who have been in grave physical danger), that it is vital to listen to what has happened to them very carefully and to show that I understand the meaning of the experience rather than constantly referring back to our relationship. In a therapy group for incest survivors I found that I constantly used the transferences in the here and now to interpret back into the 'there and then' and to restate the experience of being in the group in terms of the abuse.

The implication of all that has been said here about the changing perception of the meaning of the transference within the therapy relationship, and the need for the psychotherapist to use her own experience within the session as a guide to her interpretations, leads to the question of how we can begin to conceptualise the therapist's experience.

## The counter-transference

It has become clear that the wider view of the transference has profound implications for how the psychotherapist views her own feelings and attitudes towards the client. Returning to the example of the thoughts that flashed through my mind when my client expressed her opinion that our relationship was completely cold, my responses to her required not simply suppression on my part, but rather a process of thoughtful sifting to work out what our interaction might tell me about my client. Within this new framework I do not see my thoughts and responses as something to be laid aside slightly guiltily, but rather as a key part of the therapeutic relationship. As Brenman Pick (1988) puts it:

> If we feel at the mercy of an analytic superego that does not support us in knowing about these internal buffetings, we are, like the patient, in danger of 'wrapping it all up' competently . . . . The process of meeting and working through our own experience of both wanting to know and fearing knowing facilitates . . . a deeper and more empathic contact with these parts of the patient and his internal objects.

We are beginning to see how, in current psychoanalytic practice, it is difficult to separate out clearly transference and counter-transference, since what is being focused on is the making conscious and articulation of the interaction between the unconscious processes in the mind of both client and therapist.

Simply to accept this position is, I think, to treat it too lightly; just as with the transference, it is necessary to understand a little about its history in order to recognise what a profound alteration such concepts make to the way we think about the world. When we use them they have enormous power to help people, but they can also be abused.

Counter-transference, like transference, was initially seen by Freud as an obstacle to successful therapy. Freud did not term the analyst's whole response to the analysand as counter-transference but used the term to refer to the analyst's blind spots or the resistance in the analyst to certain aspects of the analysand's unconscious material.

We can agree wholeheartedly with Freud's emphasis on the need for anyone working professionally with other people to maintain a continuous and rigorous scrutiny of themselves and their own resistances and blind spots. It is vital here to remind ourselves that the psychotherapist also comes with her own concerns, interests, feelings, desires, history and socio-cultural background. This means, for instance, that a white psychotherapist may unconsciously have internalised much of the way in which Black people in a white society are connected with certain negative or 'dark' sides of life. Her complex and delicate task is to overtly restrain herself from expressing her own views or desires, to allow the client to develop her own images and fantasies about who her psychotherapist is and what her responses may be; yet at the same time to stay very much in touch with what she is experiencing in relation to the client and to engage in a continuous dialogue with herself about what her inner experience may tell her about the client. In order to do this she must have as much awareness as possible about her own internal world and how it has been affected by her life experiences. This is why it is so important for the psychotherapist or counsellor to undergo psychotherapy herself and to continue to monitor her dialogue with herself, initially through supervision and later through her own introspection or self-analysis and consultation with colleagues.

One of the concerns of the Women's Therapy Centre has always been that a psychotherapist's training and personal psychotherapy might not include any or sufficient reference to the ways in which the experience of her own gender, being a woman, or being a woman from a particular class and/or racial background, for instance, may impact upon her. Part of the aim of the Centre has been to join with other feminist psychoanalysts and psychotherapists to influence the profession as a whole in this respect, and it is interesting to note the following comment in the revised edition of a standard psycho-analytic text entitled *The Patient and the Analyst* (Sandler et al., 1992):

> There is no doubt that socio-cultural factors enter into the way in which transference develops . . . . The issue of gender has been examined intensively in recent years, possibly due to the influence of the feminist movement. Similarly interracial analyses have also be discussed.

In later examples we will see how important such factors may be if the psychotherapist's internal dialogue is to engage fully with her client.

Returning to my earlier example of the client who treated me coldly, I had to think carefully about how much my response to her might be influenced by my need to be the 'good mother'. It is so easy for the psychotherapist to abuse her position if she does not take this aspect of her work and training seriously, that perhaps it is not surprising that Freud did not revise his view of the counter-transference but rather continually re-emphasised the importance of the analyst's vigilance in self-analysis and awareness. Even Klein, who was responsible for widening the definition and increasing the concentration on the transference in the session, was wary of the way in which the analyst might misplace her own feelings onto the analysand if the broader definition of counter-transference was used. Segal (1964) tells of a young analyst explaining to Klein how he had felt confused in a session and so had interpreted to the analysand that the analysand had projected confusion into him. 'No, dear, you are confused', was Klein's response. She thought that the young analyst had not really understood what was happening in the material and had, as it were, blamed it on the analysand.

This crucial aspect of the counter-transference was incorporated into the new idea of the counter-transference introduced by Heimann (1950), in which it began to be seen as a means of helping the analyst to understand more about the hidden meaning of the analysand's communication. It is as if in the psychotherapy session the client's unconscious is in communication with the unconscious of the psychotherapist and will emerge in the associations of the psychotherapist within the session. There has been much debate about how this might be understood to take place. I referred earlier to the way in which a person may be seen to try to regulate her experience of intolerable anxiety by 'splitting off' parts of herself and projecting or evacuating them into another person, both to protect the self and for the safe-keeping of the split-off parts. This process of 'projective identification' (introduced by Racker, 1968) has been used to account for counter-transference.

An analogy can also be made with the mother's capacity to take in the infant's experience and re-present it in a form which the infant can handle better. Bollas (1987) makes this connection:

> We are made use of through our affects, through the patient generating the required feeling within us. In many ways this is precisely how a baby 'speaks' to its mother. The baby evokes a feeling perception in the mother that either inspires some action in her on the baby's behalf or leads her to put the baby's object usage into language, engaging the infant in the journey towards verbal representation of internal psychic states.

And just as the mother may not be able herself articulate exactly what is happening within this communication, so the same may be true for the psychotherapist. In discussing the kind of thinking which goes on about the counter-transference, inevitably I, like other writers, will make it sound as if the business of understanding is relatively straightforward. In fact, during sessions with the client, the psychotherapist needs to devote a great deal of time to being aware

of her own counter-transference response, tolerating not understanding and re-presenting what material she has to the client for her
to respond to. It is this working together on the material, this dialogue
and interaction, which can lead to an understanding which the
therapist can then formulate in a way which becomes comprehensible to others.

I want to look now at an example which illustrates some of the
facets of the counter-transference discussed so far.

> In an important session with a client, 'Clare', with whom I had
> been working for several years, she was eventually able to express
> some angry feelings directly towards me, rather than acting them
> out by coming late to sessions or missing them without notifying
> me. My counter-transference response was equally powerful,
> direct and angry. It needed some examination. We have seen that
> counter-transference, in Freud's original sense, can simply be the
> therapist's own personal response to something which she has not
> worked through herself. Checking out whether or not this is the
> case must always the therapist's first move. Having thought this
> through, I had to consider what the significance might be of the
> powerful and direct nature of my response. Was this a situation in
> which my counter-transference response represented my client's
> expectations of me – representing her father in the transference? If
> so, then I could be seen to be participating in a re-enactment of
> Clare's childhood experience within the session. Another more
> complex possibility was that Clare did not feel able to articulate her
> experience verbally so that, even though she was speaking of her
> anger, unconsciously she had to make me feel the very feelings
> that she had had as a child.
>
> These were some of the possibilities which Clare and I had to
> work on in the sessions following on from the moment at which
> she had shouted at me and my response had been: 'You cannot
> treat me like a punch-bag!'
>
> Gradually Clare became aware that she felt that she had been the
> world's punch-bag; and we began to recognise that my response
> was a re-echoing of her own feelings of rage. She could not believe
> that I could understand how she felt unless I had experienced the
> feeling myself, which in effect I did in my counter-transference.
> This is what Bollas (1987) means when he describes the work in
> the counter-transference as 'enabling the patient to manipulate us
> through transference usage into object identity'.

## Gender and the therapy relationship

Although the early psychoanalysts had been very aware of the importance of the analyst's gender, by the 1930s such factors were superseded by the emphasis on the need for the analyst to present himself as much as possible as a blank screen onto which the analysand might project his or her fantasies. It was as if the need to emphasise the nature, significance and power of the transference relationship led the analysts of that period to minimise the effects of the 'real' relationship. It is understandable that this happened in the attempt to establish a quite different way of thinking. I know how easy it is for me to be too 'concrete' and fail to be aware that at times clients will, for instance, see me as a male figure. By being conscious of gender as a factor within the therapy relationship, we become more aware not only that the gender of client and therapist may be significant but also that the client's fantasies are gendered. The more the relationship between client and therapist, between transference and counter-transference, is seen as central, the more vital it is to examine the ways in which gender affects the counter-transference of the psychotherapist.

Although the topic of gender re-emerged within psychoanalysis with the work of Chasseguet-Smirgel in the 1960s, by the time the Women's Therapy Centre opened in 1976 there was virtually no literature on the specific topic of this chapter. What did exist was the belief that it is very important for a woman to be able to choose a woman psychotherapist, and that gender plays a part; but this had not yet been acknowledged or understood in making psychoanalytic therapy at best less helpful than it might be for women, and at worst damaging. From the 1980s onwards, articles and papers have been written on this subject and, as we have already seen (see p. 22), this has been noted within the field. Interestingly enough, there has been some convergence between those who have approached the topic from a feminist starting point and those who have noted, through their clinical work with women, that the transference and counter-transference between two women may have particular qualities. Thus there is a meeting point between, for example, Lester (1990), who starts her paper on gender issues in the analytic process by stating that 'gender defines and shapes the linguistic and other symbolic structures built during development and, we believe, continues to qualify, largely unconsciously, the psychic reality of everyday life', and Pines (1993) who, in writing about her work with an analysand who had suffered from infantile eczema, acknowledges the importance of gender: 'A woman analyst's physical capacity to be a mother appears to facilitate the transference of primitive feelings arising from partial maternal deprivation.'

I am going to focus on the therapy relationship between two women, although undoubtedly gender plays a key part in all the other possible gender combinations (see Maguire, 1995). Pines, like other writers, notes that the relationship between a woman analysand and woman analyst may evoke and highlight early maternal transferences; this also implies that in the therapy relationship the client, in 'using' the psychotherapist, will involve her in experiencing these archaic feelings both as the infant and as the maternal figure. Schachtel (1986) gives a cogent description of what this means for the woman psychotherapist:

> to be in the analytic role evoke(s) for herself and for her patient all that is associated with female gender-role – pre-oedipal experience, the gender expectation of maternal or female caretaking, female sexuality, conception, 'having to mother oneself' – with the result that the level of experience evoked is inherently more regressed when the analyst is female . . . the female analyst and her patient will be traversing a transferential/counter-transferential terrain of working through differences between gender and analytic role . . . . Women have been trained to respond by doing something to and for another person that is different from the analytic role.

This certainly corresponds to my own personal experience and that of colleagues, supervisees and other writers on the subject. It is not that the male psychotherapist does not evoke early material from his clients, but rather that there is something particularly powerful in the interaction between the two women in the therapy relationship which can best be grasped in gender terms.

When a woman chooses a woman therapist she is asking for someone who is the same as her; her assumption is that someone who shares her experience of being in the world as a woman will understand her better. She is also, often unconsciously, choosing to repeat one aspect of the earliest relationship with the mother: namely that of being the same gender. As I have already pointed out, the therapy relationship may at times be very like the mother–infant relationship with all that that implies about fusion and merging in early infancy. Thus a theme which may permeate women's experience in the therapy relationship is the merging and fusion by both the client and the therapist; this may be followed by the surprise, disappointment and resistance when either party discovers that, in spite of the gender or other similarities, they are actually two separate people.

Let us look at an example which was brought to a case discussion group by the therapist, who was puzzled by her responses to her client, 'Alice'.

Alice had 'forgotten' her Monday therapy session and had returned late from a weekend away. In the subsequent session Alice remarked that she was surprised that her therapist had not known that she would be away because she thought that the therapist just knew what was going on with Alice. The therapist had felt a fleeting rage when she had come into work on Monday morning and waited for 50 minutes for her client, who hadn't even bothered to ring. However, listening to Alice she found herself absorbed in Alice's sense of their union and disappointment that the therapist had failed her test and that she did not know things unless Alice found a way of communicating them. The therapist felt that they had had a good session in which Alice had come to acknowledge how painful it was for her to see herself as a separate person from the therapist. She did not give much thought to her anger at the way in which Alice had treated her over the missed session.

What dismayed the therapist was that following this work with Alice, which had appeared to be something of a breakthrough, nothing changed. Alice went on behaving as if she did not need to speak and continued to be unable to express any angry feelings towards the therapist. The therapist thought that there had been a significant change in Alice's perception that she and the therapist were separate people and that, much as she might hate it, Alice really did need to communicate with the therapist through words. Clearly though, this was not happening. What the therapist brought to the case discussion was the sense that she had missed something crucial.

In the case discussion we focused on the therapist's counter-transference. The therapist had felt very much in touch with Alice's disappointment at their lack of perfect communication. She had felt tears come into her eyes when Alice had talked about it. Then she remembered that she had felt angry on her own behalf, both on the day of the missed session and again when Alice had returned. The case discussion group encouraged the therapist to think more

about this aspect of her counter-transference as it might shed some
light on what was happening.

This example shows how the therapy relationship between two
women may reflect some of the difficulties which arise in the mother–
daughter relationship, when the sameness of gender (existing within
a social setting which discourages the development of women's
independent subjectivity) makes it harder for women to acknowledge the differences between them and renegotiate their relationships accordingly.

Within the mother–daughter relationship the daughter must be
able to identify with her mother and also to perceive her mother as a
distinct person in her own right. The mother's own psychology may
make it hard for her to acknowledge her subjectivity, her selfish
interests, her envy, her anger and her desires. She may herself be so
fearful of the damage her anger and envy can cause that she represses
them and does not give herself the opportunity to test out the validity
of her fantasies. For the daughter to experience herself as the subject
of her own life, she needs to have a mother who can experience her
own subjectivity. In Winnicott's (1986) terms, the daughter needs to
be able to 'use' the object (her mother) in order to recognise that she
and the mother are truly different people. A similar process takes
place within the therapy relationship and may run into difficulties.

Alice's therapist found herself profoundly identifying with her
client. When tears of disappointment filled Alice's eyes, her therapist
also had tears in her eyes. The therapist understood Alice's pain at
losing the fantasy of their magical communication. Alice did need to
feel that her loss was understood but she also needed something else
from her therapist; something which traditionally might have been
seen as the more paternal role of giving boundaries. Alice needed a
therapist who could maintain her own subjectivity through recognising a broad range of her own feelings, including her anger. In the
counter-transference, Alice's therapist had lost hold of the anger she
had felt while she waited for her client on Monday morning. In so
doing she was able to use the identifying aspect of her counter-
transference and acknowledge Alice's pain, but she could not
provide Alice with an experience of her otherness or difference.
Hence Alice returned to her former state of longing for fusion with
her therapist and being unable to speak to her.

The therapist (like many women) found herself profoundly drawn
towards providing nurture and understanding for her client. More-

over, although she was able to look at the negative aspects of the transference, at a deeper level she found herself being drawn into a profound identification with her client, perhaps much as in any mother–daughter relationship. In order to be 'used' as an object, as I have already described, the object in question has to be able to perceive herself as someone having her own identity and desires – in other words, as a subject in her own right. As I have pointed out in my earlier critique of Winnicott from a feminist perspective (Ernst, 1987), women have particular difficulties in achieving subjectivity and therefore in being both the 'user' and the 'object' in the process which is meant to account for the way in which the child becomes aware of being a subject. While Lester (1990) suggests that the female analyst may show what she calls 'an excess of nurturing' in the counter-transference, Orbach and Eichenbaum (1993) relate this directly to the problematic of women's subjectivity. They agree that more is needed than the therapist's holding of the client and suggest that the client needs most of all something which, because of the nature of gendered relationships, she is unlikely to have had in her relationship with her mother: namely an encounter with another 'subject'.

Another dimension of this lack of subjectivity may be expressed in the paucity of erotic transference between female client and female therapist described in the literature (see O'Connor & Ryan, 1993). As in the previous example, it is as if the client and therapist do not feel separated enough to have erotic feelings towards one another. This has variously been attributed to the client's fear of bringing erotic feelings into consciousness because they would put her even more profoundly in touch with the power of the maternal transference, to the resistance of the therapist to her own homosexuality and to the counter-transferential pull towards the pre-Oedipal, as if the earliest relationship between mother and daughter were not sexualised. There may also be resistance to looking at the possibility that the mother and daughter continue to have sexual feelings for each other even after the Oedipal stage is entered. The denial of erotic feelings between women, particularly in the early mother–daughter relation-ship, may be an important factor in many women's feelings that they are only an object of desire, rather than a desiring subject.

The female therapist needs to be conscious of her tendency to become embroiled without knowing how to reflect on her entanglement with her client. She needs to be aware that in both the transference and the counter-transference there may be mascu-

line elements which she may easily 'not notice' or deny. She also
needs to risk giving up her nurturing role without repressing or
hiding it under doctrinaire interpretations of the negative transference. For the therapist in the above example, this meant becoming
more aware in her supervision of what she was caught up with, and
also taking to her own therapy the aspects of herself which felt
threatened by this experience. One can only hope that the therapist
herself had a therapist who understood some of the particular
difficulties involved for a woman in becoming a 'subject' and finding
her own 'desire'.

## Differences within gender

Translating the wish to provide psychotherapy for women from
different class and racial backgrounds, for women with disabilities
and for women with different sexual orientations, means looking at
how the experience of social and cultural differences, besides gender
itself, are going to be reflected in the therapy relationship. It will
already be clear that translating an 'equal opportunities policy' into
terms that can really help to give clients appropriate therapy is
complicated. (There are also important issues of access and what
needs to be done to make therapy more accessible.) Here I want to
focus on the kinds of issues which arise within the therapy
relationship, looking at examples from work with a Black client
and a client with a disability. In both examples the therapists are
caught up in the concrete and external issues because of their own
anxieties and unconscious responses to racial difference and
disability. They lose track of their clients' unconscious communication and fail to use their counter-transference to benefit the client.

The first example illustrates some of the dynamics which quickly
develop in the therapy relationship between a white psychotherapist
and a Black client, in spite of the therapist believing that she should
take issues of race into account.

The white psychotherapist was taking over a referral from a
colleague and was feeling quite nervous about how the new client
would feel about her since, due to illness, the colleague had not
been able to follow up on her assessment. The therapist had read
her colleague's brief notes, but was somewhat shocked when her

client entered the room to find that she was a Black woman. The therapist ascribed her shock to her racism. The client, 'Angela', was very wary of the therapist. She had not been expecting a different therapist and found it extremely difficult to talk to her. The therapist felt very heavy and hopeless, was amazed at the strength of her counter-transference in this first session and, feeling guilty both for her surprise at seeing a Black woman and for subjecting her to this change of therapist, she found herself desperately wanting to make things better for Angela. She was afraid of Angela's anger and disappointment, and therefore felt compelled to answer Angela's questions concretely rather than using her counter-transference to enable Angela to express her distrust and despair.

Thus, a well intentioned white therapist had found herself using her strong counter-transference responses to a Black client, not as material to reflect upon, but rather as a spur to action. She answered the client's questions under the assumption that this would help Angela to feel more secure while actually depriving her of an opportunity to explore the heavy burdens she had brought with her which must have contributed to the therapist's intense counter-transference. It was only towards the end of the session, when Angela was preparing to leave early, that the therapist was able to draw on her usual resources and suggest to Angela that she might prefer to stay and tell the therapist how rough she was feeling. Angela was at last able to express some of her distress, her disappointment and her fear that a psychotherapist (perhaps she meant a white psychotherapist) would not want to take her troubles on board.

Afterwards the therapist felt that she could not make any kind of psychodynamic assessment and that she wanted to 'work on Angela's experience of racism'. This was her way of saying that she had not felt able to contain the situation in a way which was helpful to Angela, and that she thought this had something to do with her own racism. She seemed to feel de-skilled by the experience. Ironically it was the therapist's initial fear of her 'racism' that paralysed her, preventing her from beginning to think about what that shock might be about. She needed to examine her own assumption that any client not specifically designated Black, and not speaking with an identifiable 'Black' accent, would be white. Was there something else contained in the shock? What were her fantasies about a large Black client? It seemed that she could not let herself know and thus deprived the client of the benefits of her counter-transference.

One way of looking at this might be that, as a white woman, the therapist was afraid of discovering some of the very frightening material which white people have projected onto Black people. Thus the way in which the therapist deprived Angela was by, quite unconsciously, failing to do the very thing that she thought she wanted to do: looking at Angela's experience of racism in the here and now of the therapy relationship. This takes us back to the point made on p. 20 about the detrimental effect of being at the mercy of an analytic superego. The therapist also stopped herself from thinking about the effects that the loss of the assessing therapist might have upon her client. It was as if, once she had seen her client as different from herself, she lost touch with the way in which a different person may still have similar and familiar feelings and responses. Moreover, Angela might have had particular responses as a Black woman to losing a white therapist. She might, for instance, have felt that, whatever the reality, she had been dumped by the first therapist because of her Blackness. What was there likely to be in her history as a Black woman which would lead her to have very painful memories of a lack of continuity in personal relationships due to disruptive external circumstances?

In my next example, both the psychotherapist and the client have a disability. The psychotherapist felt that she was inappropriately treating the client as if she was a child. She felt quite ashamed of this since it was precisely one of the things which she herself found annoying about how she was often related to by others. Her dilemma was that she did not know how to understand what she felt. Was she quite correctly worrying about repeating patterns of patronising behaviour towards another disabled person? Or was her client actually feeling like a child and trying to find some way of unconsciously communicating this to her therapist?

Like the white therapist working with a Black client, this disabled therapist was having some difficulties in working out the ways in which she could be similar to and yet different from her client. As we have seen, there may be a tendency for the woman therapist to have difficulties in distinguishing between being merged or exactly alike, and being similar but separate which allows for sameness and difference between client and therapist. The white therapist was so shocked by her difference from her Black client that she had difficulty in remembering the similarities between them. The therapist with a disability may feel that, because she shares the experience of disability with her client, it is hard for her to see that they are different in other ways. It then becomes difficult for her to decide whether treating her client like a child is a bad and patronising thing to do or whether it is a vital part of the therapy relationship in which the client does feel like a child in relation to the therapist/parent. This may be further compounded by her own, possibly unanalysed, feelings about being a child, being helpless, being disabled and all that this entails. It may be that the therapist herself finds it difficult to bear her client's distress just because she does have a shared experience and cannot bear to have that reignited. These are some of the issues which needed to be discussed in order to make sense of what was happening in this particular therapy relationship.

> The client, 'Isabel', had been talking to her therapist about how badly she felt she had performed at a job interview. She had been particularly unable to respond to one of the male interviewers, an 'RAF type' with silver hair and a handlebar moustache. She could see that there was some connection between this man and her father. It was at this point that the therapist had the feeling that her client was quite childlike and needed protection. The therapist imagined herself training the client up for the next interview and, although she only commented on the possible connection between Isabel's father and the male interviewer, she felt uncomfortable about her desire to 'train' Isabel in interview techniques.
> After a full discussion of the issues raised above, the therapist came to see that she was anxious about her strong counter-transference response to her client. This indicated the need for further exploration of the connection between the client's disability and vulnerability in relation to the paternal figure on the interviewing panel. The therapist also considered the possibility that her own guilt and avoidance of certain aspects of the counter-transference could have been a response to an underlying message from the client that she had gone far enough for the moment.
> In subsequent months what emerged in the therapy was that the client had indeed been attacked physically on several occasions by her father when he could not tolerate her slowness caused, in part, by her physical disability. In untangling the complex web of the counter-transference, the therapist was able to sustain the tension

in the therapy relationship until the client could talk about these events with some of the attendant emotions they had evoked. The client felt understood and was able to share a series of painful associations.

Here we have seen the importance of the responses to disability being seen as something to be examined in themselves and not reduced to more familiar and perhaps earlier material until exploration has taken place.

## Conclusions

The therapy relationship is at the heart of the therapeutic process. To understand it from a feminist perspective we must look at what happens between client and psychotherapist, acknowledging the ways in which gender and other socio-cultural dimensions are rooted deeply in the unconscious. This can only be fully understood by linking the development of the concepts of transference and counter-transference with other theoretical and clinical developments within psychoanalytic thought and practice.

### Note

1. From this point on I refer to the 'psychotherapist' and her 'client' as this is the terminology used at the Women's Therapy Centre, except when I refer to sources which are specifically about psychoanalysis when I use the terms 'analyst' and 'analysand'. Much of what I say has been learned from and is relevant to psychoanalysis, group analysis and psychodynamic counselling.

### References

Bollas, C. (1987) *The Shadow of the Object*, Free Association Books, London.
Brenman Pick, I. (1988) 'Working through in the counter-transference', in E. B. Spillius (ed.), *Melanie Klein Today*, vol. 2, Routledge, London.
Ernst, S. (1987) 'Can a daughter be a woman?' in S. Ernst & M. Maguire (eds), *Living with the Sphinx*, Women's Press, London.
Freud, S. (1912) 'The dynamics of transference' *Standard Edition*, 12:97–108.
—— (1925) 'An autobiographical study', *Standard Edition*, 20:1–74.
Heimann, P. (1950) 'On counter-transference', *International Journal of Psycho-Analysis*, 31:81–4.

Hopper, E. (1985) 'The problem of context', in M. Pines (ed.), *Bion and Group Psychotherapy*, Routledge, London.

Joseph, B. (1988) 'Transference: the total situation' in Spillius, op. cit.

Lester, E. P. (1990) 'Gender and identity issues in the analytic process', *International Journal of Psycho-Analysis*, 71:435–44.

Maguire, M. (1995) *Men, Women, Passion and Power*, Routledge, London.

O'Connor, N. & Ryan, J. (1993) *Wild Desires and Mistaken Identities*, Virago, London.

Orbach, S. & Eichenbaum, L. (1993) 'Feminine subjectivity, counter-transference and the mother–daughter relationship', in J. van Mens-Verhulst, K. Schreurs & L. Woertman (eds), *Daughtering and Mothering*, Routledge, London.

Pines, D. (1993) *A Woman's Unconscious Use of Her Body*, Virago, London.

Racker, H. (1968) *Transference and Counter-Transference*, Hogarth, London.

Rosenfeld, H. (1987) *Impasse and Interpretation*, Tavistock, London.

Samuels, A. (1993) *The Political Psyche*, Routledge, London.

Sandler, J., Dare, C. & Holder, A. (1992) *The Patient and the Analyst* (revised by J. Sandler and A. U. Dreher), Karnac, London.

Schachtel, Z. (1986) 'The "impossible profession" considered from a gendered perspective', in J. A. Alpert (ed.), *Psychoanalysis and Women*, Analytic Press, New York.

Segal, H. (1964) *Introduction to the Work of Melanie Klein*, Heinemann, London.

Spillius, E. B. (1988) *Melanie Klein Today*, vol. 2, Routledge, London.

Winnicott, D. W. (1986) 'The use of an object and relating through identifications' in *Playing and Reality*, Penguin, Harmondsworth.

# Chapter 2

# Women's development in the family

## Susie Orbach

This chapter looks at the way that cultural forces create particular structures in the individual family which then incline the psychological development of its daughters in specific ways.

First I look at the significance of culture for the way in which the individual is raised in the family. I then turn to the intrapsychic processes through which the individual makes psychological sense of aspects of their familial experience. The central importance of gender is discussed and the primary role of mothers (or female maternal substitutes) as gendered beings in the development of a girl's psychological and physical sense of self.[1]

### The social picture

The period since 1970 has been characterised by enormous turmoil and change for Western women. The Women's Liberation Movement has affected the lives of all women whether they have consciously identified with it, actively rejected it or felt that it had nothing to do with them. Women from all class backgrounds and cultural groups have observed that the public sphere has opened up ever so slightly for them: the mass media has begun to depict women in roles and situations unimaginable in 1970; there is a new public rhetoric of equality for women, while educational policy now purports to embody anti-sexist directives. Popular women's magazines aimed at women in different classes and age groups encourage women to get out there and go after what they want; corporations run assertiveness training courses. Thus young women and older women are able to think about the world and their place in it in slightly less limited categories than their mothers.

But what is apparent to me, both as a woman and as a psychotherapist, is that the new expectations women may hold are not unproblematic. Women have been brought up to feel a certain way about who and what they are, what is and is not possible, and thus they find themselves unable to take up some of these new opportunities or ways of seeing themselves without conflict, guilt and stress.

At the same time as some of the new expectations cause certain kinds of difficulties, it is apparent that socialisation to the old ways of being didn't work either: one in seven women are hospitalised as psychiatric patients during their lives; women are the major users of psychotropic drugs; smoking is still on the increase among women; alcohol misuse is on the rise among women; eating problems are so widespread among women that they can be considered endemic. In other words, something is not right in women's psychological or mental well-being. The political, economic and social reasons for this are no less complex than the psychological ones.

To better understand how women see themselves psychologically in relation to these changes and how they may or may not cope with them, we need to understand the various psychological processes that prepare women to live in the world.

## Cultural pressures and the baby

My starting assumption is that the baby enters a world with the capacity to share in it and contribute to it, with a capacity to affect and be affected by those around it. The infant is perhaps best understood as a *set of possibilities*. A baby girl raised in France to French parents will speak French, develop characteristics we associate with the French, and have body movements we recognise as French. The same baby girl raised by English parents (in an adopted scenario, say) will walk, talk and gesture like an English girl; she will develop mechanisms like the rest of her contemporaries which will engage her energy towards common goals.

Despite the obvious nature of these facts, we are used to thinking of human nature as fixed. Even if we reject crude genetic arguments about personality and desire, or Freudian notions of libido driving us, we carry around a sense of ourselves as being unique and, when pressed, we have few ways to articulate how we understand that uniqueness to have come about. We often discount our interaction with culture, the culture of the individual family, of the extended family, of our class, of our racial or ethnic background, the educational culture we experienced, as having had a part in making us the unique individuals that we are. But these enormously important contexts influence and shape us in profound and deeply idiosyncratic ways.

In saying this I do not wish to give the impression that the baby enters the world as a blank page on which anything can be written. But I want to stress that much of who we become, much of our emotional life, is shaped by the complex of influences that we engage with from very early on.

## The baby and her carer

In the last several decades psychoanalysis has made us aware of the critical nature of early relationships in general, and of the mother–child relationship in particular. However, it has abstracted those relationships, making the parental or care-giving figures into objects – objects who might fail or succeed in meeting children's needs. The subjectivity of the care-giver, her social circumstances, her psychology, is rarely in view.

In a gender–conscious psychoanalytic perspective we have to include, in the early experiences of babies, the experiences of those who parent. This means that we will recognise that the way they parent, their capacities and their emotional availability, will embody in some distinctive way their own social and psychological circumstances. A second-generation Black child whose grandparents grew up in the West Indies will be entering a culture that is both overtly and subtly racist. This racism will have deeply affected its parents' lives and will find some expression in how the child is parented. The child will be affected by how the parents try to prepare and protect it from the effects of racism. Similarly, a parent who is disabled or has a disabled baby knows that her child will face actual discrimination because of our culture's disregard for disabled people.

The parental introjection that the developing person takes inside herself will include the parent's experience of self.

This is important to have as a background when we are approaching the issue of psychological development. It is easy when talking about the internalisation of bad object relations, or the phenomenon of projective identification, or the concept of transference, to become enamoured by technical intricacies and lose sight of the social milieu in which these psychic possibilities and outcomes develop in each of us, and in our clients.

So the baby girl comes into the world. As Freud, Mahler and Stern have variously described it, she leaves the physical womb and continues to be cocooned with her mother, sucking, sleeping, excreting, gurgling as and when she feels like it. She is apparently receptive to her local environment, but everything in it has to be organised in such a way that she can digest it. She can't yet distinguish colour or know when she is eating, whether she has a mouth or a breast, whether or not she provides the food that nourishes her. These concepts are as yet foreign and incomprehensible to her. She is the recipient of care, and she relies on others for that care. Indeed, it is so much the job of her caretakers to introduce her directly to the world that certain capacities, what I have earlier called possibilities, will only develop if they are attended to. Capacities that we think of as being natural are possibilities that can take form only if they are organised and developed within the context of a relationship with another or others.

For example, a baby who grows up without language will not learn to speak. A sighted baby raised by blind parents has to be taught by people other than its parents to organise the shapes, gradations of colours and depths of field she perceives into comprehensible categories in order to see in a conventional way. A baby who is fed, bathed and changed but is not the recipient of human touch and holding may not thrive. Everything we think of as human has to be introduced to the baby in such a way that she can use it; otherwise she does not develop in a way that we recognise as human. Wild children, those who have raised themselves as in the famous 18th century case of Victor, the wild child of Avegnon, fail to develop characteristics that we associate with human beings. The way we become human is by apprehending human skills, characteristics and values in the context of human relationships. As Winnicott said, there is no such thing as a baby, there is only a mothering pair. Whenever you see a baby, you see a relationship.

## The internal world of the baby

Psychoanalysts call the emotional world that the baby enters into and constructs, the world of object relations. This is to distinguish between the people who are in the baby's actual world and the psychic internal sense she can make of these relationships. The people in the baby's world relate to the baby in one way, as carers, as parents. But the baby doesn't necessarily absorb their presence as whole people: it selects what it can use. For the baby, the parents or carers are sometimes experienced as whole people and sometimes as parts – a soothing hand, a warm breast, a pinch, a loud voice, a big smile, and so on. If we put ourselves in the baby's place we can see how small our field of vision becomes: we see a hand blurry in front of us, a coloured something or other making a noise; we receive stimuli we don't necessarily know what to do with, and we fade in and out of our world of sleep. Gradually we perceive a pattern to these sensations and objects. We begin to make a picture of ourselves in this field. We become accustomed to our mother's voice, to her hands, her smell, her feel, and to the way we are handled. We feel discomfort and comfort and we associate it with what she is or isn't doing. She comes and she goes, she tends to us sometimes but not at other times. We get used to the feel and rhythm of her caring presence. Perhaps as a baby we begin to develop an awareness that we cannot control her or how we feel. She decides to change us, to feed us. She decides to listen to our cues or to disregard them.

As the baby internalises the good and responsive caring, it grows and flourishes. Care of a kind that can be metabolised becomes the food for psychological growth and development. Its development is both physical and psychological. The baby learns to recognise repeated physical sensations and stimuli that it initiates or receives. It develops psychologically with a knowledge of itself existing in a mental sense and a physical sense. In other words, a psyche-somatic unity is being knitted together in the sense that physical experiences have a psychological component and psychological experiences have a physical component.

As the baby develops and grows, it takes in aspects of maternal care (for it is maternal care which most of us experience) through what can best be described as a psychological umbilical cord connecting the baby to its carer. It surrounds the baby in a womb-like fashion until the baby develops sufficient motor and cognitive capacities to distinguish itself from its carer. It begins to know that a certain feeling is hunger and that it is satisfied by something outside of itself – mummy's breast, a bottle or a banana. It distinguishes between being wet or dry, hot or cold. As Winnicott put it, the baby builds up a sense of itself as a person through repeated experiences which create continuity and give it a sense of being held emotionally and physically. This knowledge translates into the baby's experience that, if it cannot be attended to the moment it is in need, it can carry a memory of the details of maternal care and soothe itself in that way.

As the baby develops language and motor skills, the capacity to show what it wants and resist what it doesn't, it proceeds towards a phase many psychotherapists have seen as crucial: the phase of separation–individuation which occurs between 18 months and two years. This is a time when the toddler begins to have a sense of its physical powers, when the me/not me is becoming more distinct. It can survive when mother or any of its major caretakers leave the room. It is beginning to have a sense of selfhood, to know itself as a person with a physical beginning and end and an emotional life of its own. As it develops, it has to cope with the discomfort that it is bound to feel. How does the developing person manage disappointment while still very dependent on another?

## Psychic structures and object relationships: the work of Fairbairn

As the Scottish analyst Fairbairn (1952) understood it, one process is involved with trying to understand the whys of the perceived neglect: i.e. why did mummy not make me comfortable then; why is everything so difficult now? Of course it isn't articulated in this way by the infant, but Fairbairn speculated that a version of this kind of attempt to question and reason is occurring inside the infant's embryonic mental apparatus. With this can come a great need to protect the still much-needed care-giver. A kind of idealisation ensues in which the baby attempts to relieve the pain of helplessness by 'blaming' itself for instances of parental neglect or mismanagement. In other words, the primary care-giver is maintained as a potential giver and the disappointment is explained, forgiven or excused by the *baby itself* taking on the responsibility for the failure to receive. The baby's internal response is: 'I'm not good enough, my needs are destructive, my love and dependency is too much.'

A second process can involve repudiating the need for the care. The care that is desperately required is now negated. The baby's response is: 'I will care for myself, I do not need you.' There follows a withdrawal of what Fairbairn calls libidinal energy from the primary care-giver, and the creation inside the infant of two images of the mother who now becomes an object which is more in the child's control. One image contains a bad, mean, withholding, disappointing and frustrating mother. The other is a soothing imago containing a nourishing, all-present, ever-understanding mother. The mother is loved and idealised on the one hand and hated on the other. The powerful emotions that the baby experiences are now held within its internal world, inside the world it has fashioned, a world of object relations. This world is a retreat from the unsatisfactory aspects of actual relationships.

The satisfying experiences of maternal or parental care contribute then to the baby's growth. The unsatisfactory experiences of care can create what Fairbairn calls a schizoid split in the personality. They can propel the baby away from people into an inner world of objects that seem more controllable, and in that internal world the baby has some power and personal agency. In the most common development, it can explain its mother or care-giver's neglect by reference to *its own actions* – it is too much, too needy, too difficult. It moves out of the position of one who is a passive recipient of care and into the position of *being active* in relation to its care.

This embryonic psychic structuralisation becomes reinforced in the passage through to adulthood where, as we can see from the following example, it shapes one's internal experience in complex ways.

Jennifer is unhappily married to Bob. They have been together for 12 years and have three children who are ten, eight and four. Jennifer wants to leave Bob but she feels too insecure to do so, psychologically and financially. She is emotionally and economically dependent on Bob and hates herself for being so. She wishes she could stand on her own two feet and has enormous contempt and self-disgust for her continuing reliance on him. Although the ways in which Bob lets her down, thus fuelling her rage, follow a pattern and are therefore reasonably predictable, she hasn't come to terms with the fact of his being disappointing. She hasn't accepted who he is or the way he is. In between the instances of his disappointing her, she unconsciously resurrects him in her mind. He becomes the knight on the white horse who is not Bob but some idealised version of him, a white knight who can do no wrong, who will understand her, love her, please her and so on. Hence when he acts like himself, that is like old, ordinary, disappointing Bob, she is devastated. She hates him for falling off the pedestal that she has, without even realising it, set him on. She alternates between dislike of him for not being the white knight, and dislike of herself because she thinks that if only she were a good, less demanding wife he would give her what she wanted. In her internal world, the disappointing bits of Bob have been both idealised and degraded. The part of her that unconsciously idealises him blames herself for her failure. The part of her that hates him is humiliated by her attachment to him and tries to repudiate her need of him altogether.

Jennifer's mother, who raised her single-handedly, was a rather cold and unavailable woman. Although Jennifer dislikes aspects of her mother and feels deeply hurt by her, she would nevertheless describe her as a good person who looked after her thoughtfully and intelligently. From Jennifer's conscious point of view, the shortcomings of her childhood were circumstantial due to her mother raising her alone.

Inside Jennifer's internal and unconscious world, another reality, equally compelling, is at work. On the one hand she idealises her mother and desperately wants her to be warmer and closer. She craves from her what she was unable to give when Jennifer was little. When her mother comes to visit, Jennifer is full of anticipation that this time it will be different, this time they will understand each other, this time she will get what she needs. And yet, on each visit she is left feeling cold and empty. Her desires go unmet and her longing turns inwards as depression and rage.

Bob's ways of disappointing her are not the same as the mother's ways, but she experiences them similarly. The psychic energy first invested in her mother and then withdrawn into the world of object relations has been reinvested in Bob. When he disappoints her, she has the psychic apparatus in place to cope with it. She can't leave Bob because she feels his lack of giving to her to be her fault, just as she couldn't really reject those aspects of her mother that caused her such grief as a baby when she was entirely dependent upon her mother for care.

I shall return to the adult consequences of object relations shortly. What I want to convey by this example is the intricacy of the internal world that is operating for Jennifer, and with it, the sense of how a psychotherapist understands how the baby can internalise good and bad experiences with its primary carers. To recapitulate – satisfactory ones just get digested and are the building blocks of something we might call a core self; bad ones, being indigestible, are split off. They are then transformed in the unconscious in two distinct ways, either as an idealised relationship or as a hated relationship. In the most common constructed object relationship, the infant imagines itself as the primary motivator and cause of its own misfortune. This formation persists into the child and later the adult mind and, in time, the reinforcing of this construction means that certain feelings, emotional possibilities and relational configurations become rigidified, with some emotions impermissible and repressed.

## Winnicott's view of the baby and mother

The reason for the internal world becoming so complex so early on is connected with the infant's continuing need of the care-giver. Winnicott (1965) has a slightly different formulation of the internal world. Like Fairbairn, whose schema of schizoid phenomena and repressed bad object relations I have just described, Winnicott sees the infant as helpless and dependent on its mother for care, nurture, containment and the emotional attention required for psychological growth. His understanding of what the baby does when it fails to get the adequate care which he calls 'good enough mothering', is that it adapts itself to what it imagines its mother wants of it. It develops a 'false self' that accommodates to others in the attempt to get what it needs. Meanwhile the baby's embryonic 'true self' goes underground, eventually becoming unreachable. The baby is a mixture of fragility and resilience. It protects itself by searching for some kind of contact, even if it is only inauthentic relating that is available. So, for example, if a baby senses that appearing contented pleases its care-giver and that this gets reflected back, then it may be inclined to bury its distress. It may try to soothe itself by giving to its care-giver, by showing signs of rapid recovery when upset, or detaching itself from distress by adopting a stance of contentment.

## The baby has agency

The baby, then, is not a *tabula rasa* onto which we imprint or condition a set of responses. Rather, as Fairbairn's and Winnicott's formulations suggest, it has an ability to adapt. It has the psychological capacity to formulate in personal ways its experience of the world from the perspective of its own centrality to it. It is not just an experiencing person, but conceptualises its experiences, and from those conscious and unconscious conceptualisations it formulates and contributes to the structure of those actual relationships in which it is engaged, as well as the object relationships that it configures internally. This is an expression of its personal agency.

In addition, of course, each baby born has an enormous impact on its environment. It brings pleasure, pain or anguish to its parents. It may have been longed for or dreaded; its birth may have upset its older sibling. In those who come to meet it, it may engender love and the desire to care, or anxiety and fear. How it responds to its feed, whether or not it settles easily, whether its birth has brought a feeling of calm or panic into the home – in all these ways its presence affects those who interact with it very directly.

## Gender and subjectivity

When a baby arrives the first question on everyone's lips is 'Is it a boy or a girl?' Depending on its sex, a whole set of social interactions and constructions will follow. Gender is a key factor determining aspects of how, from birth onwards, a baby is handled, held, fed, bathed, clothed, cooed to, described, identified with and responded to. From the very first, the baby's agency is expressed in a gendered environment.

We use different words to soothe a baby girl or baby boy, we may have a different tone of voice, we have different expectations of them and we describe their activities differently in relation to their gender. A boy is a robust eater, a girl greedy. A girl who is energetic may be called a terror, while a boy is described as active. There are differences in basic aspects of care too. Boys are generally breastfed for longer at each feed and for a longer period than girls, held for longer, weaned more gradually and potty trained later.

A child begins to know itself as a subject, a distinct person who relates to other subjects, from about a year and a half. The toddler's apprehension of its gender coincides in time with its emergent identity during this phase of separation–individuation. In other words, at the same time as the toddler is realising its separateness from others and its own boundaries and capabilities, it is also knowing itself as a little girl or a little boy. Gender expresses the physical and psychological knowledge we have of ourselves as subjects in a world fundamentally divided by gender. Our entry into the female or male gender forms how we think, feel, dress, move and act. Indeed recent feminist scholarship has shed light on the fact that the modes of thought, reasoning and moral values that men and women hold are profoundly different (Gilligan, 1982; Tannen, 1990). All these characteristics are not stuck onto people but are woven into the very fabric of the creation of the person. They are established very early on in the first arena of the child's experience, in the mother–child relationship, and reinforced in the wider worlds the child enters.

## Mothering is gendered

Mothers mother. Despite the changes that are occurring in which joint parenting, lesbian parenting, single parenting, shared custody between separated parents, and so on, have made the nuclear family in which mother rears the children at home and father goes out to work a minority position, for us and our clients the norm was that mothers did the major parenting and fathers were important but peripheral figures to the hourly responsibility of bringing up children.

Since a mother or a female substitute (grandmother, nanny, aunty, childminder) has generally been the main presence in a child's early life, it means that a father's active or direct relationship to a daughter may well be filtered through the mother–daughter relationship. Father may not be an active person in the daughter's life until she has long passed out of babyhood and early childhood and is able to engage with him when he comes home at night. Up until that point, his relative absence from the ambience of early childhood may mean that who he is will have been as much conveyed to the child by her main adult companion as gleaned through direct experience. This isn't to say that a father isn't important in the formation of a daughter's psychology, but his significance is complicated by many factors: his absence or presence in the family environment, the mother's attitude towards his fathering and what she conveys to her daughter, his active pursuit of his daughter, and of course his conception of what constitutes fathering.

Psychoanalytic theory is usually told from the child's point of view. But this abstracted perspective excludes the view of the mother who mothers and of the other significant figures in the child's life. While Winnicott's work attempts to bring in the centrality of the mother and her psychology for the developing baby via his notion of the 'good enough mother', this notion is nevertheless problematic. The notion of the 'good enough mother' takes as its starting point a social milieu and psychological criteria for mothers that fail to reflect women's actual position and experience of mothering.

Winnicott's view was that a woman comes to mothering with a distinct and secure subjectivity. While the mother nurtures the baby and attends to its physical and psychological needs, stepping into the baby's skin to know what it is experiencing and requiring, stepping out again to provide it, the mother is simultaneously supported by a husband who, particularly in the first few months of the baby's life, takes care of the mother and tends to the outside environment.

This description dominates psychoanalytic thinking, yet it is a misrepresentation of the mothering position, of the mother's actual experience, and it misperceives many a mother's psychology. Few mothers are actively emotionally supported in their mothering. The labour that is part of the process of the creation of a social and psychological being is unacknowledged or hidden. The assumed subjectivity of the woman is often shaky. The confluence between the baby's needs and the mothers needs is an idealisation. To be able to give herself over to the baby, as Winnicott suggests women do, presupposes that the mother has an unproblematic, intact, highly developed and secure self to return to. Adult women rarely feel so confident in this transition. More commonly women feel insecure in themselves and lack a secure sense of self. Thus the wish for merger with the baby and the wish for a discrete subjectivity compete inside the woman. Women come to mothering with their own frequently unmet personal needs. They are not simply the baby's object, they are women struggling for human contact and subjectivity themselves. Becoming a mother doesn't stop the process towards subjectivity or the desire for it, although the requirements of mothering may impede the mother's struggle to individuate.

As to Winnicott's picture of the mother being supported in turn by the father, he is entangled in social arrangements in which women have traditionally provided nurturing skills while men have provided economic protection. It is a rare adult woman who is the recipient of the kind of emotional nurture that she provides for others. Indeed, for many women, the need to be available to their children and to care for their husbands leaves them emotionally unsupported and drained. The satisfying aspects of mothering may nourish them, but this has to be set alongside the tasks and burdens of unsupported mothering.

By and large, women have been brought up to see the emotional and physical tasks of mothering as a part of their role. Other aspects of their own self-development have been held at bay. Little girls learn to care for others through direct instruction but also through identification with the mothering person, through gaining approval for certain kinds of initiatives. In turn, women come to derive a certain amount of self-esteem from their capacity to handle their children's needs and those of others close to them. For many, there may be a conflation of personal needs and external needs. The social requirement, that a woman should see herself as a midwife to the activities of others, is in conflict with the development of her own subjectivity. Inevitably, then, women try to find a subjectivity, a sense of self, through their mothering. Not having had a secure subjectivity, they may not be able to see their children as potentially separate subjects in the world, but rather as reflections, extensions and attachments of themselves. They are in a cleft stick because mothering is the place in which women have been allowed to be subjects; but being a social subject in a circumscribed field is not the same as being a psychological subject. A woman's struggle to achieve psychological subjectivity may be stopped in its tracks or constrained by the overwhelming demands of giving to others what she still so badly needs for herself.

## The mother–daughter relationship

It is in this context then that a woman mothers. A mother plays many different parts in a daughter's life, from being the emotional base to being a role model (to be followed or rejected) to being her primary socialiser, teacher and guide, and her main, most important childhood relationship. The mother–daughter relationship which encompasses these many different aspects is shaped by the world that mothers live in and that daughters must enter. And the mother's psychology and life was shaped in the same way by *her* mother. In this social world, the two key features of women's psychology are that women should *not* be emotionally dependent but should instead provide a dependent relationship that *others* may rely on; and they should not initiate as people with their own autonomous needs but should act instead as midwives to the aspirations of others (Orbach, 1978; Eichenbaum & Orbach, 1983).

At the same time, the mother enabling her daughter to fit into the world directs her daughter towards gender-appropriate activities and towards a heterosexual orientation. By direct instruction, analogy or games, mothers and daughters engage in play which mimics the sexual arrangements of the adult world. Sometimes the mother is required to be the daughter, the father, the brother or the big sister. This kind of play is an attempt on the part of the child to fit herself into, as well as simultaneously expand, the definitions of gender and position in the family that she feels herself to be a fixed part of. The play turns frequently to marriage and through this the mother is introducing her daughter to the gender and sexual arrangements that are expected.

Within the mother–daughter relationship, the mother may unknowingly exercise restraint about meeting the emotional needs of her daughter. At the same time she may thwart her daughter's initiatives, supporting instead aspects of her behaviour that conform to appropriate notions of 'feminine' activity. This is not to suggest that mothers are consciously withholding, nor that mothers are aware of being part of a dynamic of depriving. Mothers' motivation may include the wish to give their daughters the nurture and recognition that they did not and do not receive themselves. And of course they do. But this desire, and the actions that flow from it, are in themselves mangled by the unconscious identification of the mother towards a baby girl. The baby girl stirs in the mother a multitude of identifications. She may represent to the mother her own needy and unmet parts as well as her own experience of curbing her needs and desires. When her daughter expresses wanting, she may find herself wishing to silence her without understanding where this impulse has come from. She can be alarmed if her daughter's needs seem copious. Unconsciously she expects her to contain them as she has stilled her own. This aspect of the mother–daughter relationship is especially painful. It creates an inconsistency within the relationship and as a result there is what can be characterised as a push–pull dynamic in the relationship (Orbach, 1978; Eichenbaum & Orbach, 1982). Sometimes the daughter's needs are responded to and sometimes not.

Because the daughter's initiatives are inconsistently responded to, the sense of self she internalises is imbued with a hesitation and wariness against the acknowledgement of needs and desires that arise within her or are stimulated within a relationship. She feels unsure of herself.

## The mother–daughter physical relationship

The emotional exchanges between mothers and daughters are reflected in aspects of the physical relationship. We have noted earlier how, in some of the most basic details of early life, baby girls and baby boys receive different treatment and handling around feeding and other matters of physical management. The girl acquires her sense of physicality in the mother–daughter relationship in three distinct ways: via the mother's feelings towards her own body, via the mother's experience of the daughter's body and via the actual physical exchanges between the two. If the mother experiences the discomfort so endemic in Western female experience of the body, then a version of this will be introjected by the daughter. If the mother feels confident and at ease with her physicality, this will likewise be imbibed by the daughter. The entwining of a mother's perceptions of her own body with those of her daughter's body may preclude her from seeing the daughter's body as different and distinctive. She may, without awareness, convey her own distaste and discomfort about her body to her daughter. The daughter will absorb these feelings and they will become part of her somatic formation. Jus. as a baby introjects the emotional ambience of its mother and care-giver, so she introjects the physical ambience of her mother – her mother's feelings about her body and her own body and her actual physical experience of her mother's body (Orbach, 1978, 1986).

If we reflect once again on the importance of physical relating in the earliest months of a girl's life, we will be able to see how the literal body of the mother is at times available and giving and at times uncontrollable. The elusivity and unpredictability of the mother's body is part of what is absorbed into the daughter's body in her making of her psyche-somatic self (Orbach, 1986, 1994). Sometimes the maternal body is perceived of in positive ways, at other times it is experienced as a disappointment and is internalised in similar ways to the emotionally unsatisfactory aspects of the relationship. Then, the daughter's body can feel like it is partly a bad object.

It is in regards to a daughter's body that a father's active and direct presence can often be felt. For the father's relationship to his body is not usually as problematic as a mother's to her own or her daughter's. In early childhood, a father's physical relating to a child, with the characteristic throwing of his child up in the air, carrying her on his shoulders or providing a still lap to sit on when he comes home from work, gives the girl a very different experience of her body. While in early babyhood we are inclined to think of the mother's lap as a base of security, in childhood the stillness may be sought and found in father's lap, for mother may be so busy doing household tasks that the kind of calmness which creates a sense of surety and solidity may be less available to the daughter from the mother at this point.

This physical relationship with the father, both the active and still aspects of it, contributes to a different sense of physicality for the daughter. It can be very enjoyable and a key to understanding some of what women later crave when they look to men for acceptance of their physical attractiveness.

The separate but related issue of how physiological and sexual appetites are addressed and therefore internalised by girls brings us back to other important cultural forces that are entwined in a mother's attitudes towards a daughter's body. No mother today, no parent, is unaware of the violence, and particularly sexualised violence, that is directed at girls and women. The incidence of sexual abuse of children disproportionately affects girls. The main form of sexual abuse is perpetrated by men on girls and the occurrence of rape and domestic violence are factors affecting female experience, and women's experience of their bodies and their daughter's bodies, in ways that are often overlooked. Our awareness of these phenomena is now growing. While women may still often repress their knowledge of the specific violence directed at females, they nevertheless carry a sense of possible danger for their daughters.

At the same moment as a mother transmits a joy about her daughter's body and persona, she is also aware that her daughter is potentially vulnerable, that her loveliness may be exploited rather than enjoyed, if not now then at some point later on in her life. This message – the protectiveness, the fear and the joy – is conveyed to her daughter at some level. And her daughter absorbs a version of the message. She has to make sense of these colliding ideas in the formation of her physical persona.

Of course a father's relationship to his daughter's body is no less complex. While he may be available in early childhood, he may feel confused and perplexed by an adolescent daughter's developing body and may, without wishing to or realising it, withdraw or curtail his physical relationship with her. These combined experiences reinforce and reflect the insecurity in relation to the critical area of body/physical awareness, undermining the possibility that a daughter can develop a secure body image.

## Conclusion

As a result of the emotional and physical relationships that baby girls enter into, they can develop into women who come to feel hesitant about their needs, and indeed their very selves. In the search for validation, a woman knows to look outwards, turning much of her attention outside herself, both to attend to the needs of others and to achieve the approval of others by mirroring their projections. Many women grow up with a sense of never having received quite enough and often feel insatiable and unfulfilled. In not being encouraged to develop her initiating part, and draw a sense of authenticity and strength from that, the girl, later the woman, is victimised by a constant need for affirmation from external sources. Sadly, such legitimation is only temporarily soothing. For if one has been discouraged from pursuing one's authentic wishes, one has little experience of feelings of genuine satisfaction and contentment.

The inconsistency in the mother–daughter relationship does not stop a daughter's desire for this relationship to be one in which she can articulate her needs. Indeed, the longing for mother stays with us. Mother becomes embedded in our psychologies as potentially 'all-providing' or 'all-withholding'. This split experience of the mother may become repressed but it is one carried by all Western women who are mother-reared (Dinnerstein, 1976). The wish to merge with the 'all-providing' mother juggles with the experience of betrayal at the hands of the 'all-withholding' one. This imago of mother in turn becomes projected onto women in general, and in becoming women we experience that split in ourselves.

The masculine presence, representing as it does a clear gender difference (as well as frequently a different way of life), provides the simplest form of disidentification from and access away from a girl's internal difficulties. Many daughter's relationships with their fathers contain the attempt to distance themselves from the internal image created in the female ambience by recreating themselves anew or finding aspects of themselves that are regarded differently. This is a feature of heterosexual development, where the attachment to a masculine figure contains within it not only the woman's early internalised attachment to her mother, but her attempts at separation from her and towards attachment to another whose gender difference represents his alterity to this relational configuration.

A daughter's psychology, then, is born within a mother–daughter relationship situated in a particular family, in a distinct culture and in historical time. The features that mark femininity are imbibed both directly and indirectly from the culture via all the relationships that impinge upon, affect or embrace the developing person. At present in the West, it continues to be mothers who mother. This imperative shapes a daughter's psychology in distinctive ways, providing her with, on the one hand, highly developed relational skills and, on the other, difficulties in self-actualisation. It is a picture that is manifest in many of the clients we see in therapy.

**Note**

1.  The perspective I have taken is drawn from clinical practice where, for 23 years, with colleagues I have attempted to theorise the unconscious and conscious experiences and utterances of the adult women seen in therapy.

**Bibliography**

Belotti, E. G. (1975) *Little Girls*, Writers and Readers, London.
Benjamin, J. (1988) *Bonds of Love*, Pantheon, New York.
Bordo, S. (1993) *Unbearable Weight*, University of California Press, Berkeley CA.
Chodorow, N. (1978) *The Reproduction of Mothering*, University of California Press, Berkeley CA.
Davies, J. M. & Frawley, M. G. (1994) *Treating the Adult Survivor of Childhood Sexual Abuse: A Psychoanalytic Perspective*, Basic Books, New York.
Dinnerstein, D. (1976) *The Mermaid and the Minotaur*, Harper and Row, New York.

Eichenbaum, L. & Orbach S. (1982) *Understanding Women: A Psychoanalytic Approach*, Penguin, Harmondsworth.

—— (1983) *What Do Women Want? Exploding the Myth of Dependency*, Michael Joseph, London.

Fairbairn, R. W. (1952) *Psychoanalytic Studies of the Personality*, RKP, London.

Gilligan, C. (1982) *In a Different Voice*, Harvard University Press, Cambridge MA.

McDougall, J. (1989) *Theatres of the Body*, Free Association Books, London.

Mahler, M. (1968) *On Human Symbiosis and the Vicissitudes of Individuation*, vol. 1, International Universities Press, New York.

Mitchell, J. (1974) *Psychoanalysis and Feminism*, Pantheon, New York.

Mitchell, S. (1988) *Relational Concepts in Psychoanalysis*, Harvard University Press, Cambridge MA.

Orbach, S. (1978) *Fat is a Feminist Issue*, Paddington Press, London.

—— (1986) *Hunger Strike*, Faber & Faber, London.

—— (1994) 'Working with the false body', in A. Erskine & D. Judd *The Imaginative Body*, Colin Whurr, London.

Pines, D. (1993) *A Woman's Unconscious Use of Her Body*, Virago, London.

Stern, D. (1985) *The Interpersonal World of the Infant*, Basic Books, New York.

Tannen, D. (1990) *You Just Don't Understand*, Morrow Press, New York.

Winnicott, D. W. (1965) 'The true and false self', in *Maturational Processes and the Facilitating Environment*, Hogarth Press, London.

# Chapter 3

# Women's relationship with their bodies

*Patricia Land*

A large number of women are ill at ease with their bodies; many indeed could be said to be at war with them. The reasons for this strange state of affairs are as manifold and complex as the consequences.

We will begin with the context.

Women's bodies are where mythology, anthropology and sociology meet biology and psychology. An eminent psychoanalyst has commented: 'As a psychic construction, gender and sexual identity have both biological and acquired origins and are thus at the research crossroads of several scientific disciplines' (McDougall, 1989).

The amazing fact of a woman's capacity to bring forth live human beings from inside her, and to feed them from her own body, has much to do with the present difficulty and complexity of our relationship to our bodies in a misogynistic society. Before the facts of sexual generativity were understood, the phenomenon of birth must have seemed miraculous, even magical. Awe has space not only for worship, but also for terror; and it easily gives rise to its opposite, contempt and disgust: hence the complexity of ideas of 'taboo'. These primitive unconscious attitudes may still be observed in the varied cultural forms of misogyny.

Some interesting insights into this area of cultural history are to be found in three non-psychoanalytic sources: Friedrich Engels' *The Origin of the Family, Private Property and the State*, the 'dictionary of poetic myth' by the poet Robert Graves entitled *The White Goddess*, and the extended polemic-cum-prose poem by Susan Griffin, *Woman and Nature*.

Engels refers to envy of the enormous power and creativity attributed to women, and suggests that a gradual transformation of social life must have occurred as men awoke to the realisation that the emergence of children had something to do with the consequences of intercourse, hence that they could be seen as 'belonging' to the father.

Graves traces, through a close study of ancient myths from several cultures, the ways in which tales propagandising male power and generativity were superimposed on earlier stories that celebrated the female.

Griffin explores the frantic drive to control natural forces that is so prominent a feature of Western industrial society, and suggests that its origins may be sought in envious rivalry over primary creativity. The impulse to control demands, indeed creates, an ever-increasing supply of objects to be controlled, objects which are 'other' than the subject, and which must be permitted no life of their own.

Attitudes to fertility are central to every human culture, and make of women's bodies a potential battleground over control of this precious resource. Conversely, wherever control is a major cultural issue, women's sexuality becomes a primary site of conflict. This is true of fundamentalist cultures of all kinds, and of imperialist, colonialist and slave-owning societies. It is very obvious in wars, where rape and the sexual humiliation of women become a means of making men painfully aware of their own subjugation and power-lessness.

In the West, there is an apparently liberal attitude to women's self-expression. The unconscious urge to control emerges in the demand that attractiveness, for example, be of a particular, commercially acceptable kind. A more sinister aspect may be seen in the actual risks to women of acting upon their supposed independence, for instance in moving around outside the home late at night.

The theme of control is prominent in non-Western cultures as well, but it takes different forms. Where fertility is highly valued, for example, there are often very strict controls over the public life of women, with sanctions for openly sexual behaviour and an implicit or explicit demand that a woman should have no independent existence.

What it means to have a female body is perhaps the central issue of feminism.

Attitudes amongst feminists range from a stern dismissal of meaning or consequences, so that femaleness is seen as the mere accident of birth and femininity a set of behaviours that can be unlearned, to the idea that women are by nature inherently better than men. These struggles are concerned with consequences. If we accept that our biology affects our deepest feelings about our lives, are we accepting that biology is in fact destiny? Does recognising that, for example, hormonal changes may alter our states of mind on a regular basis entail deciding that certain professions or trades are forever closed to us?

There is still much dispute over whether and how far psychological differences are influenced by our biology. The women's movement has repeatedly drawn attention to the dangers of biological determinism. However, the fact remains that our biological endowment is different from a man's, and that this has been so from the moment of conception.

Certainly in most societies, to have a woman's body means to be at a practical disadvantage in the world. A little girl learns early, in all sorts of subtle and less subtle ways, that the role assigned to her in society is a derogated one; and this has an effect on how she views her developing female form. Indeed, several women analysts in the generation after Freud drew attention to this obvious consideration, in an attempt to clarify and modify the concept of 'penis envy'.

Much work in the new feminist movement of the 1970s centred on reclaiming our bodies from the self-hatred engendered by growing up in a woman-hating culture. However, the changes often were not permanent. The unconscious is slow to change, and reluctant it seems. So are societies.

The connection is not just a verbal one. It is fairly clear, and fairly easy to accept, that social processes, mediated particularly by the family, 'get inside' each of us and shape our ways of being in the world. Perhaps the reciprocal, indeed dialectical, nature of our relationship with society is less readily grasped. But unconscious splitting processes – projection, denial, disavowal – largely shape our social world and determine political realities, crucially affecting the way society impinges on each one of us.

Splitting, in psychoanalytic terms, is what happens in the psyche when ambivalence cannot be tolerated. Its healthy original use is in early infancy, when the newborn is bombarded with impressions and develops a primitive means of sorting them out into 'all good' and 'all bad'. We learn early on, in good enough circumstances, to recognise that most of these early impressions are mediated by a person who is neither all good nor all bad but a whole being. But we never entirely give up a propensity to split our view of the world, and of ourselves, and under sufficient stress it can emerge in any of us. Indeed, some people never fully develop a capacity to hold in their minds an idea of a wholeness that necessarily encompasses imperfection and ambivalence.

This would be merely a personal misfortune were it not for the effects that unconscious splitting sets up. For the unwanted aspects of the self and of one's experiences, uncontained within the self, have to be 'put' somewhere.

In the well-parented infant this is no problem. The split-off aspects are projected into the containing parent (whom I shall refer to as 'she', since this function is usually the mother's). She, unlike the panicky baby, is able to reflect on what is upsetting her child, and to convey understanding and a soothing sense that life goes on despite hunger, uncomfortable nappies or loud noises.

However, we have to grow up and manage our own anxieties as best we can. In good enough circumstances, we carry within us a sense of a part of ourselves, derived from our early experience of containment, that can guide and comfort us. But even if we have that good fortune, under sufficient stress we again feel the need for external containment. We may find it with a partner, or with our friends; we may need to seek it in therapy. As a rule, the smaller the container, and the more intimately responsive to our particular needs, the safer we feel. Perhaps that is why society as a container so often feels crazily inadequate. Not only is it too large a unit for our imaginations, but it is the receptacle for all the projections that are not contained elsewhere: hence for all that so often goes unacknowledged even between friends, and for the raw desperation of countless people who for various reasons have never experienced being understood and contained.

The feelings that need to be contained are frightening ones – helpless rage, terror, powerlessness, smallness, inadequacy – so when these are split off on a large scale and dumped in the social structure, society itself becomes split, and the unwanted feelings are projected, sometimes violently, into those designated as 'other'. Here we return to the disparagement or active subjugation of women, of children, and of those deemed outsiders of one kind or another.

It is significant that 'outsider' groups are, like women, often seen by the power-holders in a split society as secretly enviable, embodying disavowed lusts and a hated spontaneity.

Just as fertility is central to ideas about social organisation, it is fundamental to thinking about women and their bodies. In fact, the issue of fertility can be seen as central to the life of every woman: whatever her sexuality, and regardless of whether she wants to have children, the rhythms of her procreative cycle, and the likelihood that it will come to an end before her own death, structure her physical and psychic existence.

Estela Weldon draws our attention to two major considerations built into women's physiology – and by implication and analogy, into our psyches as well – which are the literal fact of an internal space, and the so-called 'biological clock' (Weldon, 1988).

At birth, a baby girl has already got all the ova she is ever going to produce, packed away inside her diminutive ovaries. There is some dispute over whether a girl infant can be said to have an unconscious awareness of an inner space. Some child analysts have found in clinical sessions evidence of an early unconscious knowledge of a vagina. Not being able to see outward signs of her sexual identity and viability, as a little boy can, may – in the context of sexism – have an effect on her self-image.

The psychologist Erik Erikson wrote in the 1960s about some observations he had made on 300 children at play with building blocks. He noticed that girls seemed consistently to make structures in which a space contained within a wall featured, whereas boys generally built for height. The events depicted in girls' play went on inside the space; boys emphasised activity outside and around their structures, and tended to invent exciting and explosive adventures far more than girls did. Clearly, these observations are consistent with the early effects of gender conditioning, as well as with an unconscious awareness of internal space. However, it would be foolish to ignore physical reality.

To speak of our bodies as though they were separate from ourselves is problematic in itself, perhaps already evidence of a culture-bound sensibility. Freud stated that the original ego is a body ego, drawing our attention to the fact that, for the infant, there can be no distinction. The Boston Women's Health Collective put the same point more succinctly still in the title of their book, *Our Bodies, Ourselves.*

Philosophers as well as psychoanalysts and neurologists continue the ancient struggle to elucidate the nature of consciousness, and in what senses mind and body are a unit or can usefully be conceptualised as separate.

Common experience is that mind/body, psyche/soma are at the very least intimately connected, and that attempts by the psyche to ignore or bully the soma lead recognisably to trouble. Equally, to demand unconsciously of the body that it express the unthinkable pain of the mind is a recipe for confusion and despair. Women are particularly vulnerable to difficulties that involve using their bodies as a means of expressing whatever seems unspeakable. To explore this further, we need to go back to the beginning again, to the infant girl and her mother.

Nini Herman (1989) has written most movingly about the profound meaning of a woman giving birth to a woman. Like the writers I mentioned previously, she places this meaning within a cultural and historical context. For many centuries, there must have been small need for any notion that the two were different people. The daughter was a kind of continuation of her mother, embodying her fertility and expecting the same future. In times of change, of course, it is vital for the mental health of both that a potential for difference is acknowledged early on; but this recognition is harder for the mothers of girls. When the baby is a boy, his obvious physical difference at once implies separateness, despite the initial identification between mother and baby. For the mother of a little girl, the boundaries of the identification may prove hard to find and to hold on to. Hence for so many women there are the very great doubts about whether they are really separate beings, the fears of separateness, the confusions over boundaries and over the right to a life of one's own.

Being in a position, psychologically speaking, to identify with her mother has its advantages as well as its problems for the growing girl. To be of the sex that produces babies can be for the small child a source of pride and delight, and may compensate for observed differences in social esteem (These days, too, the roles of mother and father may be less clearly differentiated than of old, and mother may be seen to be as powerful in the external world as father.)

Further, at an age before words are readily available, to feel understood without them can feel consoling and, indeed, in the earliest months is vitally necessary. A little boy needs such understanding just as much as a little girl. They both also need a psychic space in which difference can be acknowledged, and a separate identity grown. It is harder on the whole for a mother to provide such space for her daughter. Each may make assumptions about their mutual comprehension. The danger for the small girl is twofold: that she will carry on unconsciously expecting such wordless communication in adult relationships, and that she will in fact be misunderstood by her primary object and develop a muddled sense of identity.

In so far as women's learned skill in being attuned to the feelings of others is seen as an advantage – and just as some women would like to repudiate it, others wish we could enable little boys to learn it too – girls have a head start in this area! Even during the primary school period, which corresponds roughly to the period known to psycho-analysis as latency, when much of the intensity of infantile sexual wishes has abated and children tend to turn their attention to interests in the outside world, groups of girls nearly always talk to one another much more than boys do, and show more interest in the lives and feelings of adults around them.

With the start of menstruation, many women have experienced a shock. It signals the end of the vaguely androgynous hopes of pre-puberty in which observed male and female roles were – at least in phantasy – a question of choice, and silly old mother had made the wrong one. It is the start of 'being a woman'. I am thinking in particular of the kind of little girl that used to be called a 'tomboy', who likes running and climbing and fighting, and is probably in unconscious identification with a traditionalist father in her contempt for the too readily put-upon mother. Even nowadays, for most girls menarche puts an end to dreams of adventure at sea or as an explorer, of a career as a racing driver or an oil-rig firefighter.

It is important to note that the image of the mother in the unconscious is deeply ambivalent, Once the all-powerful provider, she is also the source of our earliest deprivations, hence the tendency of both sexes to turn away from her in infancy, and again at puberty, in a contempt exacerbated by growing awareness of her deprecated social status. For the boy, his penis is the signifier of his separate destiny. The girl has more of a struggle to assert her separateness; menarche indeed may imply a fateful sameness.

Menstruation is not a sudden event. There have been preparations within the body for months or even years previously. The hormonal changes that will eventually result in the uterus preparing for impregnation, then casting out the unused lining in a stream of blood, and the ovaries – often several years later – beginning their rhythmic alternate release of eggs ready for fertilisation, have already had visible effects. Fine hair grows around the genital area and under the arms, breasts are budding, suddenly sweat smells. Even so, the actual bleeding is often an unwelcome surprise, as though until that moment the reality had been warded off.

It should be emphasised that different attitudes to menarche exist between cultures, and also within cultures between families. A friend who comes from Guyana told me that in her village it was usual for families to throw a party to celebrate a girl's arrival at womanhood. Another friend, from Tobago, said that, when she was an adolescent, the word got around more quietly, probably via the older women, and young men from other villages would start arriving to have a look at the newly eligible woman.

It occurs to me that the old British upper-class institution of the coming-out ball fulfilled a similar function; by the end of their schooling, most girls could be relied upon to have started menstruating, and in that setting this crucial element of readiness to mate need never be mentioned directly.

Many women remember their first period as an experience of shame and self-disgust, something to be kept as secret as possible. Even today girls are not always told what to expect; or, if told, they sometimes deny their knowledge because of conflicts over growing up.

Menarche is a moment from which there is no going back. It signals that you may not remain as a child; you are becoming a woman, ready or not. In many girls it triggers a sense of loss – of childhood, and of the range of choices that belonged to androgyny. As with other bereavements, the happier and fuller the life of latency, the more readily it can be mourned and given up. The more conflicted the child, the more likely she is to become depressed at menarche.

The onset of menstruation is closely linked to feelings about separation between the daughter and her mother, for menarche both reaffirms their sameness and insists on a future for the daughter as distinct from her mother. She is now potentially a mother herself, which means envisaging a relationship to someone as yet unknown, with all the fears and wishes this entails for both the girl and her mother. Nini Herman (1989) sees this moment exemplified in the myth of Persephone.

In ancient Greek myth Persephone was the beloved daughter of the earth goddess Demeter, who had power over the fruitfulness of the earth. Persephone was one day picking spring flowers in the company of other young girls when she was attracted away from them towards a clump of flowers of rare beauty. They were growing near the entrance to the underworld, and as Persephone gazed at them she was captured and carried off by Hades, the god of the Underworld, who took her as his wife and queen. So enraged and desperate was Demeter at her daughter's disappearance that she ceased to attend to the needs of the earth, and wandered in rags across an increasingly bleak and loveless world. After half a year, Persephone was permitted to visit her mother, having eaten a seed of pomegranate proffered by her husband which ensured that she would always be bound to return to him. Thus began winter, when Demeter mourns Persephone; and summer, when she rejoices in her company.

Menarche for the daughter comes at a time in the mother's life when she is starting to be confronted with the end of her own fertile years, when she may already be slowing down and has probably noticed wrinkles. She may feel that she is losing the sexual attractiveness that gives her social validation. A touch of envy is not abnormal in this situation, but may be hard to acknowledge. Envy unacknowledged is corrosive and may cause the mother to be dismissive or cutting towards her budding daughter, who may retaliate with contemptuous dismissal of her mother as a woman at just the time when the latter is at her most insecure, This not uncommon impasse often masks an intense hotting up of earlier Oedipal rivalries.

On a more rational level, menarche may stir in her parents realistic fears for the girl's safety, and efforts to protect her which can themselves be the vehicle for unconscious envy and thus become over-controlling and counter-productive.

These issues continue to arise and to be elaborated throughout adolescence both intrapsychically and within the family – sometimes spilling over into the family's relationship with the wider society. The Latin-derived word 'adolescence' means something like 'in the process of growth', or 'on the way to adulthood' which implies growth achieved. The physical arrival at sexual maturity and the capacity to reproduce may or may not occur in step with development towards psychological and social maturity.

Many of the psychological issues that arose in infancy and went to ground during latency now emerge anew. This is what gives adolescence both its turbulence and its hope, for there is an opportunity to rework conflicts and come to a better solution. At the same time, the upheaval may cause alarm, not just to the adolescent but to the people around her, because the physical capacity to act upon unconscious phantasy now exists. This is particularly relevant to Oedipal issues, and is what underlies the barbed intensity of exchanges in many families with adolescents.

Adolescents need containment, and are notoriously hard to contain, often attacking with well-aimed scorn the adults who attempt the task. Nevertheless, the task must be seen through. If adolescents are to have the opportunity to stay with their inner conflicts and work them through instead of acting them out, they need much support for their more thoughtful side, which may be able to bear the pain of not knowing and having to learn.

Staying with the task of containment often means, for parents, managing their own anxiety. Adolescence involves not only the final relinquishment of Oedipal wishes, with a view to seeking a sexual partner or partners outside the family; it also means the struggle to establish a separate identity apart from, though inevitably linked to, that of family member. This separate identity does not in all societies, or indeed in all families in societies where personal choice is a cultural value, necessarily imply, for a woman, a right to her own choices. However, especially in changing societies, lack of perceived choices for an adolescent girl is likely to cause her suffering.

A healthy adolescent will probably spend a lot of time with her friends, silently or openly comparing her body to theirs and to whatever is seen as the norm, practising ways of presenting herself, comparing her family life to theirs. Many girls derive huge support from friends when things at home get tough, and this can function as another level of containment. Moreover, clinging to the peer group can be a way of acknowledging immaturity and a hesitancy about moving on that perhaps needs to be respected. There were and are advantages for the young in being part of a society where to be young is to be in tutelage of some sort, and you are not expected to act as though you know everything without having to learn it.

Having to pretend to know is a common enough defence in Western society in particular. It is a risky one for adolescents, and of course tempts most of all the very ones who feel most inadequate. To put it psychoanalytically, if you have not had the opportunity to develop a secure sense of a core identity, safely contained within a skin of your own, you will seek other means of asserting the existence of a self. If you do not feel safe enough in the world to admit that you feel unsafe, you are highly likely to avoid the shaky existential experience of adolescence altogether. Some adolescents attempt to prolong the life of latency, avoiding any acknowledgement of their interest in sexual matters, or of their own stirrings of desire. Others may rush into pseudo-adulthood. For girls this often means early pregnancy.

Pregnancy in adolescence can in some cases turn a girl into a woman who, by the time her child is born, is as ready for the experience as anyone can be. But it can often be problematic. The young girl who has always felt insufficiently loved, and who in getting pregnant is seeking a being who will love and comfort her, is a familiar and worrying figure to social workers. She has so little sense of a loving internal figure, based on experience of 'good enough' parenting, that she gets pregnant in a desperate attempt unconsciously to identify both with a fantasy mother and with the baby inside.

Sometimes teenage pregnancy has the meaning of outdoing the mother as a sexual woman; or it can be a means, unconsciously via identification with the baby, but overtly through necessity, of reclaiming the mother's time and attention. When getting pregnant is seen, possibly quite consciously, as a confirmation of adult status, or as a reassurance about the safety and wholeness of the inside of the body, the need to keep renewing the assurance can be a factor in repeated abortions.

> Susan had had four abortions before she was 20. Superficially a competent young woman, she presented a lively and glamorous image that masked a desperate feeling of inadequacy and self-disgust. In her respectable family home, she had been sexually molested by her father and later by some of his fellow churchmen. Her repeated pregnancies were an attempt unconsciously to reassure herself that the inside of her body was not damaged and could still be fruitful; the abortions replicated the attack on her infant self that the abuse had meant to her, and acted out her hatred of her vulnerability, as well as her dread that for her there was no hope of being a live and lovable self deserving of nurture, or of becoming a mother who could protect her child.

Claiming her sexuality and her status as a sexual woman is a vital task for the adolescent girl, but a very complex one. Only in infancy are the psyche and the soma so deeply interconnected, as instinctual longings seek their object and cry out for gratification, and emotional needs seek assuagement through physical expression. Identification with the mother, angry repudiation of her concern, strong feelings of love and of hate towards the father, swings of wild emotion, are perfectly normal and strain relations in the most temperate of families.

In families where there is already dysfunction, the adolescence of the first child may rock things to the point where professional help is needed.

Lara's family came angrily into therapy when, at 13, she was caught shoplifting several times. She was the bright, pretty, eldest child of a high-achieving middle-class family, and was the secret favourite of both her parents. She was special to her mother because she was the only girl, and their closeness until now had, through unconscious identification, partly healed her mother's bitterness at her own unloved childhood. Her father covertly and sometimes openly enjoyed her cheeky defiance and contempt towards authority figures such as teachers (and therapists). It was painfully hard for him to recognise how powerfully his attitude was determined by his unresolved hatred of a Nazi father and his rage at the weepy and indecisive mother who represented emotionality in his mind.

The parents had married young, finding in each other someone who could in phantasy wipe away the pain of the past. They had managed with some difficulty to make room in their twosome for this charming firstborn girl, and with yet more difficulty for the three boys who followed. But the balance was understandably precarious. Lara reached puberty and started wanting to spend time with her girlfriends instead of with her parents at home. When she became interested in boys, turned her sharp tongue against her father and no longer wanted to confide in her mother, it was all too much. Not only did her emerging sexuality herald a separation that evoked terrible memories of abandonment in both parents; it also reawakened buried memories of themselves as adolescents, and raised questions about their current and future relationship. Lara's basically healthy striving towards a separate identity turned her into a persecutor in the internal world of both her parents. The unconscious choice of shoplifting as a symptom of trouble, with the implied threat of disgrace for the whole family, was both a way of expressing her anger and a highly effective way of getting her parents to acknowledge a need for help.

The perception of a woman's body as 'other', even to herself, has profound cultural and unconscious significance. Girls' sexual development seems nearly always to be more disruptive in families than boys', and I think this has something to do with unconscious notions of territoriality. We looked earlier at some ideas about women's bodies as the territory of another – the mother, the partner – and if we face the fact that unconscious phantasy works in more than one direction, it seems obvious that, for a girl to achieve her identity as a sexual being, she has to manage an escape both from her mother's unconscious identification with her and from her father's unconscious sexual possession of her, as well as to negotiate her own Oedipal phantasies.

Of course, if the father or other parental figure has in reality acted out such desires by abusing the child he should have protected, immense problems ensue, as was touched on in the story of Susan. Guilt and self-loathing become located in the child's sense of herself, partly because she is pushed into confusing phantasy with reality and therefore blames her own desires for the disaster, and partly as a result of projection by a man who cannot hold onto pain but instead acts it out by inflicting it on others.

Even when conditions are 'good enough' to enable growth, achieving a sense of a sexual self can seem complex. Part of the complexity for a woman of achieving a sexual identity is to do with the fact that a woman's sexual sensations are not as localised as those of men. Her entire body may be experienced as erogenous. Obviously this can be a source of enormous pleasure. It can also be confusing, making her feel dangerously vulnerable to loss of boundaries and uncertain as to just whose territory her body is.

Recent studies have shown that, in general, baby girls are measurably less cuddled than boys; this lack is the physical dimension of the lack of firm psychic boundaries that is so common a feature of women's inner world. When, as in infancy, body and mind are one, the experience that the body has a skin round it, that one is inside it and all others outside, is a tactile and kinetic one, but can be simultaneously translated into mental terms. The unconscious being very literalistic, a great deal of this sort of trading goes on throughout life, and what would, in a differentiated state, be analogies become, in a state of boundary confusion, concrete equations.

It is not surprising therefore that eating disorders, skin problems, sexual and gynaecological dysfunction and self-mutilating attacks on the body are all frequent vehicles of psychological distress in women.

At 52 Marina feels at odds with her body. She does not understand how it works, cannot identify what it is telling her or asking of her; she has no idea how she feels, physically or emotionally, an indication of how far back the bewilderment began, when the two aspects were as one. She radically lacks a reflective, noticing internal object. Her early years were spent among drunken adults, who were too busy scrapping to attend to childcare. When they did feed her or change her nappy, they probably did so grudgingly, as though her needs were an imposition. She had to find ways early on not to be a nuisance, assuming a rigid quietness and neatness, ignoring her hunger both for food and for cuddles and under- standing. The easiest way to manage was to become unaware of her needs.

The inability to pay attention is still with her, and is at the root of the confusion she experiences in her attempts to deal with the outside world. It is as though her concentration is so fiercely fixed on 'getting through it' (whatever it is) that there is no attention to spare for anything else. Yet in her therapy sessions she shows evidence of an acute intelligence.

It seems that the lack of warmth and the inattentiveness of her objects to her as a real live baby whose demands must be met have left Marina without a clear sense of a core identity, the source of her sensations and thoughts. Insufficiently 'held together' as a baby, either by physical cuddling or by emotional containment, Marina as an adult woman still experiences herself as a ragged bundle of needs with no-one to acknowledge them.

With no proper skin function, she had to adopt rigid structures of her own invention – obsessional tidiness, over-eating, routinised living and, during her brief, painful marriage, vaginismus. These ways of keeping at bay her terror and despair, and almost literally holding herself together, were effective in creating a façade of normality, but were the very opposite of helpful when it came to trying to bring up alone the baby daughter she was left with when her husband died. All her boundaries were 'pretend' ones, not learned from within through repeated experiences of being safely held, but self-invented by the desperate baby she still uncon- sciously was; hence, when they were not rigidly in place, they were as non-existent, and she and her daughter became very much enmeshed.

Marina's 17-year-old daughter, Lynette, having achieved seven O levels and struggling to study two subjects at A level, developed a whole-body rash that was painful enough to keep her away from school during a crucial period of revision.

An astute family doctor sent her for psychotherapeutic assess- ment, and her mother was seen concurrently by another therapist. Interpretation of their truly agonising difficulties over claiming separate identities – stirred up in both by the prospect of Lynette's departure for college – did not work magic. It was another three years before Lynette passed her examinations, during which she received intensive psychotherapy and Marina saw an experienced counsellor at the GP practice to help her sort out her own sense of self. But the rash, a 'symbolic equation' of Lynette's sense of a disturbed boundary, became less sore early in her therapy and eventually became for her something that told her there was a problem, and gave her a good clue where to look for it, when it occasionally recurred in mild form.

Even when it is truly wanted, the experience of pregnancy may introduce unexpected complexities.

Many women feel a sense of fulfilment (an interesting word, very like 'fully filled') at this time, and certainly in biological terms reproduction is what our bodies are for. A mature woman expecting a baby, especially if she is married, is also the focus of much social approval. The mother-to-be herself, however, may feel quite taken over by the whole process, and almost ignored as a person with aspirations of her own.

Many a pregnant woman has found herself identifying in a new way with her own mother This can be a time of closeness and warm rapprochement, but if the relationship is one of unresolved conflict, the feelings may be hard to manage, the identification unwelcome and felt as an intrusion.

To become and remain pregnant, the woman literally has to take in and elaborate something a man has given her. This will hold different meanings, depending on whether the man in question is her life partner or someone else, and if her partner, what sort of relationship they had prior to the conception. Furthermore, what has been taken in does not remain the same but has a life of its own, and this too must be faced and thought about.

The expected birth of a baby implies great changes in the life of a couple. There are questions for both partners about what these will mean for the relationship, and for the self within it. Can both make way for a third party?

The psychoanalyst Fakhry Davids has made the interesting point in this connection that it is a difficult task, both in the unconscious and in myth, to contemplate a generativity that depends on the linking of two people. Our primitive tendency to split our experience comes to notice yet again. Massive change is usually experienced, at least in part, as loss, even when such change is ardently desired. The changes pregnancy brings are no exception. Of course there are also real practical losses to be dealt with – of autonomy, of one's usual mobility, of the familiar body image, probably of income – but often the sense of loss is connected with unconscious material about the inviolate self and its infinite possibilities.

Dr Winnicot (1947), who was very sympathetic to mothers and their babies, assured women that it is perfectly normal to feel some antagonism, even hatred, towards a being that has brought about such momentous changes. The fact that changes in the body occur completely outside their control can be alarming to many women, however enthralling the experience may be. Early in pregnancy the breasts have swelled, and a whole new system of veins has appeared on them. The nipples may be sore. All is in readiness for lactation. Even if the prospective mother is not going to breastfeed, there is a powerful nudge towards awareness of the magical significance of the breasts, in mythology and poetry as well as in unconscious psychic life.

The psychological importance of fertility – whether disparaged or highly valued – has an effect both on women who decide not to have children and on those who find they are infertile. The meaning to an individual woman of infertility will vary according to her own hopes and expectations and those of her partner, the other options open to her, and the attitudes of her family and friends. All of these will vary with the cultural context. In social groups where fertility is honoured, the pain of sterility is particularly poignant.

Halima had been admitted to a psychiatric unit, suffering from a depression that proved hard to mitigate. She worked as an Arabic translator in an international company, had a devoted husband and, though the couple had no children of their own, was regularly the warm hostess to a wide circle of friends and extended family. Her husband, a pious Muslim, said that their lack of children was the will of God, and had left his wife free for charitable works within their community, so that he saw no cause for repining. Halima had just had her 40th birthday. After a long failure to conceive following upon numerous miscarriages, she had thought she was pregnant and was planning to tell her husband on her birthday morning. Instead, her period arrived. Having not told her secret, she kept her disappointment from him too, so as not to spoil the party. She performed her familiar role of attentive and beloved hostess that day, only to be mysteriously overcome with depression a week or so later.

In joint meetings with her husband, what Halima needed was twofold. She needed him to hear her unhappiness about having no child, and the doubts her barrenness induced in her over whether she was really the wife he wanted, without being made to feel that she was lacking in faith for being so sad; and she needed to know that he could share her sadness without being overwhelmed by it. He loved her dearly and managed both to listen without judging and to reassure her.

The personal meaning of fertility and its relationship to cultural variables has new resonances for each woman at menopause, when the end of ovulation means no more possibility of babies, ready or not. Menopause shares with adolescence the quality of transition; the path through this gateway leads away from fertility and towards ageing and death.

For some women, the end of fertility comes as a positive relief, an opportunity for the first time to enjoy sex without fear. Others may struggle for years with the sense of loss, and with the puzzle of desire that continues to assert itself despite infertility, and despite the hard knowledge of dwindling attractiveness. Sex may be in those years both comforting and poignant.

Some women, on the other hand, lose their desire along with the change in their hormone-levels, and feel cheerful about giving up sex altogether. Indeed, in families or cultures where sex is seen as chiefly a means of procreation, there may be an implied or explicit assumption that now is the time to cease having intercourse.

Each of these alternatives has consequences, both for the individual woman and for any partner who is involved, and any disagreement about something so fundamental is unlikely to be resolved without pain.

Sexuality is not the only area in which a menopausal woman is faced with change and actual or potential loss. Her self-image, no longer so bound up with sexual attractiveness or its lack, is now in question as she struggles, alone or perhaps in a support group, or with friends or a therapist, to redefine who she is and what she can find lovable in herself.

Support groups – which have been found effective as a tool for 'consciousness raising' as well as support at many stages of women's lives – can be of particular usefulness in enabling women to think about the process and meaning of growing older.

Ageing faces women with many fears – of loneliness and poverty, of losses of agility and health. It can feel like an end of options. Many of these anxieties are similar for men; but women are very conscious that they are statistically more likely to be left old and poor and alone than men, and that as women they face special health risks, notably osteoporosis and cancers of the breast and uterus. Many women perceive themselves, and are perceived by others, as the carers in their families. For them, worries about infirmity have a special poignancy, for if the carer falls sick, where is her care to be found?

Given the intense nature of these worries, and the current lack of public resources to be relied upon, it is not surprising that keeping fit becomes a preoccupation for many women in middle age. It can be seen as a sensible precaution. However, under the pressure of the still-frequent disparagement of older women, exercising can become the vehicle of denial and take the form of a manic attempt to keep at bay the inevitability of death.

Our self-image is very susceptible to what we experience as the views of others. We introject attitudes not just about ourselves, from our early environment and close associates, but about women in general, or women of a particular class or race, women with disabilities, or 'women of a certain age'. We also do our share of projecting, and then encounter our own projections reflected back. So our image of ourselves is a composite, the exact ingredients varying from moment to moment, and from one woman to another.

It needs to be said that there are clearly situations in which an external oppression sets up the potential for a truly toxic cycle of projection/introjection, and in which inner resources and family strength would have to be exceptional to prevent psychological problems. I am thinking of racial oppression, religious and political persecution, attitudes to disability, and so on.

It seems that we have come full circle and are back to the external world and its impingements on women and their feelings about themselves, having looked at the complex and dialectical nature of these processes on the way.

## Bibliography

Chasseguet-Smirgel, J. (1981) *Female Sexuality*, Virago, London.
—— (1985) *Creativity and Perversion*, Free Association Books, London.
Engels, F. (1884) *The Origin of the Family, Private Property and the State*, Lawrence and Wishart, 1977.
Graves, R. (1961) *The White Goddess: A Historical Grammar of Poetic Myth*, Faber and Faber, London.
Griffin, S. (1977) *Woman and Nature*, Harper Colophon Books, New York.
Herman, N. (1989) *Too Long a Child: The Mother–Daughter Dyad*, Free Association Books, London.
McDougall, J. (1986) *Theatres of the Mind: Illusion and Truth on the Psychoanalytic Stage*, Free Association Books, London.
—— (1989) *Theatres of the Body: A Psychoanalytic Approach to Psychosomatic Illness*, Free Association Books, London.
Mitchell, J. (ed. ) (1986) *The Selected Melanie Klein*, Penguin Books, London.
Pines, D. (1993) *A Woman's Unconscious Use of Her Body: a Psychoanalytic Perspective*, Virago, London.
Weldon, E. (1988) *Mother, Madonna, Whore*, Free Association Books, London.
Winnicott, D. W. (1947) 'Hate in the countertransference', in *Through Paediatrics to Psychoanalysis*, Hogarth Press, London 1975.
Zanardi, C. (ed.) (1990) *Essential Papers on the Psychology of Women*, New York University Press, New York.

# Chapter 4

# Envy between women[1]

## Marie Maguire

It has traditionally been assumed within our culture that women have a strong streak of covert envy, spite and malice that emerges in a particularly virulent form with other members of their own sex. In the early decades of the 20th century fierce controversy raged about Freud's theory that penis envy was crucial to female psychology. Some of Freud's colleagues accused him of male bias because he failed to see the deep envy that men felt for women. For instance Karen Horney, a German psychoanalyst, put forward the thesis that men subjugated women and excluded them from social and political power because of their envy of women's procreative capacities (1926). Contemporary feminists continue to discuss whether Freud was denigrating women or simply describing their unenviable position in societies where they are still second-class. 'No phallus, no power, except those winning ways of gaining one', wrote Juliet Mitchell, in support of Freud (1974: 96). I have written extensively elsewhere about envy between the sexes – so-called 'penis' and 'womb' envy – both of which I believe to be absolutely crucial to the perpetuation of sexual inequality (Maguire, 1995).

Nowadays, as power-relations between the sexes continue to shift dramatically, individual women who succeed in traditionally female as well as in conventionally male spheres of activity may be the prime object of envy for both sexes. Men are now losing some of their traditional privileges and their envy of women is becoming more visible. Nevertheless, in most societies it is still true that men and women have different kinds of power and control, which arouse intense envy in the opposite sex. Women have enormous psychological influence over the life of the human infant, while men still

74

continue to control most educational, juridical, political and economic institutions.

My focus in this chapter is on the ways in which envy manifests itself in the transference and counter-transference between female client and psychotherapist. I discuss a certain group of women who often seek clinicians of their own sex – those who remain trapped in an ambivalent entanglement with a deeply envied internal mother. Using some case examples from group and individual psychotherapy, I show how unconscious envy, which inhibits learning, emotional growth and creativity in all areas of life, can become a serious impediment to psychic change. I argue that whilst we can learn much from existing psychoanalytic ideas about envy, these need supplementing with a feminist understanding of women's social position and the ways this can influence psychological development.

## What is envy?

Envy – the 'evil eye' of folklore – is now, and has been historically, hidden and disguised, rarely discussed and little understood. The reluctance even to name envy is reflected in the common habit of confusing it with jealousy when, in fact, the two emotions are quite different. Envy is described in Webster's Dictionary as 'chagrin or discontent at the excellence or good fortune of another'. Jealousy is the fear that a rival will take something away, usually the affections of a third person. The crucial difference is that envy occurs between two people, whereas jealousy involves real or imagined rivalry or competition among at least three people. Envy is, then, a feeling that arises early in an infant's development, while she is still preoccupied with dyadic relationships, whereas jealousy, competition and rivalry, which are all based on and closely related to envy, arise once the child becomes aware of triangular relationships within and outside the family. Envy involves the fantasy of possessing or destroying the coveted object and is therefore a desperate attempt to protect the self from painful feelings of personal inadequacy or lack, rather than a real attempt to acquire whatever is desired. In contrast, competition, which is a component of jealousy, involves real or imagined attempts to gain the desired object. So, I might envy another woman's exciting job. If she seemed to be replacing me in the affections of a close friend, I might feel jealous and competitive.

In order to get myself a job like hers, I might well have to enter into actual competition with a number of other people.

But why exactly has envy, of all the emotions, been so strongly denied, concealed and avoided? It was listed as one of the seven deadly sins by the medieval Church and described by Chaucer as the worst of all sins. In Dante's *Inferno* the envious were accorded the most excruciating torture – their eyelids were sewn together. Melanie Klein captures the intensely disturbing nature of envy in her essay 'Envy and gratitude', where she describes envy as being an attack on love and creativity. The object of love and admiration, originally the mother, is damaged or destroyed, in fantasy if not in reality. Klein believes envy to be a purely destructive emotion, the angry desire to spoil, rob or poison that which is most needed, the source of life itself. She quotes Chaucer, 'The Parson's Tale': 'It is certain that envy is the worst sin that is; for all other sins are sins only against one virtue, whereas envy is against all virtue and against all goodness' (Klein, 1957: 189). But it is only unconscious envy which is so acutely destructive. Once she can admit exactly what she envies in other people, the envious person can begin to think about attaining what she admires, or accepting its lack.

There is a much more sympathetic social attitude towards jealousy than towards envy. In some countries jealousy can actually be used as a mitigating factor in sentencing for murder. Perhaps this reflects a universal sense that jealousy, unlike envy, implies the existence of love and an impulse to preserve it. Jealousy may reflect possessiveness, insecurity and vanity, as much as any loving concern, but nevertheless it is generally thought of as a much more presentable if not always a creditable feeling. We can allow ourselves to remain conscious of our jealousy, whereas envy is often too painful for conscious awareness; as adults we cannot tolerate the powerful and confusing infantile feelings of need, helplessness and destructiveness with which it is associated.

There is a word for envy in almost every language, and rivalry is inherent in childhood experience. The first real inequality for all of us is the experience of being small, powerless and utterly dependent on the adults around us. The painful necessity of sharing love gives rise to feelings of frustration, humiliation, rage and rivalry. If the girl can be helped to struggle with difficulties rather than to accommodate to them, her developing personality will be strengthened. Her parents' capacities to give her love and protection while, at the same time, helping her tolerate internal conflicts, will be influenced by their own childhood experiences. The help a child is given in negotiating fundamental experiences of inequality with parents and siblings will lay the basis for her capacity to struggle with the whole range of real material inequities she will encounter in later life, such as those of age, health, sex, class and race. An ability to recognise and value our own needs and desires, and to compete when necessary, may then derive from a sense of inner strength, unlike envy which springs from feelings of inadequacy. For someone who cannot compete at all, everyday possibilities are seriously restricted.

Boys and girls are equally likely to be exposed to experiences that give rise to feelings of pain, humiliation, anger and envy. There is as much difference psychologically within each sex as between them, but it is still true that most societies expect men and women to mobilise these feelings in different ways. Boys' upbringing tends to restrict their awareness of emotional life, while strengthening pseudo-adult structures which enable them to 'manage' in the external world. They may later cut off from feelings of vulnerability and inadequacy and use their aggression to compete. Girls, on the other hand, often have few opportunities to fight for what they want openly, and to see that this need not necessarily hurt others or have a detrimental effect on themselves. As a result they may develop an intense fear of competition and learn to limit their expectations and desires, to get what they want by indirect means. They may know only how to experience pleasure and success vicariously, through identification with partners or children, while deprecating themselves and playing down their assets.

I go on now to explore a range of dilemmas which often confront women psychotherapists in working with female envy. Later I discuss these issues in relation to psychoanalytic theories about the origins and effects of this powerful emotion.

## Envy in the clinical setting

It is often difficult for the psychotherapist to introduce the topic of envy to a client who has no conscious knowledge of this feeling. My first clinical example illustrates the way this subject emerged in a women's psychotherapy group. Following on from this I look at how experiences of extreme closeness, of being psychologically merged, can mask envious hostility between women. For instance, one client told me, 'When I admire someone I want to be them. When I realise I can't become them, envy sets in and I start to tear them to bits.' This woman maintained a distance from me by what she described as a 'secret armoury' of contemptuous criticism, so avoiding awareness that I had anything which she needed. In this way she also avoided feeling that she admired or envied me. In this section I trace the origins of another client's problematic female friendship back to her early family relationships. In psychotherapy, as I show through two further case examples, this highly ambivalent sense of fusion can lead to protracted therapeutic relationships, where for unusually long periods the client appears more invested in thwarting the therapist than in using the help she offers. I indicate some of the counter-transference difficulties that can arise for female clinicians who often have very exacting superegos, and may find it particularly difficult to maintain their self-esteem when faced with rapidly altering extremes of idealisation and corrosive devaluation.

First of all, how is the psychotherapist to detect and begin working with envy?

## Defences against envy

Envy does not usually appear in a straightforward way in psychotherapy since even the most envious clients are often absolutely unaware of its existence. Usually we protect ourselves against the unbearable feelings associated with envy by disowning it through a series of defences – psychological forms of protection. Fear of others' envy and retaliation is a very common defence against envy, particularly for women. Those who project their own envy outside themselves then imagine that others will find ways of spoiling anything admirable or valuable in them. Another defence against envy often found in women involves devaluing the self and idealising others. This devaluation of the self, as Melanie Klein points out, serves both as a denial of envy and a punishment for it (Klein, 1957). In psychotherapy, as elsewhere, it also greatly increases envious feelings towards others. The admired person is placed on a pedestal, seen as so special that there is no possibility of comparisons with the self which could arouse feelings of inferiority. Since idealisation is an attempt to defend the self against awareness of deprivation, rage or envy, the idealised person may later be experienced as persecuting and hateful. When this pattern is extreme, it can lead to the creation of a range of therapeutic relationships that break down rapidly because no one can live up to the idealised expectations.

Other people defend their own envy by unconsciously trying to provoke that feeling in those around them. They may be unable to acknowledge anything valuable, pleasurable or admirable in the lives of others. At the same time they focus attention on their own assets or good fortune, glamorising their lives. Ultimately this defence against envy proves counter-productive since it generates such intense anxiety about envious retaliation. Another common pattern is the habitual devaluation of what is envied, for instance by constant carping criticism. It is often very difficult for the psychotherapist to penetrate this defence since no one is ever perfect and there is always something that can be criticised. The tendency to spoil and devalue whatever is envied is both an expression of envy and a defence against it, since once the coveted attributes are destroyed, in fantasy or reality, they can no longer arouse the same painful feelings. Initially all of these defences may provide a feeling of relief from envy, but ultimately they create a new set of problems.

The following discussion about envy in a psychodynamically orientated women's therapy group illustrates the very different ways the group members expressed this feeling and defended themselves from consciously experiencing it.

One woman admitted that she dreaded being singled out for praise, as she had been in her dance class that morning. It gradually emerged that she had always feared getting special attention from the group therapist since she imagined that this would 'spoil' her relationships with the other women, who might then resent her. It was pointed out to her by another group member that she habitually denigrated those aspects of her life that might arouse envy in others. In a group where several of the other women had unsatisfactory sexual relationships and where most were unemployed or unhappy with their working lives, she took care not to dwell on the fact that her long marriage had always been sexually passionate and that she had been highly successful in the career she had pursued until her first child was born. Instead, she emphasised the aspects of her sexual and emotional life that were problematic, and criticised her previous work for personal and political reasons. She then began to talk about the way she had feared the envy and retaliation of her fragile and sickly sister. Using a childhood analogy, she said to the group, 'I'll make quite sure you don't want my teddy bear.'

Another woman in the group said that she couldn't understand this, since she herself devoted enormous effort to making other people envy her. She was aware that she boasted about the good things in her life and didn't mention the difficulties. She usually painted a glorious picture of her family life, and it had taken her months to admit the problems that had brought her to the group. 'I want you to want my teddy bear', she said. A third woman said that she was highly competitive. 'I always want everything everyone else has, and I try to get it. I want the group's attention all the time, and I want to be group therapist. I want you to admire me. I want your teddy bear and I also want you to want mine.' Another woman, who usually found it hard to talk about herself, said that she habitually idealised the lives of other women in the group. 'I always think other people's teddy bears must be better than mine. I envy you all the time, but I can't imagine anyone envying me.'

### Envy and female identity

This story was told to me in an initial consultation with a woman, 'Ms P.', whom I had agreed to see in order to refer her on for psychotherapy. It illustrates how some feelings of symbiotic closeness between women can break down into envious destructiveness.

'When I feel passionately about someone, I almost want to be that person, and that's how I felt about O. [an ex-business partner and friend]. We seemed to let down psychological barriers with each other through talking that I'd only ever let down with other people if I had sex with them. But when I tell someone else all about me I stop knowing where I end and the other person begins. I wanted O.'s approval so desperately that I began to lose track of why I was doing things. I finally realised that I needed to find myself again. But then we started to argue really bitterly. I can see now that we were always competitive. But when we were close we operated as a kind of unit. It was OK for her to be wonderful because I felt I basked in her reflected glory. When we separated we had to continually undermine what the other had in order to prove that we were better. I began to see her as a kind of monster. I felt I'd let

O. step right over my psychological boundaries . . . it was as if she'd got right into my skin, as if she was about to take me over completely. With D. [a male colleague] I also feel competitive, but it's different. I realise I can never become him and he can't become me. The sexual differences between us mean that we can only merge up to a point.'

This was an unconscious warning to her future therapist, who, she stipulated, must be a woman. Ms P. would initially fall in love with her and then suddenly become disillusioned, re-enacting both her early experience with her mother and her adult friendship with O. There is a danger here that the psychotherapist may unconsciously fear the emergence of such profound envious hostility, and so collude with the client's view of her as the perfect maternal figure. When destructive feelings break through too abruptly into an idealised transference, the client may sometimes leave suddenly, terrified of being rejected or damaging her therapist. If the psychotherapist is able, from the beginning, to talk about the rivalry and contempt behind the admiration, then her client will be in a better position to continue exploring her more negative feelings when they become conscious.

In her session with me, Ms P. described herself as growing up in an 'in-between generation. As a working-class woman who received a professional education, I had no role models.' She had also felt paralysed by a fear of maternal envy. 'If I'd got married young, especially to a middle-class man with money, and had children as well as a professional career, I think she'd have been bitterly jealous. I was afraid of losing her love.' Her father, although physically present, failed to make his presence felt in the family. 'He did try to come in between me and my mother at times, but my mother was much stronger. She always pushed him out again. So the bond was never broken between us, and I could never get away.'

Unlike boys, girls cannot compensate for early feelings of envy and inadequacy in relation to a mother experienced in infancy as all-powerful, by demonstrating that they have a different physiology and more highly valued social status. Nor is it so easy for women to develop a sense of their own value in the external world since internal conflicts, such as those I describe in this chapter, may well reinforce and interact with real practical obstacles and discriminatory attitudes. And mothers who feel isolated and undervalued often rely on their children for recognition and feel particular envy of daughters who share their gender yet may have a more fulfilling future.

In Ms P.'s early life there was no evidence of a third force, another strong adult presence that would, at a certain point, break into the mother–daughter dyad, reclaiming the mother into the world of adult relationships, and giving the daughter the opportunity to experience a different kind of close relationship with an adult. If, as often happens even when there is a father present, mother and daughter receive no external support in separating psychologically, the effects of mother–daughter envy are likely to be exacerbated.

The daughter also needs opportunities to identify with psychological qualities associated culturally with masculinity, such as the capacity to use her aggression constructively and to assert her own needs with forceful determination. This is all the more vital since attributes and activities associated with men – although culturally variable – are almost universally seen as more prestigious. But it is difficult for the girl to identify with psychological masculinity without devaluing her own sex. Children of both sexes often idealise the apparently more limited authority of the father as a reaction against the seeming omnipotence of the early mother. Many girls seek refuge from early disappointment with their mothers by idealising their fathers and devaluing their own sex.

In our society the father's role is associated with boundary-setting and helping the child to find a way out of the symbiotic preoccupations of infancy into the wider world, while mothers are expected to provide physical care and emotional containment. However, I assume that the capacity for both functions exists in women and men. So the girl can identify with an actual father or with the conventionally paternal functions or 'masculine' aspects of the mother and other significant female carers. A female single parent may be as capable as many heterosexual couples of helping her daughter to move out into the world and gain a sense of psychic autonomy. What is crucial is the mother's relationship with her internal parents, particularly her father, and with parts of herself seen culturally as male.

*Envy and resistance to change in psychotherapy*

Psychoanalysts have long been aware that accepting help can be experienced as humiliating. In 1919 Karl Abraham described a certain group of envious patients who enjoy the idea of being in psychotherapy and appear compliant, yet throughout a long treatment they absolutely resist psychic change since this would mean acknowledging the psychoanalyst's skill and professional expertise. In this way, too, the therapist is denied the satisfaction of seeing her clients change. Envy is also often linked with childhood and adult learning difficulties, since the envious person cannot bear to acknowledge that others have anything valuable to give. The Kleinian psychoanalyst Betty Joseph describes how the envious person cannot study because they cling to the belief that they already know what they are about to read (1986). A woman client, describing her learning difficulties, told me, 'I've got to find my own way, stay in control. To allow anyone to help me means I'll lose myself, get taken over.' She felt her psychological structures to be so flimsy that she would fall apart if she opened herself up to psychic growth or intimacy.

Envy interacted with guilt to inhibit psychic change in a 26-year-old client, 'Ms. J.'. She had left school early and, lacking qualifications, she worked occasionally in shops. Although men found her attractive she was unable to sustain an ongoing relationship. Instead she depended on a variety of drugs. I initially found her touchingly open and vulnerable, but I soon realised that building a relationship with her would be a painfully slow and frustrating process. She sat through her early sessions in a terrified silence, allowing herself to absorb nothing beneficial from me. Whenever she made a positive move in her life she would sabotage it immediately; after a helpful session she would miss the next.

She had a very emotionally deprived childhood, but was born with certain privileges which made her the object of envy both within the family and in the world at large. Her parents, who came from another part of the world, were extremely wealthy and well-known. Hers was a large family but as the only girl she was given some special attention by a father who ignored his sons. Ms J.'s greatly-idealised mother worked long hours in a male-dominated profession, so that her daughter was brought up by a succession of nannies. In Ms J.'s teens her mother developed a disabling illness and her father left the family. As her psychotherapy progressed it became clear that Ms J. unconsciously felt responsible for both of these tragedies

Everyday childhood competition had proved unsafe since she felt that her rival had not survived the battle intact. In her teens Ms J. had felt that her mother, whose life was becoming increasingly lonely and restricted, had begrudged her daughter her new-found popularity and her moves towards independence. Ms J. developed a deprecating manner and a habit of denigrating anything she had at home and at school, fearing particularly that she would lose her mother's love if she shone in the eyes of the world. For a long time in therapy Ms J. presented herself to me as entirely bereft of assets and resources. When she did take steps forward she would sometimes hide this from me, later admitting that she feared that I would undermine her with envious or critical comments, or reject her as too fortunate to need my help. Over the years we came to understand that her silences and missed sessions were partly an attempt to avoid making me ill or damaging a second maternal figure.

At times Ms J. evoked profound frustration in me, and there were long periods when I despaired of a successful conclusion to her psychotherapy. I often felt myself to be making mistakes with her or missing crucial issues. As the years went by I realised that, although I had sometimes been less than perfect, she was communicating to me her own profound sense of guilt about damaging or neglecting those she had loved in early life. Like many women, she felt great anxiety about being happier or more successful than her parents or siblings and therefore could not allow herself to resolve her own psychological problems until, in fantasy, she had solved theirs. Trapped in an inner world of suffering love-objects, such clients feel that they are not entitled to change until they have made all those they have ever loved – and hated – better. In a 1936 paper about those who cannot tolerate psychoanalytic 'cure', Joan Riviere argues that patients who respond – as Ms J. did – to each step forward in psychotherapy by deteriorating again, feel an extreme intensity of love and hostility towards their love-objects, now inside their internal world. The therapist must help them to face their destructiveness and go through an unusually intense death-like depression before they feel that their love-objects are secure inside themselves.

Ms J.'s psychotherapy was eventually very fruitful, but it was quite unusually protracted. Each positive move was undone many times, as she painfully worked through her fantasies of having seriously damaged each of her love-objects, living and dead. In turn I represented her neglectful, adored mother, her bookish father and her bullying but much-admired siblings, as, within the transference, each was attacked, mourned and repaired many times over. During a period when she was particularly concerned with feelings of responsibility for the past and the current problems of her siblings, Ms J. told me 'I feel guilty all the time . . . I don't have that feeling too badly today, but usually I carry it with me constantly.'

For a long time Ms J. experienced herself as the object of others' envy and was unable to acknowledge fully the strength of this emotion in herself. The first appearance of envy in psychotherapy is often in a dream. Ms J. dreamt of an envious mother who bore some resemblance to me. It was some years before she could begin to recognise this feeling in herself. Then she described a nightmare where the envious part of herself was represented by a sweet young girl who had been transformed by envy into a rotting, grimacing witch, with ragged clothes, stringy hair and a foul, poisonous smell, who lurked, snarling, behind a partition, waiting to attack. After this Ms J. began, very tentatively, to express anger and envy more directly towards myself and others. Now that she could acknowledge the effects of her own envy, she began to make more sustained changes in her life, although these were always sabotaged several times. She began to express guilt and remorse towards both her mother and myself, feeling that she'd 'wasted' opportunities to develop, both in everyday life and in therapy. She talked of how, through the therapeutic work with me, she could strengthen her identification with aspects of both parents, including her mother's strengths in conventionally male as well as female spheres. Gradually over the years she became more able to accept those assets she had been born with as well as the inner resources she had developed so slowly and painfully in herself. Towards the end of psychotherapy, she said, 'I know I've been very slow and that I've frustrated you at times. I was like that at school – slow, frustrating and bottom of the class . . . I'm not bottom of the class any more . . . my new job is at the very edge of progress in my field.' Having gained professional and academic qualifications, Ms J. now had a new sense of personal confidence, a blossoming career and a far greater capacity for intimacy.

Some families do value women highly without necessarily being conscious that they do so, and this can mitigate against the cultural contempt for their sex that girls will inevitably be exposed to later. Ms J. idealised her mother, who had managed to dominate the household emotionally, while succeeding so pre-eminently in the external 'male' world. She also told me later in her therapy that her brothers had ganged up on her not just because she was her father's favourite but also 'because I was a girl, and different from them, with something they didn't have'. In contrast, other families create a culture where women and girls are even more devalued than in society at large. With such women, envy within the maternal transference will often be accompanied by intense devaluation and contempt for their own sex. This can be one of the hardest aspects of the transference for a female psychotherapist to work with, and she may feel that her client, who may be an ardent feminist, is herself talking with the voice of the chauvinist male she so readily criticises.

This was the case with another 26-year-old client, Ms B., who had a range of difficulties in her sexual and working life. The youngest of a large family of daughters, she had consistently felt inferior and excluded from a bond that seemed to exist between her elder sisters and mother. Her problems were compounded by her attempt to escape from a disappointing early relationship with a much-envied mother through idealising her father and men in general. When she first came to psychotherapy she, like Ms J., talked of being her father's favourite. But as time went on it became clear that she had felt her parents to be so absorbed in each other that she had always felt painfully inferior to her mother and never able to rival her sexually. The only way she had been able to secure any special attention was by interesting her father in 'boyish' activities, as if she were the son he had never had. In this way she had defended herself against exclusion by the women of the family by imagining herself as an honorary male. This had left her feeling very inferior to other women who seemed to her far more confident about maintaining men's sexual interest. Ms B. was unconsciously fearful that her very precarious sense of identity would be destabilised by envious feelings and so she avoided success or competition. She also felt the lack of an image within her family of how a woman could be successful outside the home and family. For instance she told me, 'I do think men are cleverer. At university they used to get brilliant grades for essays they'd written on the hoof, while the women I knew stayed in and sweated for hours over their papers. Rationally I know that what

I'm saying isn't true. Teenage girls are doing better than boys at school and they say the future is female. But I can't help admiring men more.'

At a certain point in psychotherapy I began to feel that she was trying unconsciously to recreate her own feelings of professional and sexual inferiority in me. She found subtle ways of disparaging my work, for instance by comparing me unfavourably to more famous psychotherapists. She also spent much time talking about how attractive men found her physical shape which, she occasionally pointed out, was quite different from mine. She estimated that I was slightly older than I am, exaggerating the age-gap between us. She would then talk of how worried she was about ageing, since in her experience men of all ages – and indeed women – preferred the bodies of very young women. I often found it hard to concentrate and would feel undermined, that she was full of the vibrant energy of youth while I felt old and worn out. Eventually I talked in a peer supervision group about the way I had begun to dread her sessions which were at the end of the day when I often felt tired. The group members expressed their astonishment that she had managed to undermine me so profoundly. They pointed out that I was losing confidence entirely in my professional skills and my personal assets.

I decided that I must broach the subject of her envy of me the next time she began making subtle comparisons between us. She had previously acknowledged her professional rivalry with me but seemed quite unable to envisage the possibility that she might feel sexually competitive with me, as she had with her mother and sisters. As I talked of the possibility that she might envy me, she expressed blank incomprehension, and I wondered whether to stumble on or stop. Was I taking a wrong direction?, I asked myself. Eventually, to my great relief she seemed to recognise some of the emotional states I was describing. 'I do envy some things about you – it's true . . . I suppose I have been trying to provoke you . . . to needle you', she said. This did indeed cast light on why I had felt so extremely uncomfortable during her sessions – just as if someone was sticking pins in me and gauging my reactions. She went on to say that she had been testing me for weak spots, seeking out my vulnerabilities.

As Ms B. began to re-own her own envy of me and her much-denigrated mother and sisters, she, like Ms J., began to acknowl-edge her regret that she had wasted many of her sessions trying to provoke me enviously and was only now beginning to work on her problems. She commented sadly on how long it had taken her to work through her 'grandiosity', a defence against low self-esteem. She then had to face a terrible feeling of emptiness, of having absolutely nothing inside her emotionally.

Within psychoanalytic literature there has been remarkable consistency about the effects of envy. Unconscious envy has generally been associated with wounded narcissism (damage to the sense of psychological well-being) and is seen as an impediment to psychic change and growth. For instance, Freud's theory revolved around paternal authority and potency, which the woman envied and the man dreaded losing, while Klein, in contrast, saw the mother's psychological power as the locus of childhood envy. Nevertheless both Freud and Klein linked envy with profound difficulties in analysis, arguing that with some profoundly envious patients treatment can be ineffective or become interminable (Freud, 1937; Klein, 1957). In recent years there has, however, been controversy about the origins of envy and its centrality within the therapeutic relationship. In the following section I discuss different psycho-analytic theories about what makes some people more envious than others and look at the implication of these theories for clinical work with women.

## The origins of envy – psychoanalytic views

Although Freud focused initially on female penis envy originating at a toddler Oedipal phase, under the influence of colleagues (mainly female) he gradually came to see that all envy originated in relation to the mother. He traced the roots of the narcissistic hurt, so fundamental to penis envy, to the baby's early relationship with the mother's breast.

> The reproach against the mother which goes back furthest is that she gave the child too little milk – which is construed against her as lack of love . . . the child's avidity for its earliest nourishment is altogether insatiable . . . it never gets over the pain of losing its mother's breast. (Freud, 1933: 155)

Freud's argument was ambiguous about whether envy (which for him was mainly female) was inborn or caused by environmental factors. His colleagues Karl Abraham and Ernest Jones described envy and (in Jones's case) a particular kind of envious hatred, as developing gradually during childhood through the interaction between environmental and constitutional factors (see Joffe, 1969).

In contrast to this, Melanie Klein stated firmly that envy was an inborn drive, closely linked with the death instinct and purely destructive in its aims. Individuals are born, she believes, with 'different constitutional tendencies towards aggression and envy and with varying capacities for love' (1957: 21). These tendencies are, however, accentuated by the infant's experiences within the womb and during birth. The baby feels envy initially in relation to its first love object (which she assumed to be the mother's breast or its substitute, the feeding bottle) as a response to both satisfaction and deprivation. Envy is aroused by the baby's awareness that the source of love, comfort and nourishment on which she so utterly depends lies outside herself and cannot be controlled. Attributing considerable psychological sophistication to the infant, Klein describes her as assuming that when she is not being fed her mother must be gratifying herself with the magical richness of the 'feeding breast'.

Klein's views on the origins of envy touch on crucial psycho-analytic controversies about whether aggression is inborn or reactive and the extent to which the very young baby experiences itself as separate from other people. Winnicott also sees the mother as the focus of childhood envy, but in other ways his theories about the origins of envy are in complete opposition to Klein's. He argues that, far from being able to see itself as a separate person, the newborn baby lives in a world of undifferentiated sensations, unaware of whether the finger or nipple it sucks belongs to itself or to someone else. From this perspective the baby who feels secure, satisfied and contented will, by and large, exist in a state of pleasurable unity with the mother. For this child:

> the breast is the self and the self is the breast. Envy is a term that might become applicable in the experience of a tantalising failure of the breast as something that is. (Winnicott, 1971: 96)

If the infant is aware of sources of nourishment and comfort outside herself, then, in Winnicott's view she must be experiencing a quite serious sense of deprivation or lack.

Joffe, a contemporary Freudian psychoanalyst, in his 'Critical review of the status of the envy concept', says that babies are not yet psychologically sophisticated enough and lack the necessary sense of psychic separateness to feel what he calls envy 'proper'. The infant must, he says, not only be able to wish for something it lacks, but also be able to fantasise about what it might be like to possess the desired object, before it can really be capable of envy. He also points out that it is very difficult, given our lack of really concrete knowledge about early childhood, to delineate an exact point at which envy might arise as a separate and distinct emotion or character trait. Joffe counters Klein's focus on the destructiveness of unconscious envy by also emphasising its links with love and admiration and stressing that it can be used constructively.

In fact, Klein and Joffe are defining envy in different ways. Klein describes how the helpless infant becomes terrified that her own envious destructiveness will annihilate both herself and the mother on whom she utterly depends. This feeling is so unbearable that it is made unconscious. Klein refers only briefly to a later form of envy arising at the toddler stage which is based on early envy but also associated with rivalry and jealousy. Joffe focuses on a later, more complicated character trait which arises because some children who have suffered pain or humiliation internalise those experiences as a 'massive fantasied disability'. This creates constant envy of others who are assumed to be more fortunate.

It does seem, however, that the emotional state described by Klein may be the precursor of adult envy, and that these powerful infantile feelings and fantasies continue unconsciously to be associated with the more complicated character trait described by Joffe. We cut ourselves off from conscious awareness of envy and regard it with such universal horror precisely because of this link with feelings of infantile helplessness and with fears of destroying both love and life itself. And Klein would agree with Joffe that once we become conscious of our envy and can integrate it with feelings such as admiration and gratitude, it will lose some of its destructive potential.

Klein is obviously right in pointing out that the newborn infant has already had important formative experiences in the womb and during birth. The expectations and fantasies others have about her even before birth will also be crucial. However, as my clinical examples show, whenever a client is profoundly envious, the reasons for this can usually be located within her early history. I therefore do not agree with Klein that envy is linked with an innate drive towards aggression. Instead I would argue, as Joffe does, that the child who has been unbearably exposed to her own helplessness and vulnerability, who has suffered some significant lack of attention, feels reduced and therefore compares herself enviously with others. Her difficulties may have been exacerbated by envious parents. Although Klein herself concentrated exclusively on envy as an intrapsychic phenomenon and barely mentioned family dynamics, some of her later collaborators theorised about possible environmental causes of excessive envy. Hanna Segal, in one of her studies of Klein, gives the example of the 'excessively narcissistic mother unable to cope with the infant's projections, and keeping herself as an idealised object' who then puts the infant into a constantly devalued position in relation to herself, thus increasing the child's envy of her (1979: 147).

What are the implications of these theories for psychotherapy with women? Klein's graphic account of how this powerful emotion affects the inner world is useful in understanding the sense of emptiness, rottenness or persecution described by the women clients discussed in the previous section. She describes how the excessively envious infant who is not helped to mitigate these feelings will come to feel that she has inside her something damaged, shredded and poisonous. The source of goodness, the 'feeding breast' which she has come to experience as 'mean and grudging', has been spoiled by the aggressive and envious attacks she has made on it in her fantasies, and can no longer be experienced or internalised as an entirely 'good object'. A vicious circle is then set up whereby the envious woman's internal sense of worthlessness and impoverishment is exacerbated by each actual experience of failure, so making external progress even more difficult and increasing her envy at the success and creativity of others.

Klein's focus on the need to fully confront envy and hostility within the maternal transference is particularly relevant to those women who are terrified of separating psychically from the internal mother in case one of them is irrevocably damaged. Klein describes the client's struggle to integrate envious destructiveness with more positive feelings as the most difficult and important part of any analysis. If, through the transference relationship, the client can piece together all her different experiences of the therapist, she will become more able to see herself as autonomous from her own internal mother. Her envy will lose its destructive power as it becomes integrated with more loving feelings including gratitude for the help she has received. If the therapist, unlike the original parent, allows rage and anger without retaliating or falling apart, the client may come to feel that she can tolerate her own aggression and put it to more constructive uses.

Klein does recognise that once the client becomes more able to tolerate ambivalence and gains more sense of her own psychic separateness, she will be able to face the existence of the father's and the mother's life apart from her. However, her work on envy does focus overwhelmingly around the maternal transference. It is crucial to recognise that the girl gains positive strengths through identification with the mother. But if female psychotherapists (and male therapists with a strong identification with conventionally maternal qualities) follow Klein in viewing the mother as overwhelmingly the more enviable parent, they may fail to notice when the patient is seeing them as a male or paternal figure within the transference. As I pointed out earlier, the female client needs the opportunity to identify with the psychic 'masculinity' of both parents within the transference. This will enable her to mobilise her aggression and envy towards achieving her own desires and to experience herself more as the agent of her own destiny. She will then have the possibility of re-owning aspects of personality which are frequently projected onto men. These qualities can then be used constructively to improve her own personal life and the situation of her sex within culture.

In contrast to Klein, Joffe gives envy far less centrality in the psychoanalytic process. He views envy as a symptom of earlier difficulties which will disappear of its own accord once the underlying difficulties have been resolved. Joffe emphasises that the existence of envy can, unlike depression, be seen as a sign of hope, since the envious person still entertains fantasies about having what she desires and is not resigned to the discrepancy between what she is and what she wants to be. He argues that it is therefore vital that the therapist point out not only the feelings of personal lack and hostility but also the admiration implicit in envy, since, if the idealised attributes are preserved from destruction, they can provide a basis for identification and the envied person can then be used as a model. From the feminist viewpoint Joffe's emphasis on the possibility of emulating those we envy is also useful. As my clinical material indicates, women who feel envious and inadequate often describe the lack of positive images of femininity in their childhood. The validation of culturally denigrated characterisitics and the presence of positive role models seems to be a vital part of the process through which oppressed groups gain confidence in their capacities for personal and political change.

While working with very envious female clients, the psychotherapist must, then, be able to retain an awareness of what is being left outside the therapeutic discourse. Apparently compliant, idealising clients can then be helped right from the beginning of therapy to recognise their own envy and resentment. Similarly the psychotherapist needs to retain her objectivity in the face of envious devaluation which she may experience as deeply undermining. Ultimately it is helpful to remind the client that their envy is connected with admiration as well as with the desire to spoil. Once she acknowledges the profundity of her own envy, the client can then make some realistic decisions about whether she can act on her envious desires to change her own life. Finally the clinician must tolerate not only her client's projected envy but also her own unfulfilled wishes, which may be all too painfully inescapable when she helps other women to enjoy what she will never have. Both client and therapist are ultimately confronted with the fact that some desires can never be realised.

## Note

1   This chapter is a substantially revised version of my paper 'Casting the evil eye: envy between women', originally published in S. Ernst & M. Maguire, *Living with the Sphinx: Papers from the Women's Therapy Centre*, The Women's Press, London, 1987.

## References

Abraham, K. (1919) 'A particular form of neurotic resistance against the psycho-analytic method', in *Selected Papers of Karl Abraham*, Hogarth Press, London 1927.

Freud, S. (1933) *New Introductory Lectures on Psycho-Analysis*, Pelican, Harmondsworth 1973.

—— (1937) 'Analysis terminable and interminable', in *Selected Essays*, vol. 23, Hogarth Press, London.

Horney, K. (1926) 'The flight from womanhood', in J. Baker Miller (ed.), *Psychoanalysis and Women*, Penguin, London 1984.

Joffe, W. G. (1969) 'A critical review of the status of the envy concept', *International Journal of Psycho-Analysis*, 50:533–45.

Joseph, B. (1986) 'Envy in everyday life', in E. Bott Spillius & M. Feldman (eds), *Psychic Equilibrium and Psychic Change*, Routledge, London 1989.

Klein, M. (1957) 'Envy and gratitude', in *Envy and Gratitude and Other Essays*, Delta edition, Dell Co., New York 1977.

Maguire, M. (1995) *Men, Women, Passion and Power: Gender Issues in Psychotherapy*, Routledge, London.

Mitchell, J. (1974) *Psychoanalysis and Feminism*, Allen Lane, London.

Riviere, J. (1936) 'A contribution to the analysis of the negative therapeutic reaction', in A. Hughes (ed.), *The Inner World and Joan Riviere*, Karnac, London 1991.

Segal, H. (1979) *Klein*, Fontana, London.

Winnicott, D. W. (1971) 'Creativity and its origins', in *Playing and Reality*, Pelican, Harmondsworth.

# Chapter 5

# Fantasies and problematics of identity

*Joanna Ryan*

The issue of identity – lesbian identity, sexual identity, gender identity – seemingly never goes away. Even the most recent writings on lesbian sexuality (e.g. Doan, 1994; Stein, 1993) present the same old questions, albeit in more sophisticated forms and in changing theoretical and political contexts. What does it mean to identify as lesbian? What do or don't we have in common with others who also identify in this way, or who don't? Does it turn out to mean rather less than we originally either feared or hoped? Why can it seem so important either to do so, or not to do so?

This persistent reiteration and reworking of old questions suggests to therapeutic ears unfinished business, unaddressed themes, perhaps unhealed wounds. The diversity and plurality of sexualities, the fluidity and multiplicity of identities, the mobility of desires, are all so frequently, and so eloquently and passionately, insisted upon, that we might wonder who or what is being argued with or against. The other part of this seeming dialogue, the counter-voice, is present in a much less substantial way yet it seems to have enormous, if chimerical, power. Who does actually take up a different, more essentialist position, and in what guises, or does this recurring preoccupation reflect a more self-addressed dialogue? We might surmise that the hold that 'identity' has speaks to desires for certainty, coherence, fixity and power not attainable in most people's lives, particularly those whose sexuality is so far from and threatening to the heterosexual norm, idealised as this may be.

In what follows I outline the discursive and social context in which, as therapists, we hear and attempt to understand the many and various concerns that some of our patients tell us about in relation to identity issues. I also attempt to illustrate some of these therapeutic complexities with a clinical example.

Judith Butler (1990) has argued for an understanding of the phantasmagoric status of notions of identity and identification, which should warn us against taking these concepts as unquestionable givens or as obvious psychological realities. She also, following Foucault (1981) and other theoreticians of gay and lesbian history (e.g. McIntosh, 1981; Weeks, 1981), shows how the notion of identity is located within an historically specific discourse concerning sexuality, desire and gender, a discourse that reflects and instates certain normative and regulative functions relating to heterosexuality and the complementarity of gender concepts. Elsewhere (O'Connor & Ryan, 1993) the limitations of a psychoanalytic discourse that depends on these inbuilt gender complementarities has been described, and the necessity of different understandings of questions of identity in psychoanalytic practice has been argued for, especially in relation to lesbian sexuality. Here I wish to amplify some of these arguments.

We do not, as so much psychology would have it, just find or fail to find our true or real identities, deviant or otherwise. They are not simply 'there', waiting to be discovered or claimed, like so much lost luggage, in some inner core, true self or even biological substratum. It is, of course, true and important that some clients may voice concerns in therapy about whether they are really lesbian, or may have anxieties about not being 'proper' lesbians. Others may express enormous relief at not persisting with what has felt like a false and constrained or meaningless identity in attempts to pursue hetero-sexual relationships, and may even articulate this as the discovery of their real selves. Yet others may describe how impossible they find it to call themselves lesbian, despite persistent involvements and desires that point in such a direction. Such an ascription may seem not just abhorrent but terrifying in a more existential way.

Personal experiences in this domain may be rendered in essentialist terms, or can be heard in that way, but this does not mean that the therapist has to take up a corresponding theoretical position. Instead, further thought is needed about how such conflicts about identity and sexual orientation are understood and articulated by the therapist. As therapists, we need to reflect on our own theoretical stances in relation to 'identity' in order to respond adequately to the complex clinical material we may be presented with. In many instances the theoretical position of the therapist can matter very much to the progress of therapy; it can itself be or become a powerful source of identification, positively or negatively, for the client, so the basis of any such position needs to be clear. The impact and influence of our theoretical positions on our clients, and on what they tell us and how, is not something that in most psychotherapeutic trainings we are encouraged to think about critically, but it is often a vital matter, especially in relation to homosexuality. In respect of identity issues, the following questions, amongst many others, are relevant to the therapist's practice. Does the therapist think that there is an answer to a question posed in terms of whether someone is really a lesbian or not, that there is a true identity which a person has to find or be helped to find through therapy? How do we understand the apparent resolutions to such questions that some people do reach through therapy, or otherwise? Do we think a true identity is what's best for people?

It has often been noted by many authors how historically relative and specific is the notion of a gay or lesbian identity. Many works describe how the ascription or claiming of such an identity did not appear as a cultural form before the late 19th century. Other authors show how the rise of scientific sexology and the medical interest in sexual 'deviations' led to a fixing, proliferation and reification of these categories and typologies. It is also well recognised that the claiming of identities of this kind has been a crucial part of gay and lesbian politics, and a most important aspect of fighting the multiple forms of oppression and discrimination affecting the expression of gay and lesbian sexuality and love. Doing so, however, and coming out of a seemingly endless series of closets, can inevitably result in an over-assertion of lesbian identity and a too restrictive and excluding self-definition. The vital and often still necessary strategic importance of claiming identities, of being open, cannot be underestimated, but it is also important to appreciate how the many imperatives to identifying thus may obscure the much more ambivalent and complex subjective realities of any one person's sexual desires. That this is so does not, as is often feared, threaten the political solidarity that is so often needed; rather it points to the importance of distinguishing an identity forged for strategic reasons (of all kinds) in particular circumstances and one which is mistakenly seen as conveying a timeless ontological status or an essential psychological characteristic.

It is important also to understand the historical process of the present moment and to situate ourselves there. Many changes are taking place in our formulations concerning 'identity', most particularly a widespread process of deconstruction. This may be seen at a political and social level in the many assertions of diversity and difference within lesbian and gay communities, the discussions about what is regarded as acceptable sex, and the questioning of exclusive loyalties or styles of appearance. The demand for adherence and loyalty is increasingly open to question, as are the assumption of a common subjecthood and the notion of either gay or straight. The stereotypes and counter-stereotypes of the 1970s are challenged and replaced by a proliferation and plurality of ways of being lesbian or gay, of diverse life styles, even though the homophobia of our social structure remains relentlessly in place. There is an increasing recognition of differences of all kinds, if not without struggle.

At a theoretical level, Foucault, Butler and others (e.g. O'Connor & Ryan, 1993) have shown how the particular contents ascribed to those identities, named as deviant ones, underpin the regulative functions of heterosexually normative discourses. Such analyses challenge the 'naturalness' or 'given-ness' of any kinds of identity, as well as providing insights into the construction of such psychological concepts. Subjectively, the personal boundaries of 'straight or gay', although a powerful, perhaps unconscious, legacy, may for many women be shifting and transforming as old depictions of lesbianism jostle with new ones. For some women in some positions, the possibilities for the expression and living out of lesbian desires, and the complexities and conflicts this may bring, as well as the pleasures, have opened out enormously since the early 1970s. The limitations of our language and forms of thought to articulate lesbian desires is often described, a sign perhaps of the constant 'refigurations' that are being attempted. The demands put on anyone's personal capacities for living and loving by such involvements are part of what we, as therapists, may be made particularly aware of in work with lesbians in therapy. This psychotherapeutic awareness has also to stand in relation to another one – the much more harsh, invasive nature of the taboo on homosexuality, the stigmatisation of lesbian desire that, in widely different forms, is part of everyone's legacy, both subjectively and in terms of the dangers of the social and interpersonal world, and that can have such damaging and restricting effects. Lesbians have to find ways of sustaining love and maintaining their own sense of self-worth in a context where what is most precious to them is often unseen or unvalued, if not completely stigmatised – a considerable psychological achievement that is often unrecognised.


Z. felt herself to be persistently and chronically unable, as she put it, to 'decide' whether she wanted sexual relationships with women or men. This dilemma and seeming indecision persisted through years of therapy. Her actual sexual relationships for all this time and some years before were with women, but her constant 'indecision' was a powerful ingredient in the ambivalence that she experienced in these relationships. She vacillated between feeling not wanted and not loved by the other woman or being herself rejecting of the other as too second rate, and pushing her away. She was acutely aware of feelings of being rejected but her own very strong rejecting impulses and expressions were, on the whole, not available to her consciousness, and much therapeutic work centred on this and the fears that led her so insistently and unconsciously to push others away when any seemingly longed for closeness loomed. Her experience of this was always that the other was no good in some way, a source of unbearable disappointment to her, but this hid terrifying anxieties about her rage and her desire getting out of control were she to allow herself to sustain more engagement.

Z. often felt that the other woman didn't see her 'as a woman', and would rather be with a man or could only love her inasmuch as she approximated to a man or had some masculine qualities. She couldn't conceive of being loved as a woman, especially by a woman. Part of the appeal of the hypothetical idea of being involved with a man was that this appeared to convey more certainty and more appreciation of her as a woman, but she also felt that women found her much more attractive than men did. This confirmed how she felt that being with a woman was inferior. A long time previously she had had a sexual relationship of two years' duration with a man, which had seemed friendly and supportive but not very engaging. Most of her sexual fantasies, dreams and unfulfilled longings involved women, but some of her dreams and occasional conscious experiences involved sexual encounters with men.

Z.'s inability to decide or, as she sometimes said, to 'commit' herself in the area of her sexuality was echoed in many other arenas. For example, she had a persistent difficulty in committing herself to buying anything other than the most everyday items. The choices she was presented with felt impossible, and she would become beset with fears about making the wrong choice, being ripped off, finding what she did buy to be no good, and feeling ridiculous and ashamed.

Z. did not like identifying herself as lesbian in the sense of saying to anyone that this was how she saw herself, nor did she particularly seek out lesbian venues or make alignments with others she perceived as lesbian. She did not in any way try to conceal the fact that she lived with her woman partner, although she never challenged her family's unspoken assumption that they were 'just friends'. It soon became clear that what prevented her from being able to be more open and definite about herself, and also have the kind of sexual relationship that she ostensibly longed for, was not any particular fear about her family's attitudes but a range of deeply unconscious fears about herself in relation to others. These fears proved very resistant to therapeutic intervention and manifested themselves in ways that could easily have misled the therapist.

Z. persistently kept presenting to the therapist the possibility that she might, after all, prefer to have a sexual relationship with a man. This repetitive presentation of a possibility kept wholly hypothetical most often occurred in the context of discussions about her feelings for particular women and effectively served to cut short any greater exploration of her sexual fantasies, longings and dislikes in relation to particular people. This cutting short of any discussion or exploration in therapy of the possibilities for intimacy and physical contact with another person closely paralleled her recurrent difficulties in achieving such engagement outside therapy, but the acknowledgement and understanding of this could not be taken in and put to use by her. Instead, she would either abruptly change the focus of talk to a relatively safe subject, or feel intensely nauseous and dizzy and then black out.

Initially the therapist also felt under intense pressure to 'decide': were Z.'s great difficulties in lesbian relationships due to long-standing anxieties and conflicts about closeness and physical intimacy – anxieties which the progress of therapy was gradually bringing to light – or would Z. not be happier pursuing relationships with a man, in view of the persistence of this idea? The pressure that the therapist felt under to decide whether Z.

should be with a woman or a man was a counter-transference mirroring of Z.'s seemingly unanswerable dilemma. The therapist herself was at times in danger of being seduced by the idea that heterosexual relationships would offer Z. greater happiness and satisfaction than lesbian ones – Z.'s abiding fantasy. Or, as she formulated it, if Z.'s complex unconscious fears and conflicts about men could be worked through in therapy, then perhaps she would really turn out to be heterosexual after all. The therapist had considerable difficulty in holding onto the line of thought that would help her to understand the defensive aspects of Z.'s persistent but firmly hypothetical posing of heterosexuality as an option for her. In other words, the phantasmagoric and sympto-matic nature of Z.'s dilemmas about her sexual orientation, the motivatedly unanswerable nature of her question, were in danger of being replaced, for the therapist as for Z., by an insistence that there was a real, concrete, either/or choice to be made here, one which would have a certain definitional status as to who Z. was or what she was really like.

The therapist's susceptibility to the pressure for a 'decision' did not derive from any heterosexually normative assumption that Z.'s heterosexual fantasies betrayed a hidden, repressed or feared heterosexuality, although there was indeed much clinical material that did suggest this. Whenever Z. started to talk about fleeting attractions towards a man, strong feelings of repulsion would overwhelm her. Much emerged about her perception of the repulsive/attractive, invasive/longed-for features of her father. It seemed that he had confided in her from an early age about his sexual frustration with her unresponsive mother and his affairs with other women. She had an enormously uncomfortable but very vague feeling of unease and an urge to flee whenever she found herself in any physical proximity to him. She found him disgusting and had terrifying experiences of thinking she either was him or very like him. In one dream, later on in therapy, he was in a fortified prison surrounded by water, and she was swimming towards the prison. Although the water was full of sharks she was a strong swimmer and at last managed to swim all the way and get into the prison. Then everything went up in flames. There were other fleeting sexualised memories, fragments of dreams, where her father appeared as an object of sexual interest and repulsion. As the intricacies of her experience of her father's physicality and sexuality gradually emerged, including a hazy sense of being intruded upon, her frightening identification with this repulsive figure lessened. She became much less doubting of her own status as a woman, but her 'indecision' about her sexual object choices remained, if less insistently.

From a position such as that of Quinodoz (1989), or of others of a similarly heterosexually normative position, this exploration of Z.'s image of and relationship with her father might have added substance to the idea that her lesbianism was a defensive retreat from the mainly unconscious dangers associated with heterosexuality, a way perhaps of maintaining some sexual expression. For some time the therapist did consider this as a way of understanding Z.'s difficulties, but interpretation along these lines did not yield any movement in the 'stuckness' of her 'indecision'. This was despite the often fruitful if very difficult (for Z.) exploration of the originally inaccessible memories about her father.

Z. said that she thought that the therapist wouldn't like it if she became sexually involved with 'anyone else', but at the same time she longed for the therapist to encourage her and give her advice as to how to find a partner. She also found it very hard to imagine disagreeing with the therapist in any way and was frightened by the thought of this. Her enmeshment with the figure of the therapist, which most of the time she attempted to cover up by keeping her as distant as possible, was characterised by a mainly negative adherence, wherein she felt horribly criticised. As a child she had felt, and still felt, that she was continually having to make a choice between her parents. She reported that they were incapable of any love towards each other and were hopeless as parents, constantly squabbling and envying other families. It was as if she was anxiously rushing from one to the other but never staying anywhere. Her father just denigrated her mother and made her seem utterly no good. Her mother was very jealous of any interest Z. showed in her father, and Z. was always anxious about how her mother was if she left her for any length of time. She sensed an enormous danger in betraying her mother, but felt that she had had to take her side in the face of her father's attacks. A perception of Z.'s helpless sense of being divided up by two parents at war, not really loved by either, as a form of unresolved Oedipal conflict was also considered for some time by the therapist. In this perspective, again, it might be thought that a resolution would move Z. towards feeling able to make a heterosexual object choice.

The therapist's evolved perspective was that, whereas this therapeutic exploration could indeed lead to the greater possibility of some heterosexual encounter being realised, it could equally well enable Z. to find more satisfaction and less inhibiting conflict in her relationships with women. It became clearer that, rather than sexual orientation, Z.'s greatest difficulty lay in allowing and sustaining any close contact at all, sexual or otherwise, with anyone, man or woman. This was enacted in the therapeutic relationship, where the therapist had the repeated experience of being kept at a firm distance, of no demands being made by Z., no protest at events like breaks or unexpected absences being voiced, the lack of any greater closeness with the therapist bemoaned but seldom allowed and, if allowed, quickly 'forgotten'. Z.'s ability to keep everything distant was so great that quite often the therapist would find herself thinking how convenient it was to have such an undemanding client and also noticed how reluctant she herself felt to explore Z.'s fears of closeness within the transference. The powerfulness of this seeming reluctance was very great and was a form of mirroring of Z.'s unarticulated terror in relation to any closeness or mutual sense of connection. It was an aspect of Z.'s stuckness that seemed either too hopeless or too terrifying to address. What Z. feared most, and did everything she could to avoid, was the experience of total annihilation that would descend upon her in most interactions. Often, she said, when the therapist talked, she was obliterated, and so she frequently didn't listen. When she talked, she would blot out the therapist. It was either her or the other person; there really wasn't the possibility of two people together in any kind of exchange that would enhance both of them, rather than lead to the obliteration of one.

The great difficulty Z. had in allowing herself any kinds of wants or desires, and especially in being seen to be interested in another person, was ostensibly to do with what a third party (her mother, the therapist) was construed as feeling about this. But, like her indecision about her object choice, this also covered up her often inexpressible fears about any kind of being-in-relation to another and about the destruction of her fragile sense of existence that she dreaded so much. It was this order of anxiety that underlay her continued indecision about the gender of her object choice, and indeed this indecision functioned to keep her anxiety sufficiently warded off to be under some kind of control. This, rather than any 'identity problem', was what contributed to her seeming ambiguity about sexual orientation.

This clinical illustration underlines how, as therapists, we have to be able to sustain a complex and multi-levelled understanding of what we may be presented with – not only in respect of the perhaps more familiar notion of responding to unconscious as well as conscious communications, but also in our own abilities to situate the concepts we most habitually think and understand with, at the juncture of whole systems of discourse, with particular subjectivities embedded in these and necessarily expressed through them.

**References**

Butler, J. (1990) *Gender Trouble: Feminism and the Subversion of Identity*, Routledge, London.
Doan, L. (ed.) (1994) *The Lesbian Postmodern*, Columbia University Press, N.Y.
Foucault, M. (1981) *The History of Sexuality*, Vol. 1, Penguin, London.
McIntosh, M. (1981) 'The homosexual role', in K. Plummer (ed.), *The Making of the Modern Homosexual*, Hutchinson, London.
O'Connor, N. & Ryan, J. (1993) *Wild Desires and Mistaken Identities: Lesbianism and Psychoanalysis*, Virago, London.
Quinodoz, J.-M. (1989) 'Female homosexual patients in psychoanalysis', *International Journal of Psycho-Analysis*, 70:55–63.
Stein, A. (ed.) (1993) *Sisters, Sexperts, Queers*, Penguin Books, N.Y.
Weeks, J. (1981) *Sex, Politics and Society*, Longman, London.

# Chapter 6

# Time limited psychotherapy[1]

## Carol Mohamed and Ruthie Smith

### Introduction

Chapters 6 and 7 draw on our practice of time limited psychotherapy at the Women's Therapy Centre, undertaken during a brief psychotherapy project. Focused time limited therapy has been offered at the Centre for the past 15 years. Out of this work a more intensive project was resourced which aimed to increase the amount of therapy offered directly at the Centre and to develop our practice, assessing the usefulness of various time limited therapy models. In particular we wished to make therapy more accessible to prioritised groups of women who would not otherwise have access[2] and to explore the application and value of psychoanalytic insight into the lives of Black women. Issues in working psychodynamically with Black women, including aspects of intercultural therapy are discussed in Chapter 7.

In this chapter we discuss our experience of offering focused short-term psychoanalytic therapy to a wider client group, including women whose histories might be considered contra-indicative for brief work. We also look at the impact of time as an agent of change, separation and individuation, and ways in which time limited therapy offers, in telescopic form, an opportunity to rework earlier developmental conflicts. In pre-Oedipal issues, where experiences of mothering may have been problematic, women can be helped to connect with, validate, understand and integrate previously cut-off feelings. However, those who have lacked adequate fathering can also gain particular benefits from a time limited therapy relationship, through a re-working of rapprochement and Oedipal issues of separation, boundary setting and dealing effectively with the limitations of external reality. As a result, many clients develop self-esteem and greater confidence in their own autonomy and ability to cope. Later in this chapter, we offer case examples illustrating aspects of various time limited therapies, with particular reference to the technique of Habib Davanloo.

## Historical context of the development of brief therapies

One of the first reported cases of brief therapy in the modern psychotherapy literature was Freud's successful treatment in four sessions of Gustaf Mahler who suffered from sexual impotence (1908). Subsequently a variety of time limited psychodynamic therapies emerged employing techniques which shorten the psycho-analytic process.

However, within mainstream psychoanalysis it became a norma-tive expectation that analysis would require a minimum of 200 one-hour sessions. An extensive study at the Chicago Institute for Psychoanalysis (Alexander & French, 1946) highlighted the fact that few analytic patients actually conformed to this expectation: average attendance was shown to be between six and ten sessions. But far from perceiving themselves as drop-outs and treatment failures, the patients reported effective and lasting change and an impressive reduction of symptoms after only a few sessions. This study encouraged the further development of brief therapy models.

## The economic expediency of time limited work

The recession and the resultant reduction in public services has had major implications for policies on the development of psychotherapy services. While long-term psychoanalytic therapy is desirable in many cases, and has proved beneficial, its cost precludes the possibility of offering it to large numbers of women, unless they can afford therapy in the private sector. Indeed we are sometimes forced to provide therapy on the basis of financial constraints rather than clinical need.

Economic expediency seems to be only universally accepted argument in favour of brief psychotherapy, and 'time is of the essence' in coping with large numbers of patients. Unfortunately this obscures the fact that planned, time limited analytic therapy is not only cost-effective but is often the best form of treatment for the client:

All evidence indicates that planned short term analytic therapies are more than just a poor, barely tolerable substitute for the much-sought-after real thing, namely long, open-ended psychoanalysis (Molnos, 1995)

## The concept of time in therapy

According to Molnos, time is a relative concept. Our ideas of space and 'real' time are mental constructs and as such they have to be learned. Our consciousness of so-called 'everyday reality' is variable and there are several situations in life where time becomes distorted or even 'ceases to exist'. For example, in exploring the unconscious realms of dreams and daydreams we immerse ourselves in childhood and fairytale fantasies, and thus defeat time. When we are intoxicated by 'Love' with its remarkable idealisation of the love object, we transcend time by vowing eternal love and ignoring reality. In addition we alter our sense of time and 'reality' when intoxicated by drink or drugs, or when experiencing mystical states in which we encounter a 'reality' beyond time and space.[3]

This unconscious experience and suspension of time is the principle lengthening factor of psychoanalytic therapies, which have a tendency to become longer and longer. The idea of an open-ended psychoanalytic contract, endorsed by the wishes of the unconscious which are timeless, seduces us into a sense of infinite time. This sense of limitlessness is akin to the fantasy in which mother and child are endlessly united, taking us away from our fear of finite time and its reminder of impermanence, endings, losses, change and, ultimately, our terror of death.

The date on the calendar denoting the end of therapy is, then, the ultimate materialisation of separation anxiety. However, paradoxically, this finite sense of the time limit also serves as a major reassurance to the ego of its own existence, separateness and possibility of being an active and adult subject in the world.

### Time as the catalyst for change

In short-term therapy, which addresses itself to both 'child' and 'adult' time, the time limit provides the crucial ingredient which mediates between unconscious and conscious processes. Since the client's dreams, fantasies and idealisation of the therapist in the transference relationship are an integral part of the work, the quality of the therapeutic experience therefore includes both inner experiences of 'timeless' childlike states and also an abrupt confrontation with (relative) external reality and the need to function as an adult.

In the tension between timelessness and the time limit, union and separation become the major poles of treatment in brief therapy, which has the effect of diminishing the intensity of all other phase specific conflicts and the anxieties attached to them (Mann, 1979). The chosen focus for the therapy, together with the underlying dynamic development conflict and the constriction of the time limit, promotes a clear regression back through existential time. At the same time, this process is condensed and moderated by the enormous forward pressure to the 'real' end of time. The boundary of the time limit sharply awakens the client from her unconscious fantasy to bond endlessly with the therapist into the conscious reality of her sense of separateness. In this way, time serves as one of the greatest factors in mobilising the client's resources, acting as the catalyst for growth and change.

## Time boundaries, separation and individuation

When a client comes for psychotherapy, she does not necessarily know what a long or brief contract is. She will learn unconsciously, through the therapist's positive attitude and belief in time limited work, to mobilise her resources, tune in to the length of therapy available and work with it accordingly. The greater the ambiguity about the length of therapy, the greater the influence of 'child time' on unconscious wishes and expectations; whereas, the greater the specificity of duration (including the number of sessions and ending date), the more rapidly and appropriately is the client confronted with reality and the work to be done. This is why it is so important that the ending date is clearly established from the start of the therapeutic contract. Malan, commenting on the value of the time limit in working through endings, spoke of the 'powerful potential therapeutic effect both in telling a patient that he must take responsibility for his own life, and of reassuring him that he can manage without the therapeutic help' (Malan, 1979).

It is arguable, then, that in brief therapy, establishing the ending date before therapy begins performs a paternal function of clear setting of rules, boundaries and limits, offering the client another opportunity to work through the rapprochement and/or Oedipal phases and to emerge more fully individuated. In the move towards adulthood through the developmental process of separation and individuation, the psychoanalytic literature emphasises that recognition of the 'self' by the 'other' is vital. The child moves away from the merged, passive, dependent state with mother to a state of active independence in which an acknowledgement of the child's agency and ability to be a subject is crucial. Due to the asymmetry of the rapprochement and Oedipal phases for boys and girls, this can be more difficult for a girl to achieve. It is to the father (or other 'third party') that the little girl must look to establish her sense of selfhood, psychic separateness, and capacity to be and act in the world (Benjamin, 1988).

In this respect, and particularly because issues of dependency cannot be overly encouraged in brief therapy, we would argue that there is less focus on the maternal issues of merging and dependence and more emphasis on the therapist's paternal role. Here, through recognising and encouraging the client's ability as a subject who is capable of facing and accepting the reality of her life, the time limited therapeutic relationship becomes an agent for individuation, autonomy and change.

## Accessibility of analytic psychotherapy

We had become increasingly aware of the desperate need for a psychotherapy service for women with acute and chronic difficulties, many of whom had previously been turned away by various institutions as 'unsuitable cases for treatment' and who were finding it difficult to get help. While we acknowledge that there may be some women for whom brief and time limited psychotherapy is unsuitable, and believe that it is important to make realistic assessments of what a person might accomplish in therapy, we nonetheless wanted to address this lack or provision by broadening our therapeutic approach, adapting various analytic therapeutic models to meet the differing needs of our client group and making therapy more widely available.

We increased the number of brief and short-term therapy spaces[4] and, after making an assessment in the initial consultation(s), offered women contracts of various lengths within which to work on a focus of their choice. Contracts included: 6–25 weeks of brief individual therapy of one session per week; time limited contracts of one or two years; and combination therapy whereby women started with a few individual sessions of therapy and then continued in a one-year analytic group. Where relevant, women were referred on to alternative therapeutic services both within and outside the Centre, such as specialist projects for incest and eating disorders. Finally, to make therapy more immediately available to distressed women, our policy was to keep only a very short waiting list so that women did not have to wait long before being seen for their initial consultation and could be offered a therapy contract straight away if they wished to take up the offer.

### Working with differences

As we well know, women come to therapy with many fantasies, fears, preconceptions and expectations. However, before the woman arrives in the consultation room for her first session, there are many issues to be considered. We needed to be aware of *who* might be coming for therapy, what particular *needs* she may have and what *therapy resources* are available. We asked ourselves how we might offer a service which specifically encompasses the different needs of our prioritised groups – Black women, women with disability, lesbians, and working-class women on low incomes. In highlighting issues of accessibility to therapy, we wanted to acknowledge the way in which these women suffer various forms of discrimination.

For example, we have seen lesbians at the Centre who had previously experienced therapies in which their sexual choice was viewed as the main 'problem' to be 'cured'. This had clearly prevented them in the past from feeling safe enough to explore any issues, including those related to their sexuality.

Women with disabilities have also generally been the object of prejudice, and may anticipate the recurrence of this within a therapy or counselling situation. Sorting out the practical issues of, for example, wheelchair access well in advance of the first session is a vital pre-requisite in helping such women feel that they are coming to a 'safe' place where their needs will be understood.

A white working-class woman on the other hand may fear that therapy is a middle-class approach to dealing with problems which fails to take into account the hardships and physical realities she is facing. An acknowledgement of these realities can enable her to move on to explore intrapsychic issues which may be contributing to her distress.

Psychoanalytic theory has not specifically addressed intercultural issues and the impact of racism on an individual's life. It became clear to us that many Black women were very apprehensive of entering therapy and we discuss the wider issues of the effects of racism in limiting access to therapy in the next chapter.

To ensure that we could offer an adequate understanding of issues facing our priority groups, we explored implications for our clinical work by addressing the effects of racism, homophobia and working with disability in therapists' study and reading groups.

*Finding a way into the culture of analytic therapy*

We also looked at how we could make the 'culture' of analytic therapy more accessible to women who generally viewed therapy as elitist, middle class, white and prejudiced. From doing hundreds of assessments we were very struck by the numbers of women who had previously and unsuccessfully attempted to enter analytic therapy. They had felt alienated by sophisticated 'rules' which had not been explained to them and had left after the first consultation, feeling foolish and inadequate. Women who have never had time for themselves because they have spent so much time in looking after others may find it hard to use the unstructured space analytic therapy offers them, especially if there is little feedback from the therapist.

We needed to help clients who are largely unfamiliar with the tenets of analytic therapy to find a way into the 'culture' of therapy so that they could work comfortably and usefully within it. Brief psychotherapy models differ from long-term therapies in that they involve more active participation from the therapist. This discourages regression and dependency and enables the client to feel more confident in her power to make choices.

In some situations, we found it helpful to demystify aspects of the analytic process so that a woman who comes to therapy for the first time can understand how to participate in it fully. For instance we might explain about working within therapeutic boundaries and about the style of therapy being offered which involves non-disclosure by the therapist. This sometimes conflicted with the client's fantasies about the therapist as a friend and so, at times, discussion about issues of power in the relationship was also relevant. We might explain about the analytic space and how it is for the client to take the initiative and choose what they wish to talk about in the sessions. Here, the fragility of the client's ego would need to be taken into account: in brief therapy it is rarely appropriate to leave the client floundering for too long in silence. We might also explain how an important part of the work of therapy takes place in the relationship between the therapist and client. The client would be encouraged to recount dreams and fantasies about the therapist and other aspects of their life as useful means of getting in touch with their unconscious processes, and the use of interpretations might be explained. We applied these ideas selectively according to each individual situation, easing clients as we felt necessary into the therapeutic framework.

## Some clinical aspects of time limited analytic psychotherapy

The brief therapy we offer at the Women's Therapy Centre is neither psychoanalysis nor counselling, although it contains elements of both. The major analytic tools we employ are working with dreams, interpretations and transference, but we draw on additional techniques as appropriate to the capacity of our clients. To summarise, we use the *four pointed framework for brief therapy* widely used by practitioners as the essential structure of our practice. These points are: firstly, a planned good ending; secondly, the adoption of a realistic therapeutic focus or goal; thirdly, the recognition and working through of the underlying developmental conflicts; and fourthly, the establishment of a good therapeutic alliance and working agreement (Erikson, 1950).

### Initial consultation and assessment for time limited therapy

In our first consultation with the client we are answering these questions:

- Can brief or time limited therapy be *useful for the client?*
- What type of *therapeutic aim* can realistically be achieved?
- What *length of contract* is appropriate to accomplish this aim?

The initial meeting is the most crucial aspect of the brief therapy. An explanation is given concerning the purpose, format and length of the consultation, and the client is required to fill out a simple form giving some demographic information and to answer questions concerning her expectations of therapy. She is then offered a space to speak about why she is seeking help, and to tell us something about her history.

The purpose of the consultation is to determine as quickly as possible whether time limited therapy could be useful and, if not, which other options might be possible. According to Malan's criteria of contra-indications for brief dynamic therapy, many of the women who come to us would not 'qualify', particularly regarding their histories of early separations, destructive 'acting out' patterns, obsessions, addictions and serious suicidal tendencies. Given our client group, we had to become more flexible in the way we work and so we drew on the theories of Anthony Ryle's cognitive analytic therapy (1990), which is appropriate for more disturbed clients. In cases where brief therapy was clearly unsuitable, one outlet for women who needed open-ended low-cost therapy was through psychotherapy training programmes, and we also referred women into other resources within the community such as support groups. In particular we have observed that anorexic women and women with long-term bulimic histories need longer-term therapies.

The focus for the therapy often, though not always, develops out of the client's expressed 'presenting problem'. However, a 'psycho-analytic diagnosis' of underlying developmental issues helps us to locate the client's deeper conflicts and establish a realistic therapeutic focus within the time limit available. The 'psychotherapeutic forecast' (Malan, 1979) is important in identifying any likely areas of conflict in the therapy and in the transference. For example, if a client has a pattern of walking out of relationships angrily, due to an unresolved conflict with her mother, this may also be repeated in the therapy. This would indicate the need to explore such a possibility with the client within the first session(s), and to build safeguards into the contract.

Finally, we try to minimise possible confusions that can arise by being as clear as possible about the details of the therapeutic contract, such as the practical issues regarding session times, use of the creche, disability access, special needs and financial arrangements. However, while specific ground is covered in each assessment, the format for conducting them is personal, and each therapist has her own style and chooses how she conducts the session.

## Aspects of the therapeutic relationship in time limited work

The style of time limited work is radically different from an open-ended approach. We have identified from the literature and from our own experience particular features which have the effect of speeding up the process of therapy. In short-term work we *avoid lengthening factors* such as regression, dependency and a preoccupation with early infancy issues, although these deeper developmental conflicts can be recognised, acknowledged and touched on lightly without creating an unhelpful dependency. To this end, while acknowledging to ourselves that it is always there, we *work selectively with the transference*. In Winnicottian terms, we have to be content with 'good enough' and let go that are not relevant to the focus of the brief contract. Vital to this process is the *therapist's belief in the value of brief work*. Clients often have no concept of what is considered 'short' or 'long', so a short-term contract is offered in a confident spirit to the client, the agreement about the therapeutic goal suggesting without any hesitation that something can be done in the agreed number of sessions. Time limited therapy is quite energetic, having a certain pace to it, and while the therapist makes no promises about what can be achieved, the optimistic attitude helps to mobilise the client's positive resources

## The phases of the therapy

In the *beginning phase* there is a certain *immediacy* in being able to offer a contract straight away which maximises the client's positive motivation to seek help. From the outset, the therapist takes an *active role* in helping the client to clarify issues. The *therapeutic alliance* is achieved when a *clear contract* is established concerning the *therapeutic aim or focus* and the number of sessions and *ending date* have been set. Further clarifications on the therapeutic aim are generally finalised by the second or third session, and during this time the therapist will also be looking to determine the underlying *dynamic focus* or 'central statement' (Mann, 1979), which is the underlying (unconscious) developmental conflict. Many theorists now agree that in a large number of cases, 12 sessions allow sufficient time for working through the dynamic focus, although effective work can also be achieved in longer and shorter contracts. We encourage the client to view herself as a person who has *power to exercise choices* and, as a general point, we have found that the fewer the number of sessions offered, the more active the client needs to be in taking responsibility for her choice to take up this form of therapy. The 'honeymoon period' of the beginning phase capitalises on the client's positive motivation, and is experienced as being like the 'golden glow of unity with mother' where the therapist often becomes an intensely idealised positive transference object.

However, the *middle phase* brings with it the realisation that a relationship, once wholly unambivalent, will (once again, if it is repeating difficult experiences with a significant other) become disappointing. The work of this phase is in the reframing of negative constructs, reviewing outer world changes, and working through interpersonal conflict, either within the therapeutic alliance or by reference to other intimate relationships. The dynamic focus generally emerges during this middle phase of the work and is often the same as the one the client suffered in early life. The basic conflicts will vary according to social, economic and cultural factors, but four universal conflicts which we all experience to different degrees are: independence versus dependence; activity versus passivity; adequate self-esteem versus diminished self-esteem; and unresolved or delayed grief (Mann, 1979). These conflicts may be experienced simultaneously. They are often connected with difficulties in individuation and separation from the meaningful, ambivalently experienced object (person), who might be mother or father, or a significant other: in our experience it is often the mother. Arriving at a greater awareness of these unconscious issues helps the client to become more aware of the ways in which she operates in the world, and mobilises her to become more proactive.

The *ending*, which is kept in sight right from the beginning, introduces the harsh, unavoidable struggle over giving up the object once more, this time without self-defeating anger, or despair, or hatred, or guilt. This heralds the individuation/separation phase of growth and development. A climax (which may be more or less chaotic) will often be reached in the last few weeks, and sometimes as late as the penultimate session.

## Specific techniques in time limited analytic therapy illustrated by case examples

Making links between the client's *past* early life experience of relationships amongst family and siblings (P), their *current* (or recent past) issues in the world (C), and how these relate to the re-enactment of the client's past experiences in the *transference* relationship with the therapist (T) is a standard technique in the analytic relationship, and has been deemed essential for use in brief therapy by theorist David Malan (1979). He uses the term 'triangle of insight' to describe this process, in which conflictual relationship patterns originating from the client's early history are unconsciously repeated. Gaining insight into these patterns offers the client the possibility of resolving the conflict, and of change.

Another technique developed by Habib Davanloo (1978), which has caused much controversy in the psychoanalytic world, has proved particularly effective in short-term dynamic therapy. Known as the 'triangle of conflict' it involves, firstly, a relentless and fearless confrontation of the defences using a method of Socratic questioning which breaks through to the client's underlying anxieties, revealing true (and intensely experienced) feelings. The aim is to get to the heart of the problem as quickly as possible. For some clients, being challenged in a containing and caring way can help to release emotions which, if suppressed, might otherwise sabotage the therapy. A wide range of voice intonation is used by the therapist as a means of holding, encouraging and exhorting the client to experience her feelings in the present moment. The anxiety level of the client is quite high, but this style of work helps her to feel safe enough to disclose her hidden (and formerly unconscious) feelings, enabling a positive shift to take place so that she contacts her 'true self' directly.

We will use an example of a painfully shy client who was terrified of intimacy to describe this process. When the therapist asked her about one of her relationships she started laughing nervously. She was then asked directly, '*Why are you laughing?*' (confronting the defence) which elicited acute embarrassment and uncontrolled laughter. She then managed to reply that she always laughed when embarrassed. She was then asked '*Why are you embarrassed?* which brought out even more acute embarrassment and disintegration into tears. In asking her, more gently, '*What are you crying about?*, she replied that she became afraid if anyone tried to get close to her in intimate situations. She was then asked, '*What are you afraid of?*, to which she replied that if anyone saw what she was really like, they would think she was stupid and would not like her (underlying anxiety). In this moment of intimate contact with the therapist, where her true self had been revealed, she was asked, '*Are you afraid now?*, at which point she visibly relaxed, all embarrassment, tears and laughter gone, and said, 'No, this feels OK.'

By identifying deeper feelings so quickly, this technique offers the client considerable relief and helps her to develop confidence and trust in the therapist, leading to a naked and direct style of working with minimal resistance in the transference. The warm and open contact, devoid of defences, offers a 'corrective emotional experience' in the therapeutic relationship (Molnos, 1995), where the client feels known, recognised and accepted as they are. Though this method does indeed require a certain ego strength on the part of the client if she is to withstand it, it is nonetheless not as aggressive as it might appear, and can engender a powerful feeling of intimacy and understanding which facilitates rapid progress in the 'working through' phase of therapy.

The 'triangle of conflict' method is entirely based on psychoanalytic theory about the human psyche and its mechanisms, which is held in the therapist's mind and translated into accessible insights at appropriate moments. The therapist adopts an educational role, *teaching* the client how to learn for herself the psychodynamics of her problem rather than making interpretations in the usual sense of the term. Through Socratic questioning, the therapist elicits responses which enable the client to think more consciously for herself about her processes and understand better the way in which her mind operates. By revealing to herself her own unconscious processes, rather than having them interpreted and exposed to her by the therapist, the intensity of the power dynamics is reduced, creating more real contact and less neurotic transference. The client *learns* how her defence mechanisms block more satisfying forms of communication, while at the same time *experiencing* a new way of relating from the place of her undefended true self. Through this process both emotional and cognitive aspects of the self become integrated, and the client feels more able to think for herself and recognise her own resources and capacities for self-understanding. This helps her to develop self-confidence and esteem.

Extensive research using videos of Davanloo's therapy sessions and follow-up has shown this method to have a very high 'success' rate in the eradication of symptoms and long-lasting improved functioning of the client. However, at a symposium on brief therapy in Austria in 1986 where this technique was presented, the 200 psychoanalysts and psychotherapists present were split down the middle in a furious and vitriolic debate, and a substantial number walked out in disgust. Many of the therapists perceived Davanloo as bullying his patients. However, if one looks more closely at the interaction, one sees that the therapist is not bullying at all, but 'standing firmly on the patient's side, fighting the punishing super-ego' (Molnos, 1986).

David Malan, a key figure in brief psychoanalytic theory, and once one of the fiercest opponents of Davanloo's method, eventually altered his own way of working to become its greatest advocate, describing it as the 'most important development in psychotherapy since the discovery of the unconscious'. He goes on to describe how it is 'capable of breaking through and achieving direct access to the unconscious of even the most resistant of patients in a single interview' (Malan & Osimo, 1992).

The following case example demonstrates the combined use of the 'triangle of insight' and the 'triangle of conflict' in a nine-week contract with a woman suffering from an hysterical somatic condition.

### 'Blind with rage'

'Janice' was a white lesbian in her 20s who came to therapy in quiet but complete desperation as a result of having recently lost most of her eyesight. Hospital diagnosis and clinical tests confirmed a serious blind spot in the retina with the prognosis that it would get worse resulting in time in total blindness. Initially she presented as shy and reserved. However, motivated by the seriousness of the crisis, she was extremely open to therapy, acutely intelligent and responded well to trial interpretations.

It was very important in the therapy for both therapist and client to start by acknowledging the physical reality and severity of

Janice's symptoms so that she felt she was 'seen' and could trust the therapist. Once trust was established, the desperation of her predicament meant that there was nothing to lose by looking together at alternative meanings of her situation. She showed herself keen to explore the possible psychological aspects of her physical symptoms and to understand ways in which her body might act as a vehicle for expressing her emotional experience. A focus was arrived at to explore her blindness as a metaphor including the perspective, 'What if it were a psychosomatic condition?' In the process of arriving at therapeutic goals at the beginning, a therapeutic alliance was established, allowing the therapist to make interventions later on in the therapy which the client could receive openly and undefensively. Without this agreement, the therapist's subsequent interventions would have been experienced as persecuting and abusive.

Janice was the eldest daughter of a family in which no feelings could be discussed or acknowledged. She described her mother as a severe, cold and efficient woman, who had not cuddled Janice as a child, nor shown emotions other than critical, angry or disapproving ones. The mother, herself an eldest daughter, had been ignored and victimised by her stepmother, and she treated Janice in a similar manner. Janice retaliated in her adolescence by becoming anorexic and refusing to eat her mother's food. This was her only way of maintaining some kind of control in what was otherwise an intolerable situation. She used her body to express her distress, protecting herself by not taking anything in; this represented externally and symbolically what was taking place in her internal world.

Janice's relationship with her father was also conflictual. On the one hand he was caring and acknowledged her reality, but on the other, he denied it by colluding with the rest of the family in scapegoating and ridiculing her. She was subjected to constant humiliation and psychological abuse for being a failure and not achieving as highly as her other siblings.

When, just prior to coming for therapy, Janice reported her loss of vision to her parents, crying with distress in front of them and clearly expressing a need to be comforted, her mother was unable to respond, remaining aloof and cut off (C). This reminded Janice of the time in her childhood when it had been discovered at school that she was short-sighted because she could not see the blackboard. Her mother had denied her need (P), and it was only when her father had intervened at a later date that she was given glasses.

Interventions in the therapy were related directly to the symptoms concerning her sight and vision. For example, she *avoided looking* at the therapist during the sessions and exploration of this in the transference revealed Janice's fear that the therapist was like her cold, critical and disapproving mother, who might also deny the reality of her difficulty (T) just as she had re-experienced when she went home to tell her parents about her blindness.

As Janice began to develop further trust she spoke more openly and freely. It transpired that she found it a *strain* to *look* at people, and that her mother in particular had never been able to *look her in the eye* so that all communication was indirect. She found it easy to relate to the metaphor, offering openings for bolder suggestions from the therapist. In asking what this *blind spot* might represent in terms of her relationship to her family, it was revealed that she felt she had already been 'written off' as being stupid by her family and that her lesbianism had also not been *recognised*, as it was something that could not be '*seen*' or permitted by the family. Her *insight, vision* and *perceptions* of what was going on were totally denied and invalidated by her family, who appeared to *perceive* a completely different reality. In fact, it turned out that Janice had a very *acute perception* of what was going on in the family, but that this was unacceptable and threatening to the rest of them, since she could actually *see through* the games that people were playing and was not prepared to collude with them.

In the therapy Janice presented herself as being very placid (*dynamic focus, passivity versus activity*) and did not appear to be in touch with any anger about her situation. In the counter-transference, however, the therapist was conscious of extremely powerful feelings of rage, accompanied by murderous and sadistic fantasies about wishing to attack savagely and wipe out Janice. Reflecting to herself on these feelings (which she understood to be communications made by her client through the very early psychic mechanisms of projective identification), led the therapist to think about what this desire to 'wipe out' might mean. How did this connect with the client's 'blind spot'? What was she *losing sight of*? Suddenly the thought arose: was she *blind with rage*? Making this suggestion out loud hit home. It led to an intense rush of feelings as Janice dramatically connected up with her anger and appeared ready to explode. It was as though the veil which had been *obscuring* her feelings was removed.

Thus a further clarification of the therapy focus emerged: to explore the unexpressed anger and rage Janice felt towards her family, and to find out if there was any relationship between this and her seriously impaired vision. She uncovered an enormous amount of rage towards her parents, which she had previously been too frightened to 'see' or own as her own. As she began to release this 'healing anger' (Molnos, 1995) in the remaining sessions, her eyesight miraculously seemed to recover. Within four weeks her vision was almost normal, and by the end of the therapy it was completely restored. This was confirmed by clinical tests at the hospital. It would appear that her 'blindness' may have been an hysterical symptom in reaction to the emotional difficulties and frustrations she was facing at home, and the impossibility of her sexuality and other aspects of her identity being seen and recognised.

Instead of adopting her customary powerless passive role, the energy of her anger gave her the confidence to go home and take a more assertive and active role in challenging her parents, asking them why they had been so unkind to her in the past. The internal changes within Janice affected the dynamic with her parents, who were so surprised that they opened up considerably to her. During the nine-week period Janice was able to acknowledge and work through feelings of considerable loss and disappointment about her mother's inability to mother her, and to come to a clearer understanding of her parents' limitations.

It is worth reiterating here that there is not enough time in brief dynamic therapy for the therapist to present herself as a 'blank screen'. Such an approach could result in clients getting caught up in transference issues in which only the fantasised transference version of the therapist is apparent. Instead, the therapist needs to be active, humanly accessible and 'real', creating a very intense quality of engagement in the time limited relationship. In this case of a client 'losing sight', it seems that the therapist's role was not only as an object of transference but, more significantly, as a therapeutic ally, making a particular ego alliance which supported the healthy part of Janice which could see, in order to look together at understanding the part that was blind (in this case, unconscious and repressed). Rather than overly encouraging a negative transference in which the therapist would be experienced as persecuting and in opposition to her, Janice was able to feel that the therapist was 'on her side', working together with her to see and understand her issues. Having a positive experience of undefended contact with the therapist made it safe enough to explore, accept and integrate more fearful and unwanted aspects of her psyche in a non-judgemental environment.

We believe, along with crisis intervention theorists, that the impact of a crisis – in this case Janice's desperation in facing blindness – can have a very profound effect in making a client open and available to change at deep levels. We also note that the alleviation of somatic symptoms is a well known outcome in the documentation of brief psychotherapies. Indeed, somatising is a frequent occurrence amongst our clients, since women often project unconscious and unwanted feelings into their bodies, using them as vehicles for expressing psychic distress that they have not been able to articulate by other means.

As a final point, it is notable that Janice's mother, like many other mothers of our clients, and like many of our clients themselves, was repeating the same pattern of mothering that she had experienced in her own childhood.

※      ※      ※

As in the above and following case, many of our clients suffer from pre-Oedipal issues where they are cut off from their true feelings in some way. Connecting with these feelings is one of the major aspects of the therapeutic work. We have found that the cognitive analytic therapy (CAT) approach developed by Anthony Ryle (1990) offers a variety of accessible working tools which are useful for addressing these issues in short-term work. For example, a *dilemma* describes the polarity or the *either/or* position in which the person feels restricted by a polarised choice, giving rise to ambivalence. In psychoanalytic terms this relates to issues of separation, individuation and, in extreme cases, to the schizoid position. However, in lay terms, dilemmas offer clients a simple understanding of the mechanism of psychological splitting in an unthreatening way. The therapeutic aim is to reach a realistic resolution through integrating a third solution. For example, by exploring a client's dilemma that 'in relationships I am either close and over-dependent, or cut off and scared', the problem is *reformulated* to give rise to a new possibility and desired 'resolution': 'I am able to relate mutually with another without losing myself'.

*Snags* on the other hand describe the unconscious fantasies and defences of inner sabotaging mechanisms which prevent a person from fulfilling their potential. *Reciprocal role procedures* offer another means of understanding the mechanisms of splitting and projection, and of integrating splits in the psyche. The client is asked to identify the reciprocal roles she plays – for example, victim/abuser or hurt child/judgemental parent – by answering simple questions which help her to reflect on her past relationships. In linking her past experience with her current role(s), she can understand how this originated in her identifications with significant others in early life, and recognise the part that these images now play in her fantasies, as characters on her inner stage to which she becomes quite attached as part of her identity. She is then encouraged to own and integrate both sides of the polarity (split) within herself.

Disowning and projecting unwanted parts of the psyche onto another person or dependency object (such as an abuser, alcohol or drugs) leads to a disavowal of taking any responsibility in the situation, and retaining the powerless role of victim or hurt child. As Fairbairn noted, achieving a healthier state entails for the client 'a renunciation of compulsive attachments to objects based on primary identification and merger in favour of relationships based on differentiation and exchange' (Greenberg & Mitchell, 1983). When the 'victim' is able to *renounce* her attachment to negative identifications (which involves the cognitive process of consciously *choosing* to do so) and to own her 'abusive' part through accepting her feelings of anger, she can move on from her stuck position and utilise her energy in more constructive ways, for example by finding greater ability to assert herself and function in the world as an independent person. When working with clients with addictions, giving up the *fantasised* object that can never satisfy and *exchanging* it for a more realistic relationship (with a person who will not be perfect) is vital. In this respect, active renunciation, which acknowledges setting a limit and abstaining from negatively repeated patterns of attachment, is at the heart of the work.

In the next case, which was a ten-week contract of crisis intervention with a heroin addict, Davanloo's confrontational approach was used in combination with some of the CAT methods. Through this process, destructive anger transformed into 'healing anger' which could then be worked through. It was important not to collude with the client's 'destructive idealisation' of the therapist, whereby negative feelings would remain unconscious and become split off and projected out (or acted out) elsewhere. Earlier on we mentioned the importance of establishing a positive 'therapeutic alliance'. This does not mean that disappointments are avoided or that we wrap the client in therapeutic cotton wool. In the process of learning how to connect with previously cut-off painful feelings, clients undergo a period of mourning and sadness which ultimately leads to a more complete and integrated sense of self. Coming to terms with pain and disappointment is therefore a vital aspect of the therapeutic process. In this case, the anger (sometimes employed as a defence against sadness) later gave way to more painful feelings of loss and hurt.

### 'Tragic heroin(e)'

A young heroin addict and nursing mother was totally shocked that she had been left 'holding the baby' by a partner who had unexpectedly abandoned her when she gave birth. 'Rosa', an East European refugee, came from a background of sexual and emotional abuse and physical neglect. In her adolescence she had fled to London where she had turned to drugs, but she had managed to give it up in her early 20s. However, when her partner left, she began again to take heroin while breastfeeding her baby, and came to the Women's Therapy Centre in panic when she suddenly woke up to what she was doing. Her baby was the only symbol of hope left in a world which had disintegrated around her, whilst reawakening ugly scenes of her parents' fraught marriage, traumas of abandonment by her father who had died when she was a small girl, and fury at her mother who had failed to nurture her or protect her from systematic and brutal abuse by a stepfather.

In her first session, she described herself as a 'tragic heroine', although she was quite unconscious of the pun. This image of herself helped her to clarify her focus; she decided to work on 'empowering herself to stop acting out the victim/abuser roles' (*CAT reciprocal role procedures*). A later addition to this focus was to work on being able to assert her personal boundaries.

The only therapy space that was available at the time was a ten-week short-term contract which could serve as a useful piece of crisis intervention to help Rosa come to terms with 'holding the baby' until other resources could be determined. In negotiating the contract, care was taken to consider whether at the end of ten weeks she was again going to feel abandoned – this time by the therapist. Was she prepared to take responsibility for taking this risk? She decided that she was, and so in addition to working on her chosen focus, she began to plan what other forms of support she could establish for herself when the therapy ended. The combination of the pressures of the briefness of the contract, her intense motivation to be able to care for her baby and stop using heroin, and the desperation of her circumstances enabled her to mobilise her resources and engage intensively in the therapy.

Rosa's shocked, numb, victim-like stance in therapy soon gave way under probing questions (*Davanloo, breaking down of defences*) and her therapy soon developed into a very confrontational affair. She raged extensively at the therapist, re-enacting the abusive role one minute and the next being the 'tragic heroine' (victim). She became even more furious when, in an interpretation keeping her to the focus, the therapist pointed this out.

In the transference, the therapist was experienced sometimes as being like Rosa's emotionally unavailable and manipulative mother, whom she found it hard to trust, or alternatively as being like her abandoning and abusive partner and stepfather. Through contacting her rage Rosa began to understand and work through intense distress at the failure of both her partner and her mother, and deep grief at the loss of her father and separation from her home country. The anger served constructively in helping her to separate psychologically from her ex partner, giving her enough sense of self-respect to keep her boundaries and avoid seeing him, which, she knew, would have been destructive since she felt addicted to him as though he were a drug.

The underlying dynamic focus emerged as deep unresolved dependency issues from childhood reactivated by her current situation of abandonment and neglect which left her feeling both outraged and undeserving. She expressed these needs through addictive tendencies and unhealthy attachments in all areas of her life; she was constantly looking for an abusive person (or substance) to come and rescue her. At the same time, however, she was struggling to take responsibility for herself as an adult in the world. How could she parent a child, when she herself was motherless and fatherless, a rootless refugee, her inner world stricken with pain? The crisis of having a baby forced her to experience feelings of the desperate baby part of herself which lay beneath her angry defence, and in contacting these, she sobbed for the first time since the birth of the baby. Being able to cry surprised her greatly, and managing to entrust these feelings to the therapist helped her to feel much closer to her which brought a sense of comfort and relief. This began a process of enabling her to integrate more of her own vulnerable and dependent feelings which in turn helped her to find a way of being more in touch with and tolerating her baby's needs. Her fantasy that she would break down if she allowed herself to express her pain turned out to be false. On the contrary, the more she allowed herself to express the pain and mess of her inner life in therapy, the better she was able to cope with her responsibilities in the outside world.

Rosa managed to renounce her attachments to her abusive partner and to heroin, which she stopped using. She was very conscientious in the care of her baby whom she was breastfeeding, and was beginning to find some hope in her life. However, as therapy drew towards a close she (predictably) began to act out her anger towards the therapist over the ending. She did this by failing to eat or nourish herself (*underlying developmental conflict of dependency* – she wanted the therapist to 'hold the baby' and feed her). She was losing weight rapidly to the point that she was seriously endangering her health and that of the baby and causing great concern to the therapist. It is possible that she transferred her addictive tendencies towards heroin onto her use of food by becoming anorexic.

When Rosa complained pathetically that she was not eating, the therapist suggested that she had turned the rage and fury she felt towards her in on herself and was desperate to be fed; she was playing the victim role in the hope that the therapist would rescue her by not ending the therapy. Rosa was furious at the truth of this statement. The therapist then asked Rosa if she could cook? 'Of course I can xxxx cook', she replied, swearing angrily and ranting (*Molnos, direct, healing anger*). The therapist replied gently and firmly, 'Well why don't you go and cook and eat then?' (*Davanloo, direct intervention without interpreting*).

The following week Rosa reported that she had been very shocked by the therapist's direct and simple response which she had experienced as holding and nurturing the inner baby within herself. In this state of openness and surprise, she had felt that a real meeting and connection had taken place and, as a consequence of taking in some nourishment from the therapeutic relationship, she felt able to start feeding herself again.

By the end of the therapy, Rosa had managed to find some low-cost long-term counselling which would shortly be available, and she was encouraged to write and let the therapist know how she was getting on. She wrote a warm follow-up letter three months after her brief contract had ended, reporting that she had managed to stay off the heroin and that she was feeling much more positive about the life ahead for herself and her baby. She had maintained her boundaries in separating from her abusive ex partner, had started her long-term counselling and was attending a support group, all of which offered her the support and inspiration to keep going. She was clearly continuing to work on the issues covered in her therapy, and had achieved a significant degree of independence and 'empowerment to stop acting out the victim role'.

In reflecting on what had taken place within the brief therapy relationship, it would seem that Rosa found the capacity to trust a real, live, human, but imperfect object – the therapist – who gave her the emotional sustenance that she needed but who also frustrated her with the inevitable ending of the therapy. However, since Rosa had herself agreed to this ending, she could not turn the therapist into another abusive object. It appears that in the short time covered by the therapy she had felt a significant change within herself and her capacity to have healthy boundaried relationships, both with herself and with others, and to renounce her addictions. This formed the start of an ongoing process towards greater health.

Although it was not the explicit focus of the therapy, in both the cases outlined above, the women achieved a significant degree of psychic change by coming to terms, in part, with the underlying developmental conflict of unmet dependency needs which led to greater degrees of separation and individuation.

## Findings of the brief psychotherapy project

### Statistical findings

Of the 320 women offered consultations in the project, 290 women attended. We saw a dramatic change in the numbers and range of women who were able to obtain help from us. Broadly, our findings demonstrated that the Women's Therapy Centre had achieved its objective to become directly accessible to women from our priority groups, through self-referral (approx. 70 per cent) and referral from public agencies and the health services (approx. 30 per cent). Of those women who had self-referred, access to the Centre had largely come through reading various publications which have been instigated by the Centre's work. Where previously we had seen relatively few Black women in therapy, nearly half the women in the project came from Black and ethnic minorities. We also saw a greater proportion of women with disability, white working-class women, single mothers and lesbians than previously.

The following socio-economic factors greatly contributed to the distress of these women: poverty (65 per cent of the women were on benefits and the remainder on low incomes); lack of education (40 per cent of the women had left school at 16 or earlier); ill health (33 per cent were suffering from depression, 10 per cent had previously made suicide attempts, 9 per cent had experienced psychotic episodes and 20 per cent suffered from prolonged physical ill health); lack of support in parenting (75 per cent of mothers were single parents); and the effects of racism experienced by Black women (45 per cent) and women from other minority groups (Irish women, 10 per cent).

These factors were compounded by deep distress resulting from painful and traumatic family backgrounds: 25 per cent suffered sexual abuse as children, and 26 per cent from a history of violence. A large proportion of these came from alcoholic backgrounds. In addition, dislocation from their country of origin (21 per cent) and a high incidence of loss and separation in childhood and adolescence (30 per cent) meant that this client group was extremely vulnerable to emotional breakdown, with severe consequences not only for the women but also, in the case of those who were mothers, for their children.

*Evaluation*

It is always difficult to evaluate precisely what has or has not been achieved within a piece of therapeutic work, since changes are not usually quantifiable and the use of measurement 'scales' may be distorted by the client's transference issues, both positively and negatively. However, one of the unique features of the method in brief therapy is the use of the focus, which can in itself provide a valuable means for reviewing the therapy when client and therapist look together at what has been achieved.

Other evaluation of the work was done using client evaluation forms, follow-up sessions and letters from clients. This has demonstrated that the majority of clients experienced time limited therapy as beneficial and were able to make changes or come some way towards achieving their therapeutic aims. We also noted that the impact of the brief sessions continued after the therapy had ended, and women reported that they were still finding it useful to reflect and work on issues and insights they had uncovered in therapy. The model of offering individual sessions (up to ten) followed by a one-year group proved particularly effective.

## Conclusion

### *Accessibility*

The objective of offering more women help from analytically based therapy was achieved in a number of ways. Firstly, resources were maximised by offering time limited focused therapy contracts. This enabled us to offer direct access to therapy for significantly larger numbers of women. Secondly, we made analytic therapy available to a wider range of women from different backgrounds and suffering from different levels of distress. This included women suffering from severe physical health problems, disabilities and learning difficulties. We adopted a flexible stance which involved on occasion demystifying the analytic process for our clients and selecting different therapeutic models according to the client's capacities to work analytically. We drew on techniques which essentialised the unconscious processes in an accessible language and manner, and found particularly beneficial Davanloo's educational approach, which enables the client to break through their defended self to access inner feelings, utilise inner resources and maximise effective change.

### *Time limited therapy as an agent of change*

We found that women were motivated to use time limited therapy to make positive changes at various levels, both intrapsychically and in the improved functioning of their outer lives in the world. Those women who were working with longer time limits (such as one- and two-year contracts) were able to explore more in more depth. However, the quality of intensity of the brief contracts (such as 9- to 25-week contracts) also made a significant impact, the tensions of the time limit confronting the client with their issues in an inescapable way, crystalising inner conflicts and speeding up the process of resolution, separation, individuation and change. At one end of the spectrum, time limited work can facilitate clients' restructuring of the psyche through the resolution of underlying conflicts and the integration of a meaningful therapeutic relationship. In situations where this type of change is unrealistic, short-term work nonetheless provides a supportive framework, containing the woman's distress, helping her to review her life and make changes, and enabling her to take the next step.

In the majority of cases, time limited therapy facilitated clients to improve the quality of their existence through developing: insight, which gave them greater awareness and understanding of their behaviour; a greater capacity to be in touch with, express and recognise feelings; a greater ability to take responsibility for their part in relationships; a greater sense of power to make choices; and a capacity to take responsibility for their lives. Working with a specific focus intensifies the issues and offers an opportunity to reflect on and evaluate what has been accomplished. The follow-up evaluation forms indicated that the majority of women benefited from the process, feeling satisfied that they had come some way to achieving what they had set out to do, resulting in a greater sense of confidence and well-being.

*Working with distressed clients*

As the statistical profile shows, we were working with extremely distressed women who might not generally be considered suitable for short-term work.[5] Therapists are legitimately sceptical about offering brief therapy to clients who have longstanding difficulties such as serious addictions, manic depression and psychosis. While we share these concerns, we have found that a long psychiatric history is not necessarily an indicator that the client cannot benefit from brief work. A time limited contract can offer an opportunity for reappraisal and redefinition from old labelling, which raises self-esteem. Some women, overwhelmed at the prospect of long-term therapy in which they imagined their problems to be endless, felt encouraged by successfully completing a manageable time limited contract. On occasions this further mobilised them to utilise resources within the community such as support groups, which encouraged their ability to participate more effectively in the world. It is clear in some cases that long-term therapy would have been desirable but we have also found that brief therapy serves as a useful form of crisis intervention, containing women in extreme distress and, in some cases, helping to keep them from being admitted to psychiatric hospitals. It is also our experience that women in acute crisis can be extremely receptive to therapy and ready for change. We are not, however, in any way suggesting that brief therapy offers a 'magic cure' to this client group and would continue to advocate the need for and benefit of longer-term therapies in cases where, although helpful, brief therapy is not enough.

*The integration of maternal and paternal functions as vehicles for growth and individuation*

Theorists in time limited psychotherapy affirm the importance of the 'corrective emotional experience' whereby problems which originate in relationships can also be healed through a therapeutic relationship. We do not understand this to mean that the therapist can make up for the pain and suffering that the client has experienced. One of the most validating experiences for a client is to feel known and acknowledged, her true self recognised and accepted in both its positive and negative aspects. The therapist bears witness to the client's truth, which helps her to connect with and express the uniqueness of her deeper feelings and experience. In this, the therapist partly represents the world of mother, whose function is to help the child 'contain, think about and eventually verbalise feelings and thoughts' (Maguire, 1995).

However, time limited therapy also draws on the paternal function. This is embodied by the therapist's ability to hold firm the boundary of the ending date, which represents separation and an opportunity for the client to learn to bear her own pain and accept her aloneness so that she emerges a more authentic and individuated person.

Central to this process is the client's identification with the therapist as someone who has confidence in the client's capacity to accomplish valuable work within the clear limits and boundaries of the contract. This offers the client an opportunity to come to terms with limitations, represented by the time limit, of both inner and external realities. By recognising the client as a separate subject, capable of growth, of making her own decisions and of drawing on her own inner resources, the therapist encourages her to struggle actively to attain adult selfhood and take responsibility for her actions and choices in the world. In this way, separating at the end of therapy involves not only loss, but considerable gain in confidence and self-esteem. Integrating a boundaried relationship in this way can mobilise the client to separate constructively from a merged inner world of maternal identifications and integrate the paternal function (as it is generally understood within Western culture) of autonomy, personal authority and the ability to function in the world as a separated self.

## Notes

1.  For the purposes of this chapter, we are using the generic term 'time limited therapy' to encompass brief psychotherapy (from a few to 25 sessions), and one- and two-year therapy contracts.
2.  Our prioritised groups were Black and Asian women, women from ethnic minorities, Irish women, working-class women on low incomes, lesbians and women with disability.
3.  I am grateful to June Roberts for this observation.
4.  The brief psychotherapy project offered consultations to 320 women in the space of three years.
5.  For example, the high incidence of early separations (30 per cent) in our client group would preclude brief therapy according to Malan's definitions.

## References

Alexander, F. & French, T. M. (1946) *Psychoanalytic Therapy: Principles and Applications*, University of Nebraska Press, Lincoln NE and London.
Benjamin, J. (1988) *The Bonds of Love: Psychoanalysis, Feminism and the Problem of Domination*, Random House, NY.
Davanloo, H. (ed.) (1978) *Basic Principles and Techniques in Short Term Dynamic Psychotherapy*, Spectrum, NY.
Erikson, E. (1950) *Childhood and Society*, Pelican, Harmondsworth.
Greenberg, J. R. & Mitchell, S. A. (1983) *Object Relations in Psychoanalytic Theory*, Harvard University Press, Cambridge MA.
Maguire, M. (1995) *Men, Women, Passion and Power*, Routledge, London.

Malan, D. (1979) *Individual Psychotherapy and the Science of Psycho-dynamics*, Butterworth, London.

Malan, D. & Osimo, F. (1992) *Psychodynamics, Training and Outcome in Brief Psychotherapy*, Heinemann, Oxford.

Mann, J. (1979) *Time Limited Psychotherapy*, Harvard University Press, Cambridge MA.

Molnos, A. (1986) 'Selling dynamic brief psychotherapy and teaching the patient: reflections on a symposium', *British Journal of Psychotherapy*, 2, 3.

Molnos, A. (1995) *A Question of Time*, Karnac Books, London.

Ryle, A. (1990) *Cognitive Analytic Therapy: Active Participation in Change – A New Integration in Brief Psychotherapy*, John Wiley, Chichester and NY.

# Chapter 7

# Race in the therapy relationship

## Carol Mohamed and Ruthie Smith

### Introduction

One of the main tasks of the brief psychotherapy project, introduced in the previous chapter, was to address the needs of Black[1] women and examine the particular experiences which influence the development of the Black woman's psyche. In pursuit of this aim we looked at the issue and its implications for the therapy relationship.

In this chapter we firstly explore what racism is, and how it employs one of the psyche's most primitive defence mechanisms, the unconscious process of splitting and projection (Klein, 1946) as its means of operating. Secondly, we go on to examine the depleting and fragmentary psychological and social impact that racism has, both on the person or people onto whom it is projected, and also on society as a whole. We then go on to look at the particular ways in which the experience of living in a society in which 'Black' is associated with 'bad' and 'inferior' becomes internalised and affects the Black client's inner and outer world. These issues are complex, requiring an exploration of intercultural issues, issues of loss, separation and dislocation, and an understanding of the ways in which the (largely unconscious) 'mechanics' of racism might be played out in the therapeutic relationship.

In addressing the inter-play between external and internal experiences, psychoanalytic theory has a lot to offer our understanding of racism. However, what may sometimes be missed is a real recognition of the *fact* of racism and its impact on Black and white people, at both a conscious and unconscious level. If this is not acknowledged within the clinical setting, there is a danger that Black women's experience may be pathologised.

Written on the whole by white practitioners working with white patients, psychoanalytic theory often fails to include a Black perspective, although more recently this is beginning to be addressed. By offering a general account of the development of the psyche, which is located within a specific (Western, Eurocentric) cultural context, psychoanalysis concentrates on similarities based on this assumed context, rather than looking more widely at the implications of cultural differences. The fact that intercultural therapy is usually (if at all) presented as a topic on its own, as if it were outside mainstream analytic therapy, highlights the marginalisation of the impact of race and culture on the psychoanalytic process. In order to offer a service that we perceived to be working interculturally, we therefore needed to develop an understanding of what being 'Black' actually means.

A Women's Therapy Centre study group on race, in lecture and discussion group format, and an experiential group for our mixed Black and white staff team gave us an opportunity to explore the issues theoretically and experientially. In the tradition of the Centre we felt that it was important to maintain a dialogue between theory and what we were encountering in our clinical practice. We were questioning the universality of the application of analytically based theory and whether this was equally valid when working with Black women. Given, for example, that the structure of Black families does not fit into the Western stereotype, did the theories offer a framework for understanding the totality of the Black individual's life situation?

In seeking to understand the complexity of ways in which 'good' and 'bad', 'Black' and 'white' are expressed in the transference relationship, we concluded that differences need to be understood within the context of each person's individual experience of culture and personal history, and that the large number of variables make it difficult to generalise. However, one thing we can be sure of is that the impact of racism has a profoundly debilitating effect on society as a whole, firstly in inhibiting the establishment of a positive sense of identity, well-being and self-esteem for the Black person, and secondly in creating an impoverished sense of the white psyche, whereby aspects of the self which have been disowned become lost and are no longer available to be integrated within the self.

**The impact of racism**

*Racism as a social manifestation of the phenomena of splitting and projection*

The process of racism can be explained in psychoanalytic terms by Melanie Klein's object relations theory and her formulation of the 'paranoid schizoid' position (1946). This theory describes the primitive workings or the ego's early defence mechanisms, defining the unconscious phenomena of splitting, projection, idealisation and denigration. Klein describes how, in early infancy, unwanted negative 'bad' experiences are felt by the infant to be so intolerable and dangerous that they are 'split off' from the 'good' experiences in order not to contaminate them. These negative feelings are projected outwards into an 'object' such as the breast/world, which is then turned into a 'bad object' as a means of maintaining the sense that what is inside is good.

If we examine racism within the context of object relations theory, we might say that Blackness in this society represents the 'bad object' and that white people project their hostility onto Black people in order to preserve their own sense of goodness. The Black 'object' in the outside world (that is, the disowned parts of the white self) becomes identified as hostile and dangerous, and then becomes introjected as such. Klein (1946) argues that:

> some of the disturbed object relations which are found in schizoid personalities – the violent splitting of the self and excessive projection – have the effect that the person towards whom this process is directed is felt as persecutor.

Splitting and projection are universal mechanisms of the human psyche. However, their persecuting aspects take on very profound implications when we understand that the mechanism of racism is essentially a social phenomenon of mass splitting and projection by white society, in which the Black community receives the unconsciously split-off aspects of the white psyche. The mass persecution of Jews in the Holocaust is a very clear example of this process.

The negative feelings which are disowned and projected include greed, envy, rage, hatred and fear. These relate to the oral and anal sadistic phases of development in which issues of dependency, power and control are paramount. Whereas in the infant's phantasy, aggression is identified with biting the nipple and the expulsion of faeces, in adult life it becomes the unconscious projection of intolerable envious and 'shitty' feelings. M. Fakhry Davids (1992) argues that 'brown is the colour of despised faeces, an attitude that can be transferred to the Black person, who then becomes utterly despicable'.

It could be argued that where anal/sadistic impulses predominate, an individual is less able to tolerate differences and is more prone to prejudice, fascism, totalitarianism and racism. It is, perhaps, no coincidence that the negative expletives which white racists use against Black people include such images as 'Black shit'.

Fakhry Davids cautions the therapist that while our understanding of the persecuting phenomena of racist attack can be enriched by the perspective of object relations, in such an analytic endeavour *tolerating* rather than *disowning* that racist within us is also a vital part of the work (1992).

To summarise, in the dynamic of racism white people unconsciously identify Black people as representing the negative feelings that they cannot own within themselves and put the blame on Black people. For example, the mass guilt of rapacious white greed exemplified by colonialism is unconsciously disowned and projected onto Black people, who are then viewed suspiciously by white people as potential thieves.

We can see this schizoid mechanism at work in everyday life in the persecutory views that are projected by the tabloid press which frequently portrays Black people as dirty, smelly, lazy, violent, dishonest, stupid, oversexed and helpless. There are also many other stereotypes, such as the Black mugger/rapist, and the starving African, an object of helplessness to be pitied.

## Idealisation and denigration

In this chapter we do not have the space to enter into a detailed exploration of idealisation and denigration, but we will be referring to them later on in the chapter as defences which manifest in the transference relationship. It is noteworthy that in defining the destructive function of the psyche, which is a central concept within psychoanalytic theory, the word 'denigration' is used. We note that the *Oxford English Dictionary* definition of the word 'denigrate' is:

'defame or disparage the reputation of (a person); blacken (de-*nigrare* from *niger* black)'. As Jean White (1989) points out:

> There is a major problem with language, which is part of the very dynamic I am describing. I have chosen to use the word 'Black' as a political category and form of identification, rather than trying to be ethnically specific, but the word 'black' also applies to historically specific imagos generated in white unconscious fantasy which have no bearing whatsoever on the nature of Black people, or the reality of their experience.

Within a socially constructed reality, society's views inevitably affect the way an individual sees him- or herself, particularly when perceptions become embedded within language itself to be used quite unconsciously and uncritically in everyday parlance. In describing the nature of perception, Irma Brenman Pick (1992) illustrates this very clearly:

> It is part of common parlance . . . that we may look at someone with adoring eyes, through rose coloured spectacles, or with hate, with a mote in the eye, with black or dirty looks, or even looks that kill . . .

She goes on to say

> And if we speak of black looks or dirty looks, we imply that the look is putting something nasty into that which is looked at.

A further example concerns her definition of idealisation and denigration:

> Because of the intensity of their own early or primitive feelings, infants build up inside, initially, two separate types of picture of what we call the primary object – one ideal and the other horrendous. One might say that infants see the world in black and white, their perceptions of the outside world much distorted by the intensity of their own moods, needs and impulses.

Here, 'Black' is clearly used to represent what is dirty, bad and nasty, and 'white' represents the ideal.

### The impact of racism on society as a whole

Racism is not, then, possession by a minority of a few bigoted views: it is an integral part of British society, part of the infrastructure upon which this and most other societies are based. Joel Kovel (1988) suggests that:

> Racism is a set of beliefs whose structure arises from the deepest levels of our lives, from the fabric of assumptions we make about the world, ourselves and others, and from the patterns of our fundamental social activities.

In other words, racism touches every level of our life. Dominelli (1988) argues that:

> racism is about the construction of social relationships on the basis of an assumed inferiority of non anglo-saxon ethnic minority groups, and flowing from this, their exploitation and oppression.

Jean White (1989), offering a psychoanalytic perspective, sees racism as:

> An integral part of the functioning of white western capitalism: the projection of disowned aspects of the white psyche onto Black people. This racism . . . works psychodynamically to enable white people constantly to lose sight both of whose problem it is (our own) and how we benefit from racist social organisation and dynamics on a material and economic level, and from their socially regulative functions. I see the notion of race itself as a white creation.

The effect of this dynamic is two-way, between those projecting and those receiving the projections. Just as within the individual psyche the impact of 'splitting' damages and weakens the ego, so, too, as a social phenomenon, it has a tremendously depleting impact, fragmenting and dividing society.

## The impact of racism on Black people

*The social impact*

Black people in Britain face many social disadvantages, such as poverty, inadequate housing, unemployment or low-status work, and poor educational opportunities. This may be compounded by sexism, homophobia and other prejudices which lead to discrimination. Additional factors such as migration and dislocation from the country of birth contribute yet further to the social difficulties Black people face. Adding to this the oppression of racism, it is hardly surprising that these stresses have a debilitating impact on a person's sense of well-being.

### The psychological impact

There is a danger in generalising about the psychological effects of racism on Black people since its effects vary, depending on the person's early experiences and consequent psychological development. Nonetheless, certain trends can be identified. In the brief psychotherapy project, one of the most frequently cited 'presenting problems' was depression, and three of the most common related factors which emerged were the experience of racism, a confused racial identity, and trauma resulting from dislocation and migration. There is an urgent need for studies to explore what links there may be between the effects of racism and the high incidence of depression amongst Black women.

On the basis of statistics from the project we noted that, in addition to other life traumas which bring them to therapy, there is the added burden of racism. This has serious consequences for the Black woman's inner world and we noted the frequent manifestation of the psychological defence mechanism of severe 'splitting'. Where women might describe themselves as being 'depressed', it was our clinical view that many of these women were in fact suffering from deeper levels of distress, where their pain was so great that they had cut off from their feelings altogether. Alternatively, for some women, the only feelings that could be shown were anger and rage.

Splitting evidently has debilitating effects. For example, we observed that some clients with strong outward defences, who appeared to be invincible and self-reliant, were defended by a pride which made it difficult for them to expose aspects of themselves that were needy, vulnerable, out of control or dependent. As a consequence, valuable aspects of these women's psyches were lost, incapacitating them so that they were too frightened to trust or engage in intimate relationships. Even if they had developed a trusting relationship with their mother or family in early life, the world had taught them otherwise – that it is not safe to trust.

Behind the coating of pride, which was a response to a constant attack by society on the colour of their skin, lay fear, anxiety, a persecuting sense of inner badness, and low self-esteem. The natural defences were to shut down, cut off, be angry, not trust or rely on others, comply, and smile to hide the anger which they fear will be viewed as a 'pathology' inherent to Black women who have a 'chip on their shoulder'.

In considering the issue of racial identity it is useful to compare the radically different experiences of white and Black women in the way they perceive themselves. When a white person meets another white person on the street, they will not identify one another by their colour. Their whiteness is not considered in any way noticeable. They each see, simply, another person. On the other hand, if a white person sees a Black person in the street, they see a *Black* person, who is related to in terms of their difference to the dominant white culture rather than being seen simply as an individual.

One of the impacts of racism, then, is that a Black person *also* comes to identify themselves by their colour, seeing themselves self-consciously as *Black*, rather than simply as a person. Thus whereas for white people being white is the norm, Black people have had to embody their colour as part of their identity, and hold an awareness of that colour because of the connotations placed on it by white people. This creates a very particular way of thinking about identity – about who you are, how you present yourself and how you relate to society.

In this way, through society's largely unconscious outlook, Black people become 'objectified'. This experience may be further complicated by white people's denial (due to the repression of their unconscious racism) of Black people's difference, so that Black people often have the added experience of then feeling invisible. This illustrates how, in relating to the world, Black people have a complex and entirely different internal experience from that of white people.

In order to be accepted, Black people have also had to take on the dominant culture, which results in a key problem: the internalisation of a *positive* racial identity. In our work in the project, psychic splits in women's self-definition were evident in relation to the adjectives 'white' and 'Black' and the ways in which these are linked to the meanings 'good' and 'bad' within British culture; to be Black is 'bad' to be white is 'good'. One of the more extreme examples concerning the internalisation of a sense of badness about racial identity is illustrated by the client who was in such emotional pain that she wanted to rub off her Black skin.

Integration within the dominant culture is also a problematic issue. White people assume that Black people should integrate themselves into the white culture and take on its values, and they often feel uncomfortable if Black people *express their difference*. Those who do not conform are seen as a threat so that, for example, Asian communities who maintain their own culture are sometimes seen as 'failing to integrate'. All these examples are rooted in issues of power imbalance which is what keeps racism going. There is a denial and fear of Black people being powerful. The denial is maintained because without it there is no longer a scapegoated 'bad object' into which negative feelings can be projected.

In working with issues of race, an important part of the therapeutic work is to validate and integrate all aspects of the Black women's experience and to understand their responses within the context that they manifest. In this way, the defences are understood to be a means of survival in order to cope with a hostile external world and an entirely understandable response to intolerable prejudice.

## Cultural understanding of family experience and structures

As a starting point in working with a Black client, an understanding of her social and cultural background and family structures is vital if she is to feel recognised and understood.

### Loss and separation

Psychoanalytic theory is about the development of the self through a relationship with significant others, and at the base of this theory is the essentially Eurocentric concept of individual development. The Western notion of an individuated self concerns working through separation issues in the dyadic mother/daughter to a resolution in the Oedipus complex within the assumed context of the nuclear family in patriarchal society. This may have little to do with a Black woman's experience and, from a theoretical point or view, there are many unanswered questions when we consider the different structural model of the large extended family. The experience is quite different for those whose identity has always been closely interlinked with a community, where distinctions between 'self' and 'other' have different connotations.

For many Black women, experiences of loss and separation take place within the very specific context of cultural dislocation resulting from migration; this differs considerably from the experience of most white women. The loss of the first love-object, the mother, might be one of many separations for Black women, the role of the extended family (which may include friends and neighbours as well as grandparents, aunts, uncles and siblings) playing a more central role in children's care and upbringing, and carrying with it different implications in the process of individuation.

In order to accommodate these differences, rather than solely offering a one-to-one therapeutic relationship, Rosamund Grant, a Black therapist involved in the brief psychotherapy project, developed a therapeutic model for Black women of a few sessions of individual therapy followed by group therapy as a way of mirroring the experience of being cared for and nurtured by the community.

## Dislocation and migration

As we mentioned previously, many of the Black women we saw had a history of separations, dislocation, and a sense of alienation resulting from their move to a new country and culture. Often parents had come ahead when the children were very young, the children being sent for later on, often wrenched from happy childhoods in the Caribbean, Africa or Asia, and plunged into a strange new world and an unknown new family. Being separated during the family's relocation may make it difficult for a woman to feel rooted in or to have a sense of belonging to a society which is openly hostile.

The task of the newly arrived member of the family (who may have been loved or unloved in their previous circumstances) is mammoth. It involves mourning the loss of significant others whom she has left behind in circumstances which, in the case of traumatised refugees, might be very conflictual. The woman is faced with the over-whelming difficulties of coping with culture shock, possibly having to learn a new language, learning to make new relationships in a family which may be ambivalent towards her arrival in this country, and integrating into the new world, in a new education system or new work environment, where the rules are different.

This trauma creates psychic splits in the identity of the immigrant, who is trying to hold on to an old identity and old identifications while at the same time establishing a new identity in this culture. One client expressed this internal 'split' by describing herself as having a lively, spontaneous 'Caribbean side' alternating with a serious, depressed and withdrawn 'British side', which starkly expresses the discrepancies between her experiences of the two cultures. For some women, an important aspect of the therapeutic experience was to connect up with and express feelings which had been frozen since the trauma of relocating in this country and to mourn losses which had never previously been acknowledged.

An extremely painful aspect of a Black woman's experience is the way that racism becomes internalised. We noted that amongst the clients we saw, there were those who arrived in Britain after the rest of their family had already settled here. They expressed enormous distress over being treated as a lesser family member; in some instances they felt their status in the family to be that of a servant rather than a daughter. The Black family in Britain may have taken on the values of the dominant culture, scapegoating and oppressing the newly arrived person. Here, we turned to Anna Freud's insight into the mechanisms of 'identifying with the oppressor' as a defence against the pain of being oppressed. The last person in the 'pecking order' becomes the receptacle for everybody's unwanted pain, and the experience of colonialism becomes re-enacted within the Black family.

### British-born Black women

The psychological distress caused by having to adapt to a different culture is well noted by Furnham and Bochner (1986) and Littlewood and Lipsedge (1982). However, issues can be equally if not more difficult for British-born Black women who grow up in an environment of conflicting value systems. The 'traditional' family values of parents who are loyal to their original culture may be in direct conflict with views held by those at her British school or workplace. The daughter growing up within both cultures is faced with impossible allegiances, trying to fit in and conform at school while at the same time trying to win approval from a parent or parents who hold a very different outlook.

Healthy expressions of aggression towards her mother by the daughter may be inhibited and repressed in favour of an alliance with her, standing united against the racism they experience in everyday life. This creates further splits within a daughter, who may experience tremendous guilt and conflict over having any other feelings than loyalty and respect towards her mother.

## Factors concerning a Black woman entering therapy

The above factors which contribute to stress in a Black woman's life are issues which can usefully be explored in a therapeutic relationship. However, entering therapy has its own difficulties for a Black woman. The prevailing treatment model in this country is within the medical or psychiatric services, and is regarded with fear by the Black community. Littlewood and Kareem (1992) suggested that 'hospitalised Black patients are two to three times more likely to be involuntary patients under the mental health act', and that Black people are more likely to be prescribed higher doses of drugs and to receive electro-convulsive therapy (ECT). Psychotherapy rarely appears to be offered as a form of treatment. It is suggested within the psychiatric profession that Black people lack the verbal skills to articulate their distress, and that they tend to 'physicalise' (somatise) it instead.[2] This interpretation has meant that when Black women have sought help, they have often been deemed 'unsuitable' for psychotherapy, and physical treatments such as medication or ECT are more likely to be the outcome.

Some models of psychotherapy involve stringent selection criteria such as strong motivation, a reasonable and stable life style, a considerable degree of 'wellness' to be able to withstand the intensity of the therapy, and good verbal skills . This creates an anomalous situation whereby the most distressed clients – for example, a Black refugee learning English as a second language who has insecure housing and is trying to come to terms with living in a new country – are often the least likely to receive psychotherapeutic help, having 'failed' to meet the assessment criteria.

In order to bring more Black women into the Centre we publicised the brief psychotherapy project through the media, community and national organisations. An article in the most widely read Black newspaper brought a dramatic increase in the numbers of Black women approaching us for help. Gradually, hearing of the Centre by word of mouth, more Black women began to seek therapy.

We needed to understand what it means for a Black woman or woman of an ethnic minority to come for therapy within the context of her experience, and to be aware of issues which might make it hard for her to engage fully in the therapy. As we have mentioned, the first hurdle to overcome is the fear of stigma. It is difficult for a Black client to take the step of seeking therapy when she fears being misunderstood, labelled mad or, worse still, sectioned into a psychiatric hospital, so to facilitate the process of entering therapy, it is essential to establish *trust* and build a positive therapeutic alliance. One way of doing this was to offer an initial consultation with a Black therapist. Women had repeatedly talked of their experience of institutions with which they could not identify, so we hoped that having their first consultation with a Black therapist would offer Black women an opportunity to explore what their needs were in a safe space, thus encouraging more women to use the service. Wherever possible, if a Black client asked to continue working with a Black therapist, this was accommodated.

**Intercultural work**

Since issues for Black women entering therapy are often complex, in working with a white therapist or a Black therapist from a different culture the therapist's awareness of intercultural issues is important in order to establish a sense of *safety* for the Black client. Working interculturally is a process which requires being open and available to the client, listening and learning from her, not making assumptions, and not being afraid to ask questions in order to clarify meaning. As d'Ardennes and Mahtani (1989) point out:

> clients from other cultures have already had to overcome many barriers in everyday life, and may find the counselling environment a further struggle. Transcultural counsellors understand this, and try and meet their clients more than half way.

In order to do this, more time is required to ensure that real understanding and communication takes place. Furnham and Bochner (1986) argue that:

> in a transcultural setting, people from different cultures have different ways of: sending and receiving information, expressing their wishes and commands, and demonstrating feelings. When two people of differing cultures meet, they will need to negotiate their varied modes of communication.

For example, the amount of eye contact between peoples varies considerably, and whereas in some cultures people tend to look at one another when they speak, in others there may be little eye contact. Furnham and Bochner also emphasise that:

> Transcultural counsellors, working across languages, understand the limitations imposed on their clients by this lack of choice. In practice, this may mean that counsellors need to take longer to explore significant feelings and experiences.

Other examples concern religious differences. A Black Muslim, taking a considerable risk in venturing outside her own culture for help, would want a therapist whom she felt would be sensitive to issues concerning her religion, culture and family. Discussing these issues fully in the beginning might create a safe enough space for the woman to take up any therapy offered to her. We also need to be aware of the ways that different cultures deal with particular issues. For instance, religious attitudes to death and bereavement vary considerably: in some African cultures it is considered a mark of respect to mourn by wailing and lamenting, whereas for a Tibetan Buddhist death is respected by periods of meditation in which displays of emotion are considered inappropriate. Understanding differences is therefore vital to the process of good communication and a working therapeutic relationship.

Another difficulty that a Black woman might encounter in entering therapy concerns feelings of shame when seeking help outside her community by talking to a stranger. This may be viewed as a betrayal of the family's secrets, resulting in feelings of guilt and anxiety. These feelings may arise regardless of the colour of the therapist. As a measure of the secret distress that may be experienced within communities, it is noteworthy that the highest suicide rate is recorded in Asian women, 20 per cent of whom do so by burning themselves to death as a means of saving their family from shame.[3]

In addition to the cultural injunctions against speaking outside the family, further difficulties arise for women who speak little or no English. At the Women's Therapy Centre we found that very few Asian women were coming for therapy. In order to reach these women, an outreach programme was developed offering therapy workshops located within the community. When the Centre started running these in Asian community centres in different languages, the demand for therapy rapidly emerged, and women were very keen to talk and use the services. There was a similarly enthusiastic take-up of services when workshops were offered to Chinese and Iranian women. In these groups, women began to speak with one another about issues such as domestic violence and sexual abuse on which they had previously been silent and isolated. Women found great comfort and support from being able to share with one another. At the Centre we now employ several therapists who offer a second language, including Spanish and Greek, and various languages from the African and Asian continents.

To increase accessibility, we outlined in Chapter 6 the importance of demystifying the process of analytically based therapy. The 'rules' of the therapy need to be explained so that the client understands the nature of the framework in which they will be undertaking the therapeutic work. This helps the therapy to seem less intimidating and encourages more active participation from the client. We were surprised to find that whereas the idea of open-ended therapy seemed daunting to some Black women, a time limited piece of work seemed much more achievable and women felt contained by having a clear contract length with a known ending date.

A final and essential point in making therapy accessible to Black women is to offer a demonstrable understanding of the woman's life experience and a therapeutic relationship in which the reality of racism can be acknowledged and explored right from the start.

The statistics of the brief psychotherapy project quoted in Chapter 6 show that nearly half the women who came for therapy were Black or from other multi-ethnic communities. Following is an exploration of therapeutic issues which were highlighted in working with this group.

## Transference and counter-transference in intercultural work

The term 'transference', widely used to describe projective phenomena, is not exclusive to the therapeutic relationship. However, in analytic therapy, working with the client's transference and the therapist's counter-transference is a central tool and provides an important medium of communication.

In any therapy the divided aspects or 'splits' of the client – both good and bad – will be projected onto the therapist, and the feelings that arise need to be worked with and understood. When working interculturally, we need to be particularly sensitive to the way in which this is played out, so that we can differentiate both the clients' and the therapists' intrapsychic projections and fantasies from those issues which arise in relation to colour and the reality of racism.

## *The issue of power and race in the transference*

Psychotherapy is often viewed as a white, middle-class form of treatment, so it is with some justification that Black people may be suspicious and wary of entering into it. One way of addressing this is to make explicit and talk openly about the client/therapist dynamic. There may be a reluctance to acknowledge the existence of a power imbalance in the therapeutic relationship, but it is inevitable if one person is in need and the other, in her role as professional, reveals little about herself. This dynamic is compounded when the therapist is white and the client is Black.

It seems inconceivable that a Black client's very real experience of racism would be pathologised by the therapist in the therapeutic relationship. Unfortunately, this is often the case. Dr Jaffar Kareem (Littlewood & Kareem, 1992) suggests that 'a Black person's experience may easily be denied by a white therapist simply because it is outside of the therapist's particular experience of inner and outer reality.' The following case serves as an illustration of this.

A Black client told of a painful encounter with her white therapist. The client was telling her therapist about an instance of overt racism she had experienced from a white doctor. The therapist, unconscious of her own racism, was not able to accept the reality of the Black client's experience. As a consequence she was unable to work with either her client's feelings or her own in the counter-transference. Instead, she interpreted that her Black client was projecting her aggression onto the doctor. By denying and invalidating the reality of the client's experience of racism in the world, and 'blaming' the Black client's psychology, this therapeutic intervention served only to increase further the client's existing distress, which was damaging to her.

It is only by acknowledging the external reality of a client's experience of racism that it becomes safe for the client to explore intrapsychic issues and disentangle inner and outer realities.

We consider it important that the white therapist is aware of her own power and the way it is viewed by her Black client, and conscious of her own racist conditioning. To deny it is to hold onto it, which may result in it being unconsciously transmitted in the dynamic of the therapy relationship, with the Black client experiencing herself as bad and powerless, and reinforcing her own feeling that the white therapist is a powerful judgemental superego figure. If the white therapist is able to take on board the idea of herself as an oppressor, or representative of oppression, it may prevent the pathologising of the client's rage and introduce the possibility of working with the positive potential of anger.

In the project we felt that the responsibility for bringing up issues of difference and race lay with the therapist. If these issues are ignored, important work in the transference is denied. We are not suggesting that only Black therapists can work with Black clients, but rather that the therapist needs a heightened awareness and capacity to differentiate both her own issues and those of her client so as to be fully emotionally available to interpret the feelings in the transference and counter-transference. In order to do this she needs to have thoroughly worked through her own personal issues about race. For a white therapist this means exposing herself to and facing her own racism, which is uncomfortable, embarrassing and painful, particularly when most white therapists are fearful of 'getting it wrong'.

For example, if a white therapist has not fully acknowledged to herself feelings of guilt about being the 'white oppressor' her feelings might paralyse the work. On the other hand, it is not helpful if a white therapist gets caught in the trap of thinking that she is not good enough to work with Black clients because she has not experienced the extent of their oppression. The therapist aims to be able to talk about uncomfortable feelings in a direct and undefensive manner, without overloading the client with unnecessary items from her own personal agenda. The following case illustrates this.

> A South American woman was trying to come to terms with the loss of her partner who had been tortured and murdered during a fascist coup. She was expressing excruciatingly painful moments of grief, powerlessness and rage which the white therapist found almost unbearable to tolerate, experiencing herself in the counter-transference as a torturing white oppressor. For a while the therapist felt too paralysed to speak, helpless because of her own overwhelming feelings of guilt. The situation seemed hopelessly

stuck. The dynamic in the therapy could only shift when the therapist had been able to acknowledge these feelings to herself, and separate out what were her own issues in the counter-transference and what were those of her client. This enabled her to think more clearly about what was going on and understand that she was picking up, through the process of projective identification, the client's own feelings of stuckness, helplessness, power-lessness and guilt for surviving. Having been able to sift through and differentiate what were her own issues, she was then able to regain her capacity to speak and offer interpretations that were meaningful to the client.

### The dynamics in intercultural relationships

In addition to the mechanisms of splitting and projection outlined earlier in this chapter, another feature of the therapeutic relationship will be the client's use of the defence mechanisms of idealisation, denigration and projective identification. The ways in which these are played out will be influenced by the dynamics of race in the therapy relationship. If a white client is working with a Black therapist, a different dynamic will ensue than if a white client is working with a white therapist, a Black client with a Black therapist, or a Black client with a white therapist.

A *white client* will know that a *Black therapist* would have to be good at her work to have arrived at her position. Initially the Black therapist may be idealised and perceived as the 'good object', so that all of the good aspects of the client are projected on to the therapist, requiring a denial of her 'bad' aspects. Idealisation is used here as a way of denying more uncomfortable feelings which are happening in the transference.

The client who experiences the therapist as constantly raising issues about colour, or who feels that the therapist has a 'chip on her shoulder', may well also be operating on a level of denial. The fear expressed by white people about a Black person's anger – for example, seeing Black people as potentially violent – relates to the white person's underlying fear of the fantasised retaliation that might ensue if the Black person gets in touch with their anger at all the 'badness' that has been pushed into them by white people. Because racism operates at the level of schizoid functioning, it is inevitable that working with the issues will create a sense of persecution. As Klein (1952) describes it:

> The drive to project (expel) badness is increased by fear of internal persecutors. When projection is dominated by persecutory fear, the object into whom badness (the bad self) has been projected becomes the persecutor par excellence because it has been endowed with all the bad qualities of the subject.

What is being confronted in the therapeutic relationship where *the client is Black* is the client's experience of being Black in a society that is not only openly hostile, but also sees the Black individual as the embodiment of what is bad and unwanted.

When a *Black client* asks to be seen by a *white therapist* we therefore need to understand the context of this request in which the Black woman has internalised negative views concerning her Black identity. As a consequence, she may be distrustful of a Black therapist, who is 'denigrated' and viewed as inferior and second rate, or as having 'sold out' to the white institution and its white values. In such a situation, it would be important to explore these issues with the client and to be aware if the Black client employs the defence mechanism of idealising her white therapist.

When a Black client is in therapy with a white therapist, issues of identification, which can be complex in all therapeutic relationships, need to be thought about specifically from the point of view of race and the meaning for the client in working with a white therapist.

> One Black client who was in crisis initially came for a few sessions to try to resolve a particular issue. It later transpired that she had spent many years fostered by a white person who had consistently undermined and verbally abused her, almost using her as a 'slave' around the house. When asked how she felt about her therapist being white, the client replied that she would rather work with a white therapist because she was frightened of Black people, having spent so many years trying to deny her own Blackness. Her answer revealed clearly how much she had internalised racism towards her own Blackness. It was very important that the white therapist did not collude with this view, but instead address the negative identification and suggest to the client that her Blackness was a vital part of herself which she needed to reclaim. When the brief contract ended, it was suggested that the Black client might seek out some further therapy with a Black therapist, so that she could continue to explore the issues.

Issues of splitting, projection, idealisation and denigration become even more complex when *the client is of mixed race*. The following example demonstrates the complex and debilitating ways in which a client may express splits and find it difficult to come to terms with fundamental issues of identity.

'Sharon' was of mixed Black and white race. In her initial consultation she asked to see a Black therapist to whom she expressed anger that her father had had sex with a white woman and had allowed a child to be created that was neither Black nor white. Sharon had been adopted at birth by white parents. She expressed confusion about what and who she was, describing herself as feeling unable to relate to the rest of the world. She did not know how to identify herself and made a split between different aspects of herself, seeing the Black parts of herself as 'bad' and the white parts as 'good'. The brief psychotherapy project felt it appropriate to team her with a Black therapist, and a two-year time limit was agreed in which to work on the focus of race and identity.

Her behaviour was intensely destructive and self-demeaning, which, she felt, gave her an opportunity to express the feelings about what she considered to be her 'unacceptable' Black side. She felt that 'everyone hated her because she was Black'.

The 'good' parts of herself were split off onto her career as a freelance journalist. This was seen to be the 'acceptable, white, good' part of herself. She talked of how easy life is for white people because they get the things they want. She felt that she was deprived of getting what she wanted because half of her was Black.

The therapy revealed that unconsciously she was denying the Black part of herself and wanting to be white, and this case shows very painfully the very deep and damaging effects of racism and the ways in which it becomes internalised within the psyche. In the two years, Sharon was able to explore her internal splits and begin to integrate a more positive view of herself as a woman of mixed race.

When a *white client* is in therapy with a *Black therapist* the white client may not outwardly express her disappointment at having a Black therapist, but it may be a feature of the transference relationship. There is a tendency for the white client to unconsciously endorse the idea that white is good and Black is bad, and so a Black therapist will easily become the object of the client's racist projections. As part of the therapeutic process, the Black therapist may well be presented with the fantasies and prejudices of society, and has to act as the container for these as well as the unconscious split-off parts of the client's ego. These will have to be worked through in the therapeutic relationship. The Black therapist will therefore need to have examined her own experiences of racism, so that she is able to work with the negative projections of her white client without retaliating.

> A white client working with a Black therapist made no reference to the obvious fact that the therapist was Black and she was white. However, this was very alive in the material. The therapist eventually interpreted the client's blindness to the difference in colour between them as the client's need for them to be the same. The client became very angry, and declared that she had never in any way viewed herself and the therapist as different. She added that she had in fact been glad that the therapist was Black, because she felt that a white middle-class woman probably wouldn't understand her. In the transference relationship, the deprived inferior parts of herself were projected into the Black therapist and she related to her in this way. Together they were, as it were, sisters, fighting the oppressive hostile world – she needed the Black therapist to be as powerless as herself. Acknowledging this would have meant taking back her projection and making conscious her racism, which would have been felt to be intolerable.
>
> During a session she experienced the therapist as making interpretations that 'got inside her' and made her angry, forcing her to face feelings she couldn't bear. In the following session she described a dream in which there was an annoying blackbird which insisted on singing on a branch outside her bathroom window and wouldn't leave her alone. She struggled to make associations but could only describe how furious and intruded upon she felt by the bird.
>
> The therapist compared the blackbird in the dream to the client's relationship with her mother who 'got inside her' in a consuming and destructive way that always felt intrusive. The song was not sweet, but invasive and persistent. Like her mother, the bird had its

own agenda – it had its song to sing which left no space for what she wanted or needed. It did not consider her, or care about whether or not she wanted it. It would not leave her alone. In her associations, the client went on to describe how she felt 'contaminated' by her mother after contact with her by telephone or visit.

Similarly, the client felt that the therapist was equally uncaring and invasive. Interpretations in the relationship were often experienced as attacks. The therapist was accused of not understanding her client and of being preoccupied with her own thoughts or conclusions. Like the client's mother, she was expressing her own agenda. The client often expressed rage, lamenting how useless her therapist was. In the countertransference the therapist felt impotent, confused and herself intruded upon, as if the client had launched a violent assault against her. This was a feature of the transference relationship. The client projected very powerfully into the therapist a picture of her internal world. Not surprisingly, her external world mirrored this. Life was a constant battle with authorities, friends and relatives. The world and the therapist were like attacking, retaliatory persecutors.

The dream could provide an interesting insight into the mechanism of racism, using Klein's ideas about the paranoid schizoid position. The colour of the bird in the dream was clearly significant. It was important that the therapist recognised this as a primitive communication about her client's psyche. If the bird represents the Black therapist in the dream, it also suggests a denigration or the therapist into whom something bad was evacuated.

The blackness of the bird may therefore represent 'explosive faeces'. Klein (1946) describes how:

> As urethral and anal sadistic impulses gain in strength, the infant in his mind attacks the breast with poisonous urine and explosive faeces, and therefore expects it to be poisonous and explosive towards him.

What may be so frightening about the bird, representing both the mother and the Black therapist, is the persecutory anxiety of the retaliating 'bad object', which, to use the client's language, left her feeling contaminated. This fearful experience is mediated by the relationship to the 'good breast', that is, the mother/therapist's capacity to meet her baby/client's needs, to contain the frustration, and to make those needs her primary agenda.

The therapist needed to be able to separate out the complexity of issues being presented in this material and to understand what was being communicated through the client's racism. It was vital that the therapist was able to contain and digest all of the feelings and be available to the client's inner world, while at the same time tolerating her racist attacks so that she could make what was clearly unbearable bearable to the client. This was done not by interpreting her unconscious projections as racism, but by addressing the underlying issue of her invasive and depriving mother. Had the therapist focused on interpreting the racist aspect of the attack she would have been experienced by the client as being like her mother/therapist, following her own agenda. Instead, the therapist did not retaliate, but contained and dealt with the internal 'shit'. In this way, the client was able to resolve the deeper agenda about her relationship with her mother.

It is the work of all therapists to endure and make sense of their clients' negative projections. However, Black therapists not only have to contain the client's negative projections, but also tolerate the additional burden of receiving unconscious racist attacks without retaliating.

This process of working with racism in the transference relationship can be extremely painful for the Black therapist. As Lennox Thomas (1992) points out, it is important 'to be very aware of countertransference feelings of distancing from the patients who are seemingly abusive or racially demeaning'. While the therapist may wish to protect herself from receiving abusive and racist projections, this could block her ability to work with the issues that the client is bringing.

When a *Black therapist* works with a *Black client* there are many variations in the way the relationship may be experienced. We have encountered many situations in which Black clients working with Black therapists have felt heard and understood. However, the issues are not always straightforward.

For example, some Black women may be frightened of airing their 'dirty linen' in public for fear of betraying their family and community, and so find that working with a Black therapist offers a safe place to explore issues which might otherwise feel too painful and exposing to express to an 'outsider'. On the other hand, some clients, given the closeness of their community and their lack of experience of the safety of confidentiality, express the fear that if they see a Black therapist who comes from the same culture there will not be enough privacy for them to talk freely.

The ways in which Black people internalise racism also offer complex material in the therapeutic relationship. Black clients who have not managed to establish a positive identity concerning their race and colour will project this onto their Black therapist. The issue becomes more complex when the therapy relationship is between Black women from different cultures. The psychoanalytic theory of identification with the aggressor offers an understanding of the way a 'pecking order' may occur between different cultures. For example, an African woman who has experienced racism at the hands of a Caribbean woman will bring fears about this into the therapy relationship if her therapist is from the Caribbean.

Finally, internalised racism about skin tone is so deeply ingrained that different shades of skin colour are often experienced problematically in the therapy situation. One such example was when a Black therapist's 'light' skin tone was idealised by the client as being more favourable than her own darker skin.

## Conclusion

In therapy we are generally working with clients who have experienced social and economic distress, but many Black clients would say that racism is the most painful experience of their lives. We therefore felt that it was vital in the brief psychotherapy project to attempt to go beyond just nominally 'offering a service', we needed to reach out to Black women to make therapy *really* accessible.

In working with Black women, we have sought to understand how racism intensifies the issues that we all struggle to work through in our psychological development, such as the splitting into good and bad, the tendency to idealise and denigrate, and coming to terms with loss in the often problematic experience of separation and individuation. Melanie Klein's ideas offer a useful framework for beginning to understand this complex process.

We note that, in comparison with white people, Black clients have a fundamentally different perception of the world and of their own identity when living in a predominantly white culture. In speaking of difference there is an assumption that white people are the dominant culture and Black people are different in relation to that. A Black person is firstly identified by their colour, and secondly as an individual, so that being Black is an integral part of the identity. White people on the other hand will not identify themselves by their colour, but will identify themselves as *themselves*. This is a key psychological difference between Black and white people which needs to be accommodated within the therapy relationship.

For therapists working interculturally, we feel that it is crucial that race is brought into the open in the transference relationship, although it is important that unconscious issues of racism are not overly focused on at the expense of deeper underlying issues. Therapists who are conscious of the issues will be fully available to their clients and what they are bringing. In order to be able to do this they need to acknowledge and work through the persecutory anxieties associated with the schizoid phenomena of racism, and be fully aware of ways in which they might have 'cut off' from their own feelings about it. Splits can be healed and integrated only when the terror and rage have been worked through, to arrive at the 'depressive position' which offers the possibility of reparation and hope. Klein (1952) describes how:

> further development on the line of integration and synthesis is initiated when the depressive position comes to the fore. The various aspects – love and hatred, good and bad – of the object come closer together, and these objects are now the whole person.

Integrating the ego in this way makes for an increased understanding of psychic reality and a better perception of the external world, as well as for a greater synthesis between internal and external situations.

Although we have not conducted a formal follow-up study of the women seen in the project, the positive feedback we received from women who came for a follow-up session or from our client 'end of therapy' forms has led us to understand that many women experienced the therapy as helpful. One Black client said that it was very important to her that the reality of her life and experience had been heard and understood. The fact that the demand for therapy from Black women continues has left us hopeful that analytic psychotherapy has something useful to offer Black women in helping them to find their voice.

## Notes

1. For the purpose of this chapter we are using the word 'Black' to denote all women of colour, including Asian women and women from Black ethnic minorities.
2. In our experience we have not found any evidence to suggest that Black women are more likely to somatise than white women. Furthermore, somatisation does not preclude a woman from benefiting from brief therapy, as the case example of a white woman in Chapter 6 illustrates.
3. BBC Radio 4, May 1996.

## References

Brenman Pick, I. (1992) 'The emergence of early object relations in the psychoanalytic setting', in R. Anderson (ed.), *Clinical Lectures on Klein and Bion*, Routledge, London.

d'Ardennes, P. & Mahtani, A. (1989) *Transcultural Counselling in Action*, Sage Publications, London.

Dominelli, L. (1988) *Anti-Racist Social Work*, Macmillan, London.

Fakhry Davids, M. (1992) *The Cutting Edge of Racism*, paper presented to the Applied Section of the British Psycho-Analytical Society on 28 October 1992.

Furnham, A. & Bochner, S. (1986) *Culture Shock: Psychological Reactions to Unfamiliar Environments*, Methuen, London.

Klein, M. (1946) 'Notes on some schizoid mechanisms', in *Envy and Gratitude and Other Works*, Virago, London 1988.

—— (1952) 'Some theoretical conclusions regarding the emotional life of the infant', in *Envy and Gratitude*, op. cit.

Kovel, J. (1988) *White Racism: a Psycho History*, Free Association Books, London.

Littlewood, R. & Kareem, J. (1992) *Intercultural Therapy: Themes, Interpretations and Practice*, Blackwell Scientific Publications, Oxford.

Littlewood, R. & Lipsedge, M. (1982) *Aliens and Alienists: Ethnic Minorities and Psychiatry*, Penguin, Harmondsworth.

Thomas, L. (1992) quoted in Littlewood & Kareem, op. cit.

White, J. (1989) 'Racism and psychosis: whose madness is it anyway?', unpublished paper.

# Chapter 8

# Working with adult incest survivors

## Sue Krzowski

There are some existential realities, 'facts of life', that each human being needs to face at a psychological level if we are to live to our full potential: our aloneness and separateness in the world, our inevitable dependency on others, the limitation of our human powers, the passing of time and our own mortality, the fact of our conception, birth and relationship to our biological parents, the fact that culture requires us to live as male or female according to our sex. We might add to this fundamental order of things to be negotiated the incest taboo. In most cultures children and parents are forbidden to have sexual relations with each other and children are required to find a sexual partner outside the family. Why is this? Does it do any harm for parents to have sex with their children? If so, how is it harmful? What is the function of the incest taboo from a psychological point of view?

In this chapter I want to explore some of the psychological consequences for the daughter when she is sexually abused as a child by her father. I will argue that psychoanalytic theory can help us to understand the symptoms and difficulties that these women bring to therapy. I will suggest that the relationship to the internal maternal object, and in particular its containing function, needs to be addressed in the psychotherapy before Oedipal issues in the incestuous relationship with the father can be worked through. I have arrived at this conclusion from my experience of working with and supervising incest survivors in both individual and group therapy. I will include some individual case material to illustrate my point.

In Britain, it was the Women's Movement, starting with consciousness-raising groups in the 1970s, that enabled women to break the silence about their own experiences of sexual abuse as children. As groups of women came together to examine different areas of their lives under patriarchy, including their sexuality, it emerged that many of them had experienced sexual abuse in their childhood but for most of these women it had remained a shameful secret. The largest group among them were those who had been abused by their fathers or stepfathers.

For some incest survivors the memory has been repressed and kept out of consciousness, while for others it is a constantly intrusive, waking nightmare. Rape Crisis, Women's Aid, the Incest Survivors Campaign and other women's organisations mobilised around these issues and began to bring them into the arena of public awareness, so that political action could be taken to address the problems. This process is ongoing and has seen many twists and turns. For feminists the emphasis was on understanding why the majority of abusers of both boys and girls appeared to be men, while the majority of children who reported abuse were female. As public denial began to break down, the emphasis was on the search for someone to blame – feminists, social services, mothers, the child victims, therapists. Little attention was paid to the abusers themselves. More recently there has been a growing recognition that boys are abused more frequently than we had thought and that women, even mothers, sexually abuse their children, although they appear to be in a minority. The blind eye begins to see.

Slowly as a society we are beginning to acknowledge that there is a problem which will not be solved by denial. Child protection has become an area of concern and the focus of government policy and resources, however inadequate. By the beginning of the 1980s the central register of children at risk had begun to include children at risk from emotional and sexual abuse as well as physical injury. However, the therapeutic needs of adult survivors, as well as the ongoing needs of children and their families after disclosure and its immediate aftermath and, in a small proportion of cases, a court case, have not received the same attention or provision.

Many adult women survivors approached the Women's Therapy Centre in London and we began to try to address the therapeutic needs of these women from a psychoanalytic point of view. This was not without its conflicts. In our study group we were involved in looking at psychoanalytic theories and clinical practice from a feminist perspective, as these chapters have elaborated. But feminists have been critical of Freudian psychoanalytic theory in relation to childhood sexual abuse, and not without reason.

It seems ironic that Freud's investigation into hysteria, which introduced him into just this area of sexual trauma, led to his discovery of psychoanalysis but also to his turning away from the evidence of prevalent childhood sexual abuse in his female patients, and his seduction theory which was based on this, towards the unconscious phantasy world that he had discovered. It was in this respect that he was criticised by feminists. This issue has been well documented elsewhere and I will not go into it here. However, in rejecting Freud there is a danger of throwing the baby out with the bathwater.

Freud, a man of his time, we may assume had his own resistances to acknowledging the frequency of childhood sexual abuse and its implications. Nevertheless, psychoanalytic theory, and in particular the theoretical developments since Freud, offer us an insight into the internal processes of the psyche that can help us to understand the psychological legacy of childhood sexual abuse. It has been my experience when working with incest survivors that it is the complex impact of the real abuse upon the unconscious internal phantasy world that is so devastating and damaging for the child's subsequent psychic development and later adult relationships.

Psychoanalytic theory provides a framework for understanding that our relationships to our parents, at a time when we are at our most vulnerable and dependent, are the medium in which our emotional development takes place. The emotional quality of these first relationships is crucial in shaping and texturing our relationship to others and to ourselves throughout our lives.

When a child, male or female, is sexually abused by a powerful adult, there will be issues that they have in common with other such children, but there will also be differences in the nature of the relationship to the abuser and the psychological impact that it has on the child. In the relationship that I am focusing on the abuser is a parent, the father, someone with whom the child has a relationship of extreme dependency, someone who has unlimited access to her, someone of a different gender.

When Michelle came to therapy she informed me that she had seen several therapists already. This is not an unusual feature. Although she had felt that each of them had helped her in different ways, Michelle was still suffering enormously and when things got really bad she would cut herself on her chest and arms. She had made several suicide attempts which she assured me had been cries for help in times of despair – she had not wanted to die, but to escape from her distress.

When I asked her what she hoped to get from this therapy which she had not got from the others and why she thought it would be any different this time, she was insistent that what she needed to do was work on her relationship with her mother. She complained that the Freudian analyst that she had seen three times weekly had only been interested in her sexual relationship with her father and had not understood that her real problem was with her mother.

This complaint had a familiar ring to me. When I first started working with incest survivors I was continually surprised by the persistence with which they seemed to need to talk about their rage and disappointment with their mothers before they could begin to work through their experience of being sexually abused by their fathers. This pattern was equally true for women in groups as it was for women in individual therapy.

Michelle was her parent's first child. When she was 18 months old her brother Sam was born. When Michelle was four years old her paternal grandmother moved in with the family. From this point on her father frequently sexually abused her. Michelle told her mother who took no action to stop the abuse until puberty. Only then, worried that Michelle would become pregnant, did she threaten to expose the father to the rest of the family if he did not stop. The father stopped sexually abusing Michelle and started physically abusing her mother.

Interestingly, it was Michelle's theory that her father abused her because she reminded him of his dominating and controlling mother. She thought that, when abusing her, he was getting his revenge on his mother.

Michelle described how she would become obsessed with older women, 'mother figures', in her life. It was when the woman she was currently secretly obsessed with had unwittingly disappointed her that she had become so distressed that she felt the need to seek help again.

In the early months of the therapy, while describing devastatingly painful scenes of sexual abuse in her childhood, Michelle would seem strangely excited and have a chillingly triumphant smile on her face. She would be extremely tense and anxious but showed no emotion in these sessions. In the counter-transference I would feel enormous pain and be overwhelmed with tears after she had gone. I also felt very concerned and protective towards

her. It felt almost unbearable to have to know what awful acts
human beings are capable of towards vulnerable children.

As long ago as 1924, Ferenczi, describing the impact of an adult's
sexual act on a child, wrote:

> The weak and undeveloped personality reacts to sudden unpleasure not
> by defence (repression), but by anxiety ridden identification and by
> introjection of the menacing person or aggressor.

Ferenczi recognised that an intrapsychic process was taking place
which was not merely a repression of a memory into the
unconscious: something more complex was happening. He goes on:

> The same anxiety compels, however, if it reaches a certain maximum,
> compels them to subordinate themselves like automata to the will of the
> aggressor, to divine each one of his desires and to gratify these; completely
> oblivious of themselves they identify themselves with the aggressor.
> Through the identification or let us say, introjection of the aggressor, he
> disappears as part of external reality and becomes intra- instead of extra-
> psychic; the intra-psychic is then subjected in a dream-like state as is the
> traumatic trance, to primary processes, i.e. according to the pleasure
> principle it can be modified or changed by the use of positive or negative
> hallucinations . . . . When the child recovers from such an attack, he feels
> enormously confused, in fact split – innocent and culpable at the same
> time – and his confidence in the testimony of his own senses is broken.

Ferenczi understood that when a child is sexually abused it is an
overwhelmingly traumatic experience, a threat to the self. The child
takes the experience in but, because it cannot be contained,
processed and integrated, she is forced to defend herself psychologically in a more primitive way. The experience has to be taken
control of and split off. In the process, a part of the child's self
becomes split off. The abuser becomes an internal object in an
abusive relation to the child self, which will find representation in the
child's phantasy world and unconscious expression in her future
relationships.

> The triumphant quality to Michelle's stories worried and puzzled
> me. I was pleased that she was able to disclose to me events she
> had never told anyone about before. She monitored my reactions
> very carefully and was beginning to trust that I would not reject
> her or diminish the seriousness of what she was telling me and

what it had meant for her as a child. However, the triumphant quality persisted until I understood that in a part of Michelle's mind the role of the therapy was twofold – to protect her friends from being burdened by her distress and to be a tool in her secret accusation of her parents. She reasoned that her need for therapy was proof that her family was dysfunctional and that there was something wrong. Michelle had reproduced in her relationship with me a dynamic in her family in which her sexual relationship with her father protected her mother and gratified him while neither parent took care of her emotional needs. Michelle had come to expect nothing for herself. From this position inside herself she expected nothing for herself from the therapy either. There was no place in this scenario for her therapeutic needs to be considered or for me to be someone who might help her to recover from her childhood experiences, someone who could make a difference. I was being put in the position of someone who would collude with this 'abusive' use of the therapy. After interpreting this situation and the implication that change from this point of view might seem like letting her parents off the hook, the therapy moved on.

During this first part of the therapy Michelle showed hardly any of the emotions appropriate to the incidents of abuse she was describing, while in the counter-transference I was filled with them. Michelle needed me to contain the feelings she could not yet contain for herself. While communicating the physical details of the sexual abuse with words, Michelle communicated the emotional feelings through projective identification. She complained of feeling a dreadful frozen emptiness.

Melanie Klein (1946), herself influenced by Ferenczi, extended our understanding of splitting, projection and projective identification as a normal psychic defence mechanism which belongs to a primitive (paranoid–schizoid) mode of functioning in early infancy, but which, if it persists as a predominant mode of functioning, can lead to a weakening of the ego, difficulties in further psychological development and, in extreme cases, psychotic illness. It is in the relationship with the mother that the internal capacity to contain psychic experience and think about it in a meaningful way develops. In writing about Bion's (1962, 1963) development of Klein's theory, Hanna Segal states:

> The infant projects into the breast his anxiety . . . . A mother capable of
> containing projective identification unconsciously processes those projec-
> tions and responds adequately to the infant's need. When this happens,
> the infant can reintroject his projections, modified by understanding, and
> he also introjects the breast as a container capable of containing and
> dealing with anxiety. This forms the basis of his own capacity to deal with
> anxiety. (Segal, 1989)

This internal object with its quality of containment will have a
symbolic representation, an image, in the internal world which will
be associated with the mother or part of the mother that the baby
relates to – her breast. In theory there seems to be no reason why a
father could not provide this capacity, this 'maternal' function, if he
were able (male therapists certainly need to have this capacity), but in
reality child-rearing in early infancy is still predominantly the role of
mothers.

Segal (1975) suggests that the mental stability that comes from the
taking in of a containing experience can be disrupted in two ways –
either from the mother's incapacity to bear the infant's projected
feelings or from the infant's excessively destructive omnipotent
phantasy. I believe that, in the case of childhood sexual abuse, it is
also disrupted by a premature and ongoing traumatic sexual
relationship with the abuser, in this case the father. The intensely
traumatic, abusive experience repeatedly overwhelms and breaks
down any internal capacity the child has to contain her own
emotional experience, and constantly forces her back into paranoid–
schizoid defences which are a normal response to trauma. The sexual
abuse is a traumatic experience on many different levels – physical,
emotional and in the child's internal world.

At the moment when the child is being sexually abused, her
mother fails her. Not only does she fail her daughter by her absence,
but the experience is so overwhelming and anxiety-provoking that
the child's internal maternal object must also fail her. It is impossible
for a child to cope with such an experience. If the mother has in fact
not been able to provide the child with a good enough experience of
containment, then this function will, of course, be all the more fragile
and likely to break down.

We might also consider what it is that the daughter is containing for
her father who must surely be in a primitive state of mind when he
treats his daughter as a part object, oblivious of her subjectivity. With
what unconscious projections is he violating his daughter's psychic

space while violating her body? Brendan McCarthy, who has worked with abusers as well as survivors, offers us some insight.

> The younger the child at the incest encounter the more deeply disturbed by the experience will she be. It relates also to the impact on a very young child of her father's sexual need and her role in containing and managing it at a time of limited understanding. Not only does she replace her mother in the Oedipal configuration and suffer the guilt ridden consequences of doing so, she is also confronting a regressed and overwhelmingly needy father in search of a primitive reunion with his mother's body, so the child also in her passive aquiescence becomes the lost maternal object for the father, coping with his sphincteric loss of control. (McCarthy, 1988)

I am suggesting that it is because the relationship to the internal mother, the function of containment, has broken down, as well as the relationship to the external mother, that these clients are so preoccupied with the relationship with the mother in their therapy, and that containment and firm boundary keeping are crucial clinical issues in this work.

> In the next phase of the therapy Michelle began to do what she said she had wanted to do: she began to work on her relationship with her mother. From the moment her brother was born, when she was 18 months old, Michelle experienced her mother as rejecting her. She felt that her mother taunted her not only by withdrawing her attention but by now showering it on her baby brother. Michelle had been intensely jealous and envious of her brother but her mother had not been emotionally available to help her to manage these feelings; on the contrary, she had been extremely punitive, confirming Michelle's perception that she was evil while her brother was all good. She still longed for the mother that she had lost.
>
> In her early teens she had found an alternative set of parents in a couple who were neighbours. During the therapy the woman announced that she was pregnant. Michelle was distraught and broke off her relationship with them without any explanation. She described in her session how she had attacked herself by hitting her womb with a heavy object and cutting her chest. In the counter-transference I felt like a powerless witness to Michelle's attacks on herself, the powerlessness she must have felt as a child in relation to her father and mother, neither of whom protected her from abuse.

I could not stop Michelle physically from abusing herself but I could speak up for the vulnerable, feeling part of herself that she was attacking by interpreting what I was witnessing and how I understood it to be linked with her past. We understood that the womb that she attacked inside her also stood for her mother's womb, the womb that had produced the baby brother who took her mother away from her. I pointed out that, whatever emotional cruelty she felt that her mother had shown towards her in the past, it was she who was now treating herself in a cruel and abusive way. It was our task in the therapy to understand why she was doing this and what meaning it had for her, so that she could find a less self-destructive way of expressing her powerful feelings by putting them into thoughts and words.

She had a very disturbed weekend during which she had violent fantasies of attacking herself, although now she did not carry them out but brought them to her sessions. We were able to understand the link between the violent fantasies her friend's pregnancy had provoked in the present and her mother's pregnancy in the past. She was shocked when she realised the link between the two. After working through these feelings she was eventually able to go to the baby's christening party to find a delightful little girl she rather liked.


Bion (1967), who developed Klein's ideas, saw projective identification in two ways: as a mechanism for projecting unwanted aspects of the self into the breast to defend the ego, but also as a means of primitive pre-verbal communication between mother and infant which can be seen as a model for the unconscious communication in the transference and counter-transference between client and therapist. Bion called the mother's capacity to take in and think about her infant's projected anxiety states 'maternal reverie'.


The reverie, the thoughts, that Michelle needed me to be able to take in and to think about were of the emotional experience of a little girl being repeatedly sexually abused by her father and let down by her mother. I needed to be able to contain and to identify with the almost unbearable set of feelings that Michelle communicated to me unconsciously through a process of projective identification, until she herself was strong enough to experience these feelings consciously and to acknowledge her own identification with her internalised objects, including her own abusive aspects.

The summer holiday was a turning point for Michelle: having introjected an experience of being contained by me, she was now more able to contain her own feelings. This new capacity seemed to be symbolised by her moving out of a shared household where she had been unhappy for some time and into a self-contained flat. Michelle felt empowered to protect herself and her own interests.

Having worked on her relationship with her mother, the focus now shifted to the sexual relationship with her father. In parallel with the therapy, Michelle attended an incest survivors group, during which she made a poignant drawing of her child self removing a gag from her mouth and her adult self removing a blindfold from her eyes. She was ready to face her feelings about the abuse. Michelle would now be in tears in the session when she talked about her memories.

After the group Michelle plucked up the courage to write a challenging but compassionate letter to her parents telling each of them how she felt that they had hurt and damaged her as a child. Her mother's reply came quickly in a very defensive letter, while her father remained silent for some time.

Michelle desperately wanted a response from him. The waiting was excruciating but she allowed herself to experience an extreme vulnerability during this time, seeking support from friends and continuing to manage her feelings without resorting to cutting herself.

The incestuous relationship with the father makes Oedipal development extremely problematic. In father–daughter incest the father breaks the incest taboo. In doing this he not only violates the daughter's physical body but he also violates her mind. He breaks the boundary between unconscious Oedipal phantasy and the reality that incestuous relationships are prohibited. He makes concrete and actual a relationship that should remain in the realm of internal phantasy and of the symbolic order. He thus deprives the daughter of reality testing and of a possibility for development through relinquishing Oedipal ties.

Laplanche and Pontalis point out that, in concentrating on the triangular Oedipal relationship, we are led to examine all the poles of this relationship, including the unconscious desires of both parents towards the child and the relations between the parents.

> It is the different types of relation between the three points of the triangle which – at least as much as any particular parental image – are destined to be internalised and to survive in the structure of the personality. (Laplanche & Pontalis, 1988)

In incest the generational boundary between the parents and the child is broken and the daughter is symbolically displaced upwards into the parents' generation and the position of child–mother and father's partner in the sexual couple, while the mother is displaced downwards into the child's generation becoming, in effect, an adult–child and sibling. The daughter's childhood comes to a traumatic end when, robbed of her innocence, she is catapulted into precocious sexual knowlege and pseudo-adulthood. In her internal world she is guiltily trapped in the triangular Oedipal relationship to her parents.

Klein saw the resolution of the Oedipus complex not so much as an age-related stage as a developmental task in which the child must find her place internally in relation to the points in this triangle and with respect to the sexual desires of all three. Klein (1935) linked the entry into the Oedipus complex with the onset of the depressive position and the development of new psychic capacities, including the capacity to symbolise. When the child begins to see the mother as a whole person with an independent existence, she becomes aware of the mother's relationship to the father. The father has always been there from the child's conception in the mother's mind if not actually present. But it is only as the child reaches this stage of development, moving on from the two-person relationship with the mother, that she becomes aware of the three-person relationship between herself and her parents. The relationship with the father as a third term – i.e. someone who is different from and other than the mother or the child – has the potential to facilitate the child's separation from the mother. On a symbolic level the father and his internal representation signifies the capacity to differentiate, structure and order and the entry into the realm of social relationships, language and culture.

When the father commits incest he denies his daughter the opportunity to use him in this symbolic way. He pushes her back into the primitive realm of body-to-body relating that she has so recently experienced with her mother and that she is struggling to develop out of. It is the frustration of Oedipal desires that leads to new development, while their exploitation and appropriation by the father only pushes the daughter back once more into the maternal realm.

In the therapy relationship the client needs to have an experience of being contained by the therapist in order to develop or re-establish an internal space in the psyche into which some of the split-off, projected feelings can be reintrojected and integrated, strengthening the ego's capacity to contain psychic pain. It is only when a containing maternal object has been internalised that rage and hatred towards the father about the abuse and Oedipal issues of guilt and sexuality can be faced.

Eventually, Michelle received some ackowlegement from her father that what he had done had deeply affected her life. Michelle felt that something had been resolved for her; for the first time the abuse could become a memory in the background of her mind and, although she would never forget it, it was no longer something she was preoccupied with daily. She felt that she could relate to her parents as an adult equal now that the abused child in her had been acknowledged by them.

Michelle was unusual in that she was able to get acknowlegement from her father that he had abused her. Renegotiating relationships with real parents can only be helpful. But many daughters do not have this opportunity or are unsuccessful in their attempts.

However, as I have tried to demonstrate, what must also be renegotiated in the therapy is the psychological legacy of the sexual abuse, the relationship to the internal objects and their representations in the client's unconscious phantasy. We must keep in mind the *interrelationship* between reality and phantasy, rather than preferencing one to the exclusion of the other.

## References

Bion, W. R. (1962) *Learning from Experience*, Karnac Books, London 1984.
—— (1963) *Elements of Psychoanalysis*, Karnac Books, London, 1984.
—— (1967) 'Attacks on linking', in *Second Thoughts*, Heinemann Medical, London.
Ferenczi, S. (1924) 'Confusion of tongues between the adult and the child', *International Journal of Psycho-Analysis*, 30:225, 1932.
Klein, M. (1935) 'A contribution to the psychogenesis of manic-depressive states', *International Journal of Psycho-Analysis*, 16:145–74.
—— (1946) 'Notes on some schizoid mechanisms', *International Journal of Psycho-Analysis*, 27:99–110.
Laplanche, J. & Pontalis, J.-B. (1988) *The Language of Psychoanalysis*, Karnac Books, London.

McCarthy, B. (1988) 'Are incest victims hated?', *Psychoanalytic Psychotherapy*, 3, 2:113–20.

Segal, H. (1975) 'A psycho-analytical approach to the treatment of schizophrenia', in M. Lader (ed.), *Studies of Schizophrenia*, Headley, Ashford 1975.

—— (1989) 'Introduction' to R. Britton, M. Feldman & E. O'Shaughnessy, *The Oedipus Complex Today*, Karnac Books, London.

# Chapter 9

# W is for Woman

*Valerie Sinason*

This chapter is an account of work with one woman with a learning disability, which, I hope, highlights some universal issues that are relevant to work with both men and women in this client group. I have the permission of Ms 'Rita Atir' to give an account of our time together and have changed all names and some other details to ensure her privacy. 'Atir' is 'Rita' back to front and, for reasons that will become clear, I wanted to provide her with a last name.

## Background and referral

Ms Rita Atir was 25 when she was first referred for a psychotherapy assessment by a social services department as a result of her difficult behaviour. The referral letter stated that she smeared faeces, was doubly incontinent, cut through electric cables and floorboards and, when in such a disturbed state of mind, could also be violent to those around her. She had limited language, could not read or write or use money and needed a high level of attention and surveillance. Together with her severe learning disability she also had a physical disability and was a wheelchair-user. The referral was sought at this point as her residential placement was in jeopardy and her mother was insistent that she should not be placed in a hospital.

Background details given were very scanty. She was the oldest child born to a first-generation English family of four daughters and one son. She was the only one with a learning disability and was considered to be the only one who had been sexually and physically abused by her father in early childhood. Placed in care at the age of 11 she experienced a succession of short- and long-term placements. However, she maintained some contact with her mother (who had remained with her husband and other children).

Although an adult, in the referral letter she was only referred to as 'Rita'. There are many different styles of name and titles prevalent at the moment, both personally and professionally, and, so long as they are thought about, each have their own possibilities and boundaries. However, when the referrer and I are both formally addressed and an adult client is addressed only by a first name, a significant imbalance has occurred, a denial of adulthood.

It is indeed a tragedy that there are adults who cannot function as autonomous adults with all their faculties. However, not to deal with that loss by linguistically denying adulthood perpetuates it. There is an additional gender pressure on the learning disabled woman to remain a 'good' non-sexual girl.

My practice with all such patients is to say 'Hello, my name is Mrs Valerie Sinason and you can call me Valerie or Mrs Sinason. What would you like me to call you?' It is grist to the therapeutic mill to interpret the choice or variations made when relevant, but that is a later and different task.

On phoning the referrer for more details a tone of despair could be heard. Rita Atir had caused several fires in past placements and there was serious concern as to whether the adult carer and other residents were in danger in the current home. Smoke alarms had been placed in all rooms, the kitchen was now locked at night and the families of other residents were frightened and angry at this deterioration in the environment. Indeed, the social services department wanted Rita Atir to be placed in an institutional setting with 24-hour nursing staff on hand but had been curiously intimidated by the mother's fury at such a prospect. 'The mother will only let Rita stay in a family setting which is all-female. No institution and no mixed home.'

After arranging an initial meeting time for Rita and her adult carer, who I will call 'Terri Ret', I had many questions and impressions in my mind. Where a child does not grow up normally and the status of their adulthood is in doubt, the normal developmental separations cannot be worked through. The mother–daughter relationship here looked painfully loaded. As well as good attachment, what other possible components were in the links between them?

Could it be that the power of her wish to keep her daughter in an all-female setting was connected with an omnipotent idea that she could thereby eradicate past male abuse? Was she punishing her daughter sexually by restricting her adult freedom? Why were social services bolstering this wish?

## First meeting

When first meeting with an adult who cannot manage to live alone, I see them for a short time with their main carer. This allows me to check publicly the reasons for referral so that the patient, who often cannot read, properly understands why they have been referred. It gives me the chance to check, where necessary, the meaning of the patient's signs or sounds and also to get a preliminary idea of the patient in the context of their environment. Finally, as psychotherapy is a treatment for which consent is crucial and as people with learning disabilities can appeasingly consent to whatever they consider their carers/parents want them to do, such a meeting gives me a chance to evaluate such issues.

Rita Atir, a slim Black woman with shoulder-length hair, was sitting in a wheelchair smiling blandly when I entered the waiting room. Terri Ret, her adult carer, stood at her side rather nervously but hopefully. She was white, large and in her late 50s. The two women wore matching tracksuits, evoking questions in my mind about the cross-over from attachment to symbiosis. I said that my name was Mrs Valerie Sinason and that they could call me Valerie or Mrs Sinason. Terri said that she always used first names and she was Terri. We shook hands. Rita grinned broadly at me and said 'Ms Rita Atir', then burst out laughing mockingly. 'Rita Atir. Me Rita. Say Rita.' She giggled at me and fixed me powerfully with her eyes. I said that I would say Rita if that was what she wanted but I was surprised to hear her laugh at her whole name. 'Me Rita. You Valerie', she said in a more serious tone. I said that was right – she had got my first name correctly and had put it together with her first name seriously, so that was what we would call each other right now but another time we might want to be Ms Atir, Mrs Sinason and – 'Ms Ret' interposed Terri. 'Ms Atir. Rita Atir. Rita. Valerie. Terri. Terri Ret.' As she turned

the wheels of her wheelchair with considerable strength on the way
to my room she said the different names over and over as if savouring
such possibilities for the first time.

Our own names are such a basic aspect of our identity, often being
the first words we learn to write, that they deserve serious attention.

Inside the room I invited Rita to choose where to sit in her
wheelchair and she then ordered Terri to sit on the armchair next to
her. With a wry smile Terri obeyed. I commented that I had never met
them before and they had never met me before but they knew each
other. 'You don't', laughed Rita. I agreed and the mockery left Rita's
face. She was checking, right at the start, whether I would mind
experiencing not knowing, exclusion, mockery; experiences that, I
felt, she was vastly painfully knowledgeable about. I asked if she
knew why she was here today. 'Yes. Terri say. You say, Terri!', she
ordered. Rather shyly Terri said that she really liked Rita; she had
known her for three years and Rita was very polite and friendly and
had a good sense of humour. However, in her room she was
regularly violent, smashed things, and smeared and wet the bed.
Recently this had extended to the kitchen and now there was a really
big fear for the safety of everyone in the house.

The smile had gone from Rita's face and she looked vulnerable and
frightened, scanning Terri's face avidly. I commented on this. 'Stay
with Terri', said Rita imploringly, looking at Terri. 'Well, you know
how much I care about you, Rita – but I can't manage when you are
such a naughty girl.'

'Naughty' is a painfully frequent term applied to adults with a
learning disability, reinforcing the erosion of their adulthood. It is not
surprising that it should be used. Faced with appalling signs and
symptoms of emotional disturbance that could, in some cases, as with
Rita's firesetting, also cause danger to others, the word 'naughty'
reassuringly offers the possibility that such actions are conscious and
can be changed.

I commented on what a hard time it was for both Rita and Terri,
who liked each other but were both frightened as to whether they
could manage this violence together. Once the deep fears concerning
abandonment, separation and violence were on the map, Rita began
to be interested in seeing me by herself. After four sessions with the
three of us together, individual treatment slowly began. In following
Rita's needs, it became clear that she needed some time on her own
and some time with Terri.

## First session on her own

Rita wheeled her way to me, really excited, giving Terri a cheerful wave goodbye. Inside the room she looked around and giggled. She opened her handbag to show me her purse which contained 30 pence, paper and a pencil. I said that she wanted to show me she had her own bag with things that mattered to her in it. She nodded. 'Got money, paper, pencil.' I said they were important things to have. I considered that, in feeling safe to have time on her own, she was able to show that she was a female with internal space and resources.

Taking out her own pencil but using a piece of paper from my desk she drew round the outline of her hand. Lifting her hand to look at the results she saw, with an expression of dismay, a lopsided circle. She had not been able to differentiate the fingers. I said that, when she felt pleased with herself and her resources, she wanted to make her mark on things and show what she could do, and then she could be disappointed at what she couldn't do. I added that I did not know her well enough to know what she couldn't do because of her learning disability or physical disability and what she couldn't do because of her feelings.

After a while she said 'Mummy'. I asked what she was thinking about mummy. 'Worried. What she doing?' I said when she was away from people she worried about them. She nodded. 'Terri. What she doing?' I asked what she thought. 'Don't know. Worried. Terri come here.' I said that she wanted time for herself but then got scared of being empty and not having things working properly, and then she felt worried about how other people were. 'Terri', she repeated and I said that we could get Terri if she wanted. She giggled excitedly. 'Me get her. Me bring her.' I agreed and opened the door so that she could wheel herself out. I then had to open one further door for her and left her to negotiate the rest of the journey. I stood outside the door of my room until she and Terri returned.

While standing there I considered the problems architecture caused. With automatic electronic doors Rita would have been able to be more independent. I also wondered about her mention of 'Mummy'. In proudly showing me her wish to write and her possession of femaleness (her handbag), did she fear an envious maternal attack from me? Was she fearing that I, a new mother-figure, would be as disappointed by her handicaps as her real mother was, and did that fear cause her to handicap her real drawing possibilities?

When they came in Rita said to Terri, 'Knock on door. My room.' Terri knocked on the door and Rita looked very proud. 'Come in. Sit down', she said. I said that she was proud to know this room and to invite Terri into it. I did not consider the timing right to consider her appropriation of my room. 'Tell her Terri', said Rita insistently. I said that there was clearly an important reason for Rita wanting Terri to come to the room.

'Well – her mother rang to invite her over for this weekend and Rita went and smeared everywhere and cut up her newest dress.' Rita's face looked crumpled and Terri was trying to report neutrally but looked exhausted. I commented on how upset and tired they both looked. Rita burst into tears and Terri said it was always hard when Rita's mother rang and she visited her. The mother complained to social services if Rita was not dressed neatly and would probably not like the new, more modern adult clothes Terri had brought her, so social services might tell Terri to keep Rita in short white socks. And it made her angry that Rita's mother could ring up whenever she wanted to see Rita and interfere and she, Terri, had to clean up all the mess.

As Terri spoke, Rita was looking at her with real protective concern. I realised that Rita, in addition to other reasons, had brought Terri into the room to give her a space. Terri faced from her mother and social services the same feelings of being on trial that she felt with Terri and her mother and perhaps, too, with me.

## Sessions 10–30

A pattern developed of Rita wanting half an hour on her own and a further two minutes with Terri present. She would go to bring Terri back to the room and decided to negotiate the corridor doors herself. At times this meant waiting for someone to come along and open them for her; at times it meant showing a hidden reserve of strength in her arms and opening the doors herself.

The theme in these sessions centred on her relationship with her mother – the external one and the internal representations of her mother in her own mind.

As she felt safer to explore her relationship to me – the mother in the transference – hints of her sexual abuse began to emerge. She expressed feelings of guilt and triumph towards her mother, as well as fury and hurt over the abuse, which had been sadistic. Her violent behaviour began to diminish.

## Session 31

Rita wheeled herself to the table, took a piece of paper and, looking very shyly at me and covering the page, drew or wrote something which I could not see.

I had the feeling that something very important and precious was happening. 'Not cross Valerie?', she asked, looking worried. I said that she was doing something important and private for her and letting me see that she could do something important and private, but that she was worried there was a jealous Valerie about who wouldn't like it. She laughed relievedly.

After a few moments she shyly handed me the piece of paper. To my amazement there was a capital R. Rita looked at me tensely. 'R for Rita', I said with emphasis. She broke into a triumphant, joyous smile and then sobbed. 'It's right. R for Rita. You read it. Again!' I looked at the piece of paper and said, with performance emphasis, 'R for Rita'. 'It's there!', she exclaimed, 'on the paper! My letter! You can read it!' 'That's right', I said, 'And do you know everyone who can read letters could pick up that piece of paper and read that letter.' 'Yes', she enthused. 'R. Everyone's R.'

For a woman with a severe learning disability, the fantasy power of letters can be even stronger than for the normal beginner reader. If your private personhood has been abused and it is hard to think, how do you cope with having a name, an identity, built of public letters that are stitched together?

After that session Terri told me that Rita had said her first complete grammatical sentences. 'Thank you for taking me to the Tavistock. It clears my head.'

## Session 32

Shyly looking at me, Rita wheeled herself to the desk and started to write. She handed me a page of V's. I felt deeply moved. 'V for Valerie?', I asked. 'Yes', she said. Then, publicly, she wrote R's next to them. 'Valerie and Rita.' Then she giggled. 'Miss Rita Atir and Mrs

Valerie Sinason.' I said she was remembering our very first meeting and how our names sounded next to each other and that I had asked her how she would like to be addressed.

## Sessions 33–40

Each session involved Rita writing. Always starting with R for Rita she could now add V for Valerie and T for Tavistock and Terri.

I decided that I would let her use my old portable typewriter as she found the pencil quite hard to manage and did not want to use felt-tips. As a former English teacher of deprived pupils, I had been impressed by the way seeing a word printed gave it extra objective weight and pride, and Rita had often spoken about her mother being a secretary and managing a typewriter. I had used the typewriter as a piece of equipment for several learning-disabled patients and none of them had damaged it.

## Session 40: the typewriter

Rita picked up how to use the typewriter very well and soon she could feed the paper in and manipulate the carriage return herself.

She very quickly typed R for Rita, V for Valerie and T for Tavistock and Terri. Then, looking very intently at me, she typed a D. 'D?', I asked. 'Yes.' 'D for dog?' 'No.' 'D for door?' 'No.' We carried on in this way for a few minutes. Then Rita announced, 'Get Terri.' They both returned in great excitement. Terri had been thrilled at the growth of admitted intelligence in Rita and the fact that the writing had continued at home.

'What good typing', she said admiringly. Rita beamed. 'What is R for?' 'You know', said Rita severely. 'True. It's Rita', agreed Terri. 'You tease me', grinned Rita. 'V for Valerie?', asked Terri. 'Yes.' 'Who could T be for?', she asked teasingly. 'It's you! You!', grinned Rita. 'I know', said Terri. 'But D? What is D for?' 'David', said Rita sadly. There was a silence.

Terri looked thoughtful. 'I think David was a friend of hers from boarding school.' 'Friend', said Rita. She cried. 'David. Friend.' She sobbed very deeply. I said that she missed her friend David. 'Yes.' I said it must be very hard keeping up with an old friend when she could not write letters to him or use the phone. 'Yes', she said. 'David', she said. She looked at me imploringly. 'David', she explained. I asked if she wanted to see David again. 'Yes. You get him.' Making the therapeutic comment 'You would like me to be able to find him' did not feel correct here. I was well aware of the awful invisible plight of people who could not read or write or phone being moved away from each other with no choice and often nobody checking up on those precious relationships and helping to maintain them. I turned to Terri and asked if she thought that there was any way of finding out where David was. 'I'll try', she said, clearly moved. 'Yes. You!', said Rita.

## Session 41

Rita came in and typed R, T, V and then D, and looked intently at me. 'David?', I asked. 'Yes. Get Terri now.' She got Terri. Terri had phoned the boarding school. Rita had left it nearly ten years ago but there had been two teachers and a school secretary who remembered her and Terri found out that Rita and David had been close friends for eight years. David had been suddenly moved to a new school when he changed foster placement and their contact had dramatically stopped. The address of David's new home was provided.

Rita started saying a few more words and surprised Terri by her repeated insistence to 'Phone David.'

## Session 43

Rita did not type but said 'David' and cried. She cried for more than ten minutes, deeply. I said nothing and was deeply moved myself. My only intervention was to pass her a tissue at a certain point. This was not to stop, muffle or erase her tears but to provide her with comfort as she was physically uncomfortable with the sniffing her crying had caused.

When her tears had stopped, I gently asked if she had found out anything. 'No letter. No phone. Get Terri.' Terri said that no-one had replied to her letter but all was not lost; she had also found out the address of David's college and was going to write there too.

## Session 46

In the last ten minutes, with Terri in the room, Rita sat typing noisily. Terri said that she sounded like a proper typist like her mother. She was thrilled at that. She said that she had nothing to ask this time but wanted Terri to talk. Terri proudly said that they could tell me something about David, and Rita was deeply excited. They had traced him and would be able to phone him on Sunday.

Rita took a deep breath and then, for the first time, typed the letter P. 'P?', I asked. 'Papa', she shouted. 'Pest', she shouted and angrily laughed. Then, for the first time, she pushed the carriage return the wrong way. I said that thinking of a man she liked, David, whom she had missed, had made her think of another important man in her life, her papa, whom she might miss. But thinking of him also made her think of painful things. Then there was a pest in control that affected her learning. She laughed. That was the only error she made in her typing.

I said that she was showing us how much she knew and perhaps she knew even more letters and wanted to read more . She said 'Yes.' I looked at Terri and Rita looked at Terri. 'Evening class', proclaimed Rita. We all laughed. I said Rita liked to have us all in the room so that she could show us what she needed.

## Session 47

In the waiting room Rita surprised me by standing next to her wheelchair. She was smartly dressed with a new bag. 'Can walk sometimes', she said gleefully. With Terri smiling proudly at her she unsteadily made her way to my room. Inside she looked at my old bag pointedly and said, 'See my bag Valerie?' I said 'Yes' and commented that she had a smart new one and she thought I could do with a new one too. She giggled appreciatively. 'Valerie old bag!', she chuckled. I laughed too. I was thrilled at the linguistic move in this younger woman!

She proudly opened her bag in front of me and showed me her small change, pointing accurately to the coins she would need for the drinks machine. 'Get drink first', she said. She correctly worked the machine and proudly returned to the room.

She reopened her bag and checked the contents of her purse. 'More money left', she said. I commented that even though she had paid for a drink, and got it herself, she still had money left. I was aware of her growth in female adult confidence and the way she was enjoying holding back her news.

She took a comb out of her bag. 'Comb', she said. She asked me to point out C for comb on the typewriter. She typed it and combed her hair again. 'Hair nice Valerie?' I said yes, it was. She had combed it and she knew the letter for comb and how to comb her hair and feel attractive. 'Me see your man Valerie?', she asked and laughed uproariously. I smiled and said that now she felt so attractive that she thought I ought to watch out.

There was a radiant pause. 'Get Terri now', she announced. Then she brought Terri in. 'Tell about David', demanded Rita. Terri said that she had phoned the home placement number for David on Sunday. She had asked to speak to David and told him that Rita would like to speak to him. David had sounded very pleased. Then Rita and David had spoken on their own for half an hour and Terri had come back in when Rita called her to make an arrangement.

'McDonalds!', shrieked Rita. 'They are going to meet in McDonalds next Sunday at 3p.m.', explained Terri. 'His carer – whatever she is – says I have to be there too – but I can sit at another table. She did not honestly sound too pleased. But Rita and David sounded ever so pleased and Rita has not done any of her naughty old things for ages.'

## Session 48: first meeting with David

Just before I went to the waiting room to get Rita there was a knock on my door. It was Rita. In an adult way she had come to the room by herself for the first time. She looked adult, female – and sad.

'Hello Valerie', she said. 'Came myself.' I wondered to myself what the experience of seeing David in company had been like; was coming to me by herself a step forward in independence as a result of seeing David or an attempt to deny the hurt of not managing to see him independently?

'You have', I said. 'Please come in.' She sat on an armchair very seriously. 'Get Terri', she suddenly announced. I said that of course she could, but it seemed that the moment an adult Rita came into the room someone else did not like it and needed her to get Terri. She thought for a moment and then agreed, 'Yes. But still get Terri', and left.

When Terri came back Rita did not make any verbal demands. She just looked at her politely. 'Do you want me to tell or do you want to say what happened?', asked Terri. 'You say', said Rita. 'Well, we have seen him. It was a strange week. Rita kept everything tidier than anyone I have ever known but on the day we were going she could not find anything and kept changing her clothes. I told her she was just like I was when I went on a date.' (Rita laughed.) 'She drove me mad. She couldn't do up her buttons, find her coat. She was crying and saying she couldn't go, but go we did. He recognised her right away but she did not recognise him.' 'So tall', said Rita proudly. 'He was', agreed Terri – 'Six foot.' They both giggled.

According to Terri, after that first moment they could not stop speaking. Terri had given them money and sat in a corner several tables away from them. David's 'carer' had allowed him out for four hours (at 26 years old) and Terri explained that, even though it was a long time to sit on her own, she was so thrilled that they had finally met, and so sad that they could not make their own independent arrangements, that she did not mind.

'We get married', said Rita. 'Me and David to get married.' 'Yes', added Terri. 'He told me he wanted to as well.' Rita sat still with the most beautiful smile on her face. 'Love David', she said. 'David friend.' She sat musing – 'D . . . R . . . T . . . V . . .'.

She walked across the room and pointed to the phone. 'T for typewriter and telephone', she said. I agreed and asked if she was able to use the phone. 'No, and David no', she sighed. Terri told me that David had said he would phone Rita next week, but Terri did not know if he knew how to use the phone and said that Rita did not know how to use it even though she had tried giving her lessons. 'If David not ring – me ring', said Rita firmly.


### Session 49

Rita opened her bag proudly and took out a brand new phone book. She thrust it into my hand imperatively. 'You want me to phone someone?', I asked, trying to sound neutral but having a cowardly feeling at the same time. 'Yes. David.' I repeated that she wanted me to phone David now, whilst gaining time to consider what to do. 'Please phone', she said with real courtesy. 'I can't. David can't. You must for me.' I said that I would dial for her and be her fingers, and then the phone call would be hers. I dialled while she held the phone but it was engaged. I felt guilty at feeling relieved as I put the phone down.

'Phone again?', she asked. 'Try now. Might be free.' I did. 'Ringing now', she said. She was then enormously anxious about having to speak to someone who clearly did not understand her or did not want to understand her. Her voice became quite mumbly as an attack. 'Daywid', she mispronounced. The woman must have said that he was out because Rita then said 'Oh', and then passed me the phone. I said 'Hello', and a quite cynically amused voice said 'Hello'. I explained that I was helping Ms Rita Atir to phone her friend Mr David Divad. Was he there? 'Mr Divad', said the woman, with mocking inflection, 'is at his special needs college and doesn't come back until 5 p.m.' I asked her, without any real trust, to tell him that his friend had rung.

For a moment Rita sat looking carefully into my eyes. 'She won't tell him', she said in a suddenly wise, adult way that made me momentarily think I was hallucinating. I said I agreed. 'I'll get Terri now.' For the first time Rita took charge of the subject matter completely. 'I phoned David. Not in. At college. Nasty woman.' Terri said, 'Well done for phoning!' She then turned to me and said, 'She knew he would be at college but she felt safer ringing from your room since she first mentioned him here and all the way here she has been saying "Valerie will be pleased to see me".'

## Session 50

Unusually, Rita came in with Terri right at the start. Terri looked apologetically at me. 'Terri in. Talk about David. Talk about your man. Me go to toilet.' She then left the room. We looked amazed at each other as this was the first time she had ever left us together in the room without her present.

Terri said that her ex-husband had visited from Ireland and Rita had been very angry that they had had private time together. She had also been very frightened that Terri would go back to Ireland with him. David had not rung and for the first time Rita had openly behaved in a rivalrous way with Terri. She had also used sexual swear words which Terri had never heard her mention before.

Rita returned after knocking politely on the door. She looked very pleased with herself as she sat down. 'Sorry Terri', she suddenly said. 'What for?' 'Bad words.' 'Ah.' 'What sort of bad words?', I asked. 'Called Terri a fucking cunt when her man was there.' I said that perhaps it had felt very hard that Terri had a man there who might be fucking her cunt when she and David were not able to be together fucking.

There was a shocked pause and Rita cried. 'David. Want David.' Terri put an arm round her. 'It is really hard, love.' 'Toilet', said Rita. Terri and I sat in silence until she came back a few moments later. 'Better now', said Rita. I said that today was the first time she had left Terri and I together and perhaps she wanted to pee on us and all our words. She roared with laughter and said 'Yes!' I said that she should talk and asked what she was thinking. 'Piss on your husband Terri! Piss on your Ireland! You piss on me leaving me. Papa piss on me. Wet my bed. Me in trouble. He wet my bed. Valerie goes on holidays with man. Piss! Fuck! Cunt!' She was shouting loudly, coherently and bravely.

Terri and I sat in silence and then Rita cried and she and Terri hugged each other with Terri crying too. 'I am not going to Ireland you silly cabbage. I left Ireland. He's a no-good man my ex, just like your papa and we're better off without them.'

There was a long silence. Then Rita lifted her tear-stained face to look at me, wanting words from me. I said that first there were all three of us in the room, then Rita went out and there were two people in the room. Nearly all the conversation seemed to be about who were the twos – the couple – the mum and dad – the man and woman – and who was the left-out one – the baby. It was easier for Rita to think of pissing on all the men and making a two with Terri – a mother and daughter or two women – than to keep up any hope that Terri could have a man and care about Rita, and that Rita could have David and care about Terri, and that I could go on holiday with a man and still think about Rita.

It was almost time to finish. Just before she left Rita stood up and looked at Terri very seriously. 'Marry your man Terri. Give another chance', she said as she prepared to leave the room. Terri looked amazed. I said that Rita wanted Terri to be properly married and wanted to be able to marry herself, and commented on how hard it was trying to keep in touch with David.

## Session 51

Rita came in looking very purposeful. 'Letter', she pronounced. She took paper, an envelope and a pen from her bag, gave them to me and said, 'Write to tell David to come here.' She handed me a separate piece of paper with David's address written on it. I said that she wanted David to come here with her and she said, 'Yes.' I said that I would be her secretary and asked her what she wanted me to write; she said, 'Dear David, I want to see you. Come to the Tavistock with me. My friend Terri will phone you.' I handed her the letter. She signed it with a large R, carefully folded it and put it in the envelope – something she would not have been able to do a year ago.

I said that it was possible that David could not read and we did not know how sympathetic the person reading the letter would be.


## Session 52

Rita proudly took off her jacket showing a short-sleeved jumper. She lifted up her jumper showing a brand new, well-fitting bra. 'See what I got Valerie. Bra. Woman clothes. You have bra.' I said yes, I did, and we were both women with breasts. She nodded. When Terri came in Rita announced, 'You didn't ring him.' Terri nervously told me that she had not rung David because Rita's mother was very angry to hear that she had met a male friend – even though Terri had been present as chaperone.

'She is responsible for the adult fostering and she really doesn't want Rita to have a boyfriend until she is dead.' I said that, well, that did make it very hard for Rita because her mother could be alive for another 40 years! Rita laughed genuinely.

I said that this was a very important problem. 'Want see David. Get married', said Rita. I said that she really did. 'Want phone. Want see.' I said that if she was able to learn to phone David herself she would be able to do so without needing Terri's help, and if David learned to phone her by himself he would not need the help of his foster-mother.

Rita wiped a tear from her eye and looked at the floor. Her body slumped. I said that we could see how hard it was for Rita to bother to learn and be brave and say what she wanted when she then had to face these difficulties. Rita then sat up sharply and said to me, 'Phone David now! Here!' Terri burst out laughing – 'You cheeky thing!'

I said that just this once more I would let her ring from my room. I would show her the numbers and she would speak, but I would not do this again because what was needed was a meeting with her mother. Rita shot up out of her chair with none of her physical disability showing. She looked in her diary and showed me the number. I wrote the numbers out large and asked her to point to their equivalent on the phone. When she had it right I told her to press. When the worker answered she said 'David?' The worker said, no, but he would get him, and soon they were laughing and chatting away.

After a few minutes Rita said to him loudly and earnestly, 'Learn phone me. Phone me. Learn', and put the phone down. 'Phew', she said. I said that she really wanted him to be brave like her. 'Yes.'

## Session 53: the first dream

Rita came with a briefcase and a large pack of pristine A4 paper. Sitting at my desk she took the pile out, put one piece in the typewriter and, sounding extremely business-like, commented as she typed M, 'Phone Mummy.' Then she typed T for Terri, D for David, V for Valerie and SS for social services. 'MTVDSS. Phone and write. Get Mummy, Terri, David, social services here with you Valerie. Me hold case conference. Me want to see David. Me woman. See my man.' She then said, 'Get Terri.'

When they returned Terri said, 'Rita told me her dream this morning. It is the first time she has ever told me a dream that wasn't a nightmare about her papa.' She had dreamed about me and her and her mother. Rita nodded delightedly and told me the rest of the dream. 'Terri and Mummy and you and David and social services at the Tavistock and we were all talking nicely.'

I said that that meeting sounded like a good idea. Would Rita like to make the arrangements? 'Yes. You dial and I speak.' We worked out a date and in the room Rita phoned her mother, the social services department and David. All agreed to come except David who said that he did not know how to and his 'lady' would not bring him.

## Sessions 54–8

These sessions focused on Rita drawing up her own formal agenda of what she wanted discussed. She made several points: 1) as a grown-up woman she could see any man or woman she wanted; 2) she did not want to see her mum just because her mum was free – sometimes it was not a good time for her; 3) she did not want to wear baby clothes just because her mum did not like her being grown-up; 4) she did not like Terri behaving stupid because she was frightened of her mum; 5) she did not like social services telling Terri what to do and being frightened of her mum; 6) she did not like Terri telling her to tidy her room but she wanted to stay with her.

## Session 59: Rita's case conference

Rita was thrilled when she arrived at the Clinic and saw her guests in the waiting room. She practically ran to the room telling people where to sit. I explained that we were all here at Rita's request and all the things on the agenda to be discussed were Rita's, and commented that everyone must be concerned for Rita to be willing to meet today.

I asked Rita to introduce everyone because she knew them all and I didn't. Unlike our first meeting where she had exchanged names and laughed mockingly, she was extremely serious and formal. 'My mother, Mrs Attir, this is my therapist Mrs Sinason.' She went through all the items on her agenda from memory and deeply impressed everyone. Rita's mother was an attractive woman in her 40s who looked extremely proud of this daughter. 'Why honey-child', she interposed, 'I didn't want to hurt you about no man. I just don't want you left with babies and no-one to help you – especially with you not reading and managing those things.' Very slowly Rita went to her folder and showed her mother her page of typing. 'That is my typing.' Her mother looked in amazement and her eyes glistened. 'And I am a typist. It runs in the family. You are my type.' Both women giggled with a similar tone and the rest of us shuffled with unshed tears.

## And after that?

There was no fairy-tale happy ending, but there never is. Rita's relationship with her mother improved dramatically and she had permission to see David, but David, humiliated at his inability to phone and without the supportive network Rita had, gave up. Terri did return to Ireland with her ex-husband and Rita had to be placed elsewhere, too far to come to therapy. She managed phone contact for a while and I was relieved that, despite a period of deterioration and bedwetting, her spirit returned. A year later a card came with a great big R on it. When I opened the card I saw 'To Va from Ri'. She was adding on letters to her name – the equivalent of a degree!

## Discussion

Rita came for once-weekly therapy for a year and a half. She was a woman with a severe learning disability caused by brain damage that had affected some of her physical capabilities too. She came from a deprived social background and had experienced physical and sexual abuse as well as multiple placements and the accompanying multiple losses. However, her relationship with her mother, although difficult, maintained her hope in and ability to make attachments.

As with many such patients, her organic disability had been blamed for the emotional disturbance caused by trauma which I have called 'secondary handicap', and after a year of therapy her self-injury and violence to others had dramatically decreased.

There are many issues to consider in her treatment, both clinically and politically. However, in concentrating on the compelling narrative of her attempt to bring back the major good male attachment figure of her boarding school, which, for me, was the most painful as well as hopeful narrative in her treatment, I have tried to highlight the terrible predicament such patients are in.

If you are not able to read, write, phone or travel, your autonomy when it comes to social life is severely restricted. You rely on escorts, social service minibuses, the kindness of volunteers. If you live in a large mixed group home, or in a village for the learning disabled, or in a well-resourced hostel, you are able to develop peer friendships by yourself. The right to develop friendship, sexual or otherwise, is a basic emotional and social need. However, the politics of learning disability sometimes militate against that.

In this example, I have shown how social services used a parent as a means of avoiding the adult needs of their client. I could equally have presented one where the parent wanted their child to have a friendship or marriage but the fear was located in the social services department.

In my long-term work I have found that there can be a terror in the client and in the network around them of allowing a link between two people. In fantasy and in reality a parental intercourse has been seen to produce disability. By maintaining such clients' asexual lives, the non-handicapped community is omnipotently trying to avoid the disaster that has already happened. Until therapeutic interventions can deal with the fear of that coupling, the nature of the disability itself, the fear of abandonment and dependency needs, the learning disabled adult is doomed to a frozen life of Peter Panhood – short white socks, beaming false smile and scars from self-injury hidden under Crimplene asexual clothes.

# Chapter 10

# Working with older women

*Barbara Daniel*

## Introduction

This chapter draws upon work with older women referred to an NHS psychology department. Many of the women had longstanding psychiatric histories and would present from time to time with a crisis. But both old and new referrals had an identified psychological problem for which their referrer sought a psychological, as opposed to a psychiatric, intervention. Depression was the most frequent diagnosis although its expression in each was always quite unique.

The thesis presented in this chapter is that the link between internal and external worlds becomes increasingly important as we adapt to the experience of advancing age. Ageing presents the individual with a 'different' sort of emotional business to which he or she must attend, which is not simply a continuation or completion of psychic development. This is best addressed in the meeting of internal and external worlds, for such growth may well be dependent on a facilitating cultural environment.

I suggest that we need theories which explore, describe and represent this meeting; for the tasks of old age may be best facilitated where this link is properly understood and the external culture provides the individual with opportunities for activating this phase of psychological growth.

Finally, I make some brief comments on race. The case-load of women with whom I worked were predominantly white and were experiencing for the first time the particular closeness of a therapeutic relationship – with a Black therapist.

Ageing is a complex notion. At one level it is no more than a series of progressive changes in an individual's life. We have chosen to mark off periods along this 'life-road' and term them ages and stages of development. But not only is there no universal consensus on chronological states, we may also not know what meaning any particular chronological age has for an individual.

An example of the difficulty in this area can be seen in attempts to define middle age. This has been variously put at 35, 40 or 45 years. That someone of 35 should be thought to have stopped growing up in favour of growing old would seem to be unnecessarily reductionistic. When we come to people's self-definitions of age the situation is no clearer. What is the person trying to convey who fixes you with a gaze and announces, 'I'm 50 years old!' or 'I'm 75 years old, you know!' To what extent and/or to what internal indicators are we to attend? Is it the greying hair? (I am now due respect); the loss of physical elasticity? (I am due protection); or do they wish to highlight the summit of intellectual prowess or career endeavour? (I should be elevated to the head of the corporation/ table). Again, it might be to call attention to current psychological issues (e.g. internal states of mind).

So, when we talk about ageing or being aged, do we mean the assimilation of 'age' as a particular sort of experience, or its external trappings, viz. chronological age. Obviously it's not an either/or debate and should not be posed as such. But such questioning serves to demonstrate the complexity of the area.

It also becomes directly relevant in defining the nature of the task in psychoanalytic work with older adults. Is the individual coping with different psychological issues by virtue of advancing chronological age, or are the presented issues a reworking or continuation of earlier psychological issues? I have termed these two positions 'different business' and 'unfinished business' and will argue that such work is different business, although it includes unfinished business.

Sociological data suggests that there are observable, external changes which are indicative of an internal change process. Individuals demonstrate a change in the self-concept which appears to arise from within. Shifts can be discerned as early as around the age of 40 years and onwards. Men become more accommodative and affiliative, while women become more powerful within the extended family group, as well as more oriented towards agency in the outside world. This amounts to a reversal of the traditional cultural roles of men and women. Where individuals experience difficulties, these reflect their failure or reluctance to assimilate to the potential of a new life phase. Thus men may show disturbances linked to fears about the emergence of a new feminine side to their natures, and women about an emerging aggressive side.

Erik Erikson (1950) has a theory of progressive ageing which is dependent on the cultural and social context. The final or eighth life stage is reached with no diminution of liveliness. There are tasks to be done in establishing and guiding the next generation; living in a co-dependent relationship with the young. The emotional task is to accept one's one and only life as 'something that had to be and that, by necessity, permitted no substitution'. This model proposes an ongoing process of internal and external changes inseparable from the cultural context.

Jungian psychology proposes that there is an inexorable inner process which pushes towards completing the life cycle in appropriate or archetypal ways. (An archetype refers to an innate readiness to handle experience in terms of certain well-known repeated patterns.)

Around the ages of 35–40, the human psyche has begun its preparation for the course of the second half of life. The shift of the psyche into this mode is inevitable because we follow a path analogous to the course of the sun which is governed by an inexorable process of expansion and then contraction. This cyclical process is normal and natural. The period of contraction is fundamentally different from what has gone before. This is a period of reversal, a new phase. Individuals may accommodate to this inexorable change or they may react against it.

The Freudian perspective does not convey the idea of ageing as a change process but rather as a phenomenon to be encountered. Freud proposed that we face ageing within the personality structure with which we have faced the world. We collide, as it were, with age. This idea serves as a backdrop to post-Freudian (that is, Kleinian) views, which hold that there are specific psychological issues to be addressed in old age. They are, in essence, a re-presentation of earlier developmental tasks.

The experience of age, the phenomena of age, revives these tasks, or rather the need to deal with them. For example, experiences of loss, loneliness, helplessness or the fear of helplessness, are held to be some of the vicissitudes of ageing. The way in which the individual deals with such experiences reflects their underlying psychopathology. A window is thus opened onto previous life cycle crises and stages of psychic development. The reappearance of developmental tasks allows for another opportunity to address them.

One of the unavoidable facts of this life period is that there is an increase in experiences of loss; research consistently shows a high percentage of depression in the elderly population; and some individuals complain of feelings of excessive loneliness which are not alleviated by access to family or other significant others. It soon becomes evident that these feelings are of a different order.

The fear of helpless dependence may be seen as reviving dim memories of the helplessness of infancy with its related anxieties. We must note, however, that women of the generation of my clients have also lived lives with expectations of a continuity of values and roles within which to express them. With the loss of these roles, some women experience profound dislocation.

The external losses and internal disruptions combine to push many older people into crises which are expressed either somatically or as deep depressions.

## Clinical cases

Four case examples are presented. The first two brief histories both address issues of the specificity of roles as outlined above. The case of Mrs Turner illustrates issues of loneliness and the symbiotic relationship of mother and daughter. Mrs Turner's view of herself could not be shifted from that of a mother. The work with her was brief and 'success' had to be limited to the fact that she was no longer receiving psychiatric help. Mrs Harper, too, illustrates these women's circumscribed roles. However, she was a client who seemed to have more ego strength than Mrs Turner, and appeared to have made a number of internal and external changes as a result of a short period of therapy.

Work with Mrs Cato, a client who was referred not in crisis but with longstanding unresolved problems, most closely approached 'standard' therapy. This client needed to do a lot of integrative work before she was ready to deal with some of the existential issues of ageing and the end of the life cycle. Some integration was achieved by the end of her therapy, which lasted about one year and is the longest of all the therapies presented here. At the end of this time, we see some reparative attempts. She found herself a voluntary job in a primary school, where she could not only use her skills but also receive acceptance from the children.

My final case history reflects for me in almost classic terms the end of the life cycle. This client, Mrs Bone, had been thrown into crisis following a physical age-related illness. The crisis, however, was very much one of dealing with the end of life, but not so much in questioning what it was all about as in reviewing and coming to terms with what it had been.

## Clinical implications

I believe that all the cases raise issues about how to work with this age group, and about the therapist–client relationship. Young therapists working with clients who are very much older than they are sometimes fear that they lack wisdom or knowledge or that their clients might not trust their youth. However, within the transference the therapist may assume any age. Thus, for my client, Mrs Cato, I was most often the adult who was bountiful but could also be withholding. For a brief period in the therapy with Mrs Bone, I was in that reverse Oedipal relationship which some therapists suggest is the usual configuration where the therapist is younger. By this is meant the analysis of the Oedipal situation but in reverse. The client has to accept the therapist as the representative of the younger generation and the future. This requires dealing with and overcoming envy of the younger person. In fact, the person of the therapist is less important than the need for the older person to do the work of the therapy.

Flexibility is another notable feature of my work with these clients. Sessions did not need to happen each week or for exactly the 50-minute hour. Indeed, therapists have commented on the older person's ability to continue the work between sessions, and have suggested that in some cases one sees a weakening of resistances so that insight occurs as if the time was right. Often, however, there are physical constraints which restrict weekly sessions or the length of sessions. I worked with my two older clients in their own homes. This sometimes entailed accepting hospitality but I found that this did not destroy the analytic frame; I carried the frame in my head and not in my consulting room.

I have mentioned the different sorts of work done in old age. My experience with these clients also suggests that something occurs which is like working through layers. Mrs Harper concluded her therapy at what she felt was an appropriate time for her. Mrs Cato had reached a point of some integration but had not begun the sort of life cycle review that Mrs Bone appeared able to do so readily. Mrs Bone herself moved from one layer of integration to the next.

## The case histories

*Mrs Turner*

Mrs Turner was a 63-year-old widow who had lived a successful life focused on her nuclear family. Some years after her husband's death and her daughter's departure from the home she had begun to experience repeated depressions. During these times she found it impossible to live in her own home. She would insist on and plead for her daughter to remain at home with her, and be reduced to the tearful helplessness of an anxious child. Although Mrs Turner recovered sufficiently to be discharged, she only remained free from frequent slides into depressive states by being taken to live in her daughter's house. There, she could experience the day-to-day liveliness of the family home where she took on board her daughter's domestic and family issues as though they were her own.

Mrs Turner had been an unwanted illegitimate child who had seen her only means of being accepted and of retaining the safety of a home as by being a good responsible 'little mother'. She had never dared to admit openly to any angry feelings about these experiences.

*Mrs Cato*

Mrs Cato was a 68-year-old widow whose referrer wrote a despairing referral to the department. She wondered if anything could be done to improve this lady's disturbed relationships, to improve her quality of life in the present as opposed to her 'obsessive' focus on past wrongs. Mrs Cato was the youngest of three siblings. She had one adult child who was now married with a family of his own. The presenting problem was that she was estranged from all her family. She felt that they had isolated and rejected her deliberately and as a consequence she was depressed and lonely. Her older sibling had stolen the love of her son and she felt expelled from this maternal relationship. She felt hated by the family.

Her story revealed that she had been an unwanted child and that her mother had made repeated attempts to abort the pregnancy. This painful fact so dominated her unconscious world that her 'way of being in the world' repeated endlessly a craving to be wanted and loved as well as engineered experiences of rejection. Hatred and anger towards her mother had become converted into tales of ideal parents and an idealised childhood. The inference she drew that her own child did not want her as a mother suggested to her that she was hated (a mirror image of her own earlier experience). This generated tremendous anger and a counter-hatred which had to be denied because, if she allowed this to show, she would in reality be further ostracised. She made desperate efforts to be good, to be perfect, and to have everything around her perfect. Nevertheless, these 'unpleasant' emotions broke through, expressed in her desire to punish. Since this urge, too, was alarming, it had to be denied and deflected away. She reported an incident where the family's feelings of warm gratitude towards her had changed to coldness because they had somehow decided that a gift she had made to them had been grudgingly given. Now these warm feelings had become cold. How could they have such a thought? She could not rest until she had expunged this thought from their minds. Therefore, she bombarded them with phone calls and letters scolding them for daring to think such a wicked thing. For, in effect, this would mean that she was seen as wicked – an untenable prospect – and she would have once again lost the opportunity to be loved.

This client was clearly struggling with a gross split between an internal mother who was idealised and one who was hating and destructive (hadn't wanted her born). It seemed more often than not that it was the destructive 'mother' who was in the room, stretching to its utmost my ability to hold my patient.

A relatively mild example of how she brought these feelings into the room is the session in the which she told me that she thought I had been thinking that she might have brought all her troubles on herself. When I asked what could have caused me to think this, she replied that I might have had a thought from what she had told me during the previous session, that she was domineering.

During the following session, Mrs Cato became tearful and upset at the fleeting realisation that there would not be a magical solution to her problems. She found herself admitting this. The admission was followed by a burst of anger – 'There, I've said what you wanted me to say!' Thus, I became the domineering part of her and an object into which she could discard those unwanted aspects of herself. But since I was not an inanimate object but a person, one with whom she was having a relationship, this was also an attack on me in my role as transference object/person. Hence this exemplified the attacks she had made on other people with whom she had a close relationship.

Attacks could become quite destructive as, for example, when she pointedly told me that she was working like 'a nigger'. She then missed the following session. When she returned, she was at pains to point out that she didn't mean to hurt me but she did tend to make these 'hurtful slips' – the grown-up version of the table that just jumped up and hit me! These destructive attacks caused fear of retaliation but also of harm done. She would find it difficult to leave the room, wanting to stay by my side and to seek reassurance not only that I was still OK but also that I still loved her. Where I could contain without retaliation these undesirable parts of her personality, they could be explored, faced and ultimately reintegrated into a more whole personality rather than one that had to be either good or bad.

## Mrs Harper

Mrs Harper, aged 78, was referred for grief work and for behavioural help with a fear of travelling alone. Her husband had died nine years previously and her referrer thought that she had many unresolved feelings about this. Her history of an adventurous past and a love of independence was contrasted with a current portrayal of herself as incompetent and unsociable, relative to her late husband. It was in him that all competencies and positive features resided. She was now afraid of travelling and exploring any area further than her own house. Even this was never explored at nights. She was afraid of a future of being alone and had conjured up a picture of loneliness and helplessness which filled her with anxiety if she allowed it ever to come into her mind. This had resulted in one of her adult children being 'unable' to leave home. Both avoided any reference to this arrangement. Mrs Harper, however, was clearly a mentally alert and competent woman who filled her day with activities described as 'keeping the place orderly'. She was often admired for her physical fitness and intact intellect. The tension between what she was (someone trapped at home) and what she might be (an adventurous woman) was evident from the beginning of our contact. But with the sense of agency lodged in her dead husband she was left in a state of frustration and anger at having to take difficult decisions. This surfaced as a general anger about the dangerousness of living in London, and difficulties in making decisions about her home. She felt cheated and angry at her husband for 'going'.

In therapy, she began to play with the dangers of independence and the emergence of a more steely side to her personality. By the end of therapy, she could insist on her right to manage her own property, and had made incursions into an occupation traditionally reserved for males in her family – growing exhibition flowers. She could say openly that she was 'alone but not lonely'. She found in her grandniece a prototype of her own past experiences when young and alone in London, and was able to extend magnanimous support to her. It is particularly interesting that Mrs Harper continued to occupy her time with caring, although in a newly vigorous way. She added to what she had already been doing practical tasks such as altering the length of someone's walking stick.

## Mrs Bone

Mrs Bone was a frail widow of 86, whose frailty was due in part to a heart attack she had suffered during the previous year and from which she had substantially recovered. Now, however, she seemed to have disengaged from her usual activities, and had begun to speak of her life as being pointless. She was assessed as having clinical depression reactive to her physical illness and she was referred for psychological treatment.

The first point of note is the effect the referral had upon the team: it generated a concern to restore her to her previous level of fitness. We were all filled with admiration for the quality of life she had maintained. Here was a woman who had remained active in her church, maintained a home with apparently little help, taken up painting when already in her 70s, was lucid and intelligent and in touch with the world. In our unexamined concern to 'restore' Mrs Bone, we fell into the very danger against which Zoja warned, namely that of attempting to readjust the elderly person to an 'efficient and productive' life.

> My initial interventions were systemic. I wanted to examine the various systems of which she was a part in order to see what changes could be wrought to improve her quality of life. I explored the family structure and organisation. I looked at current and potential systems to see what supports could be generated there. Such a systemic response is not wrong in itself. It is often the most appropriate intervention. However, in this instance, my response and that of my colleagues was tantamount to an insistence that Mrs Bone should fulfil our phantasy of everlasting life and vitality. For a period, therefore, a collusive phantasy was maintained. My future-oriented mode was met by Mrs Bone's insistence that there was nothing wrong with her apart from a number of physical problems, the sequelæ of her past illness.
>
> This denial was eventually punctured for both of us when, in spite of the practical supports that were made available for her to resume outside activities, there were many reasons why this could not happen. I began to understand that she was having difficulty with a psychological and not physical effort. I let her know that I could understand this and her acknowledgement led to increasing trust and greater personal revelations. She began what was in effect her life review – specifically her life as the 'one and only life cycle that had to be'. She revisited areas of her life that had been curtailed by circumstances. Because of the wars, she had had a late and childless marriage. She explored the inevitability of this in the face of the prevailing world situation. She would have liked a son; and while she noted with regret that this had been denied her, she also discovered in her memories evidence of having been accorded the parental role by non-biological 'children'. This memory gave her pleasure.

Here we see well-represented 'ego-integration', an acceptance of life as it has been lived. There is a relative lack of envy, an acknowledgement of loss and similarly of what has also been good. This integration was also represented in the recovery, for a short period, of physical and psychological strength. For instance, Mrs Bone played the piano for the first time for two years and was able to visit her general practitioner whom she had avoided for a year because of stored-up anger against the medical profession. But this phase gave way to a more important one for her. Her physical appearance fluctuated between extreme frailty and variable robustness, and this seemed to mirror her psychological state. Concurrently, I discovered my own avoidance of what was before my eyes – that not only did Mrs Bone want to die but that at 86 years it was highly likely that she would die in the near future. When my unconscious accepted her wish, this was tantamount to my letting go of her and allowing her to be free to really occupy the therapeutic space that had been offered but that I was crowding. I began to understand that she wanted to talk about dying and was not afraid to talk about it; and, I believe, this helped to facilitate my own facing of the inevitable.

But how does one face such a prospect? How does one talk about such a prospect? Searles (1965) says that our psychoanalytic literature seldom mentions grief about the prospect of one's own death. He suggests that the ramifications of feelings which flow in response to facing the facts of individual mortality are perhaps the most complex we might experience, and the patterns of responses are bound to be unique. Where the personality is less whole or mature, he suggests, the individual may be unable to gather the range of diverse emotions and/or see them as relating to the here-and-now situation. Instead, these feelings may be spread over different people at different points of the individual's remembered life. So, for example, the individual remembers rage at this person at one time, sorrow about another person at another time, and so on.

The next phase of therapy was a moving one – in essence a period of grief and mourning. Mrs Bone recalled her family of origin, the family tragedies which had caused her sadness while at the same time defying explanation. She reviewed the ages at which family members had died, noting that both her mother and grandmother had died in their 90s. She recalled her mother's sayings about life (that she had done the best she could) and of death (she used to say 'gone to glory'). She recalled moments of the deaths of people she had known or heard about; some of these were quite irreverent and she thought about how she would ideally like to die. As she thought about her own death, she contrasted the early death of Jacqueline Du Pré and her own longevity, asking why people like her carried on. At times, she railed against this longevity and mused on euthanasia. She wondered what it all was for. At other times, she was fleetingly resigned to following her mother and grandmother into her 90s. She veered between thinking that she might be lucky to be without a sibling because she would avoid wondering who would go first; and she admitted that she had hoped for a simultaneous death with her last sibling. For the first time she admitted to feeling isolated. Sometimes she felt 'very old' and at such times she dreaded the thought of becoming helpless and needing to be looked after.

She talked of the preparation she had made in the earlier period of her heart attack. She had made a will then, with thoughts about the pleasure it would give to her next of kin. But she had been robbed of this by the interference of medical technology which had resuscitated her. Now the situation had changed, and the opportunity to confer a gift that would have been appreciated had gone; her relatives now no longer needed her help. She was bitter about this. The period of grieving seemed to end with a resignation that death was not going to be as imminent as she had hoped. She began to acknowledge her 'luck' in having intact cognitive powers, friends and other supports. Her house resumed its importance to her and she decided to remain in her own home at all costs.

When I look again at the process just outlined, I wonder whether Mrs Bone's recall of the inexplicable family tragedies was not also a symbolic comment on the inescapable existential fact of mortality, an inexplicable 'family' tragedy. However, clearly she struggled to accommodate this enormous step within her mind. The protest, anger, despair and resignation stages of grieving are clearly represented. We can also glimpse something of what Jungians have referred to as following an archetypal pathway. When she reflected on how one actually took this step, she reached back to form links with her mother and grandmother – how had they managed it? Moreover, in almost classic terms, she talked of the preparation she had previously made for death in the giving of gifts to loved ones. Zoja has pointed out how preparation is an intrinsic part of this archetypal process. The will in previous generations used to be a witness to an inner preparation for death. In Mrs Bone's case, it was also a way in which she had hoped to bestow psychological gifts to others, a further archetypal need of this life cycle stage and of which she felt robbed.

This period also touches on another provocative issue, that of a conscious or unconscious intention in death. Interestingly, there appears to be some meeting of Jungian and Freudian perspectives. In the former, death, the end of the life cycle, is a natural stage to be entered into. The individual 'entry into' death and old age is its preparatory stage – an initiatory phase. Where the elderly person has been able to follow the necessary preparatory pathways, then this final stage cannot be wholly unconscious. Searles, offering a Freudian perspective, also suggests that the meaning of death cannot be wholly unconscious and symbolic since the *fact* of the end of life has to be faced; and that this reality is associated with realistic anxieties. It seemed to me that Mrs Bone's struggle expressed this process, which is both conscious and unconscious. The wish for a simultaneous death with a loved one, as expressed in regard to her sibling, speaks of the very human dilemma of the knowledge that 'either we shall die before our loved ones or they before us' (quoted in Searles, 1965: 514). The dread of helplessness which she invoked may be, as previously stated, associated with the more unconscious fear of being abandoned to a state of helpless dependency.

Mrs Bone's therapy went through further stages. In the succeeding stage, she addressed the theme of being an outsider. This was a central theme with its roots in the past but addressed very much in the present. It was also the area of her therapy which most closely equates with work with younger clients. Shortly after this period, she suffered a heart attack which necessitated hospitalisation, from which she subsequently died.

This work with a very old client raises questions about the stance of the therapist. What makes it possible to do such work? It has been suggested that the therapist needs to have worked through her feelings towards her own (elderly) parents so that she does not either idealise her patients or use them for her own purposes. For my part, I found that it was made possible by knowing what I had to give; my psychoanalytic understanding *could* make sense of some of her pain of which she had to speak in code. When I had understood this and conveyed it in a way that did not compromise her dignity, she could take what was offered. I also accepted her wisdom and could take from her. My client was a relatively 'whole' person and could experience gratitude.

While the ideal relationship between older client and younger therapist is held to be the 'reverse Oedipal constellation' (the older person works through their feelings of rivalry with the younger person), this may not be attainable where the older person is filled with excessive envy. Such envy makes it difficult for the client to accept, without the urge to destroy, the younger person's gifts. Thereby is also lost the opportunity for the coming together of the two poles of the archetype, old and young, and the recognition of the interdependence of each. Searles has noted that it is helpful to the elderly client to have some sense of having helped the younger therapist in her own journey. I found this to be true in two ways. First of all, in Mrs Bone's confrontation with the end of her life I, too, could look death in the face without flinching or the wish to avert my eyes. Secondly, after her death I was invited to attend her funeral and did so. This involved being at her house with other mourners as the cortège passed and stopped briefly outside. I experienced a feeling of genuine sadness. But I also knew that it was as if I were attending by proxy other funerals of my own loved ones from which I had unavoidably been absent.

## Issues of race

The women with whom I worked were all white and English and I am Black and of Caribbean descent. The gap between our histories and experiences could not have been greater. Until relatively recently, these women had all lived in a fairly homogenous cultural environment with little close contact with Black peoples.

The difference in race (or, more rightly, colour) between ourselves as client and therapist is immediately obvious. (The difference in age is also, of course, immediately obvious.) When both therapist and client register this colour difference at their first meeting, they also both know the stereotypical cultural associations which are a part of each of these definitions. For example, the notions of white equalling power and high status, and as something to be desired; and Black equalling low status, undesirability and powerlessness.

The issue of race in therapy is the issue of a difference which has been immediately registered. The client will go on to use race in whatever way is meaningful for her and it will be for the therapist to see how she uses it. Like any part of the verbal content of the therapeutic process, it can have various levels of meaning, any of which come into focus at any time.

For my client Mrs Cato, I was more often than not the bad object to whom she was tied in an ambivalent relationship. Her use of race consequently was more often hurtful. As described in her case history, in one session she wanted to impress on me how unjustly she had been treated by those people whom she held dear, and said that she had worked 'like a nigger' on their behalf. I registered a feeling of shock at the time. She missed the next session and, when she returned, she was anxious about having hurt my feelings but, she said, these hurtful things slip out. After the session I could not write up my notes – I had no memory of exactly what was said or what had led up to the attack. I, too, seemed to have wiped it from my memory. For this client, I represented the bad object who was to be both hated and loved. When she became afraid of the damage she might have done, she would seek to repair this by reassuring me that she did have good thoughts about the group to which I belonged. Such reassurance would, if delivered by a younger client, be considered (in today's terms) politically incorrect.

The shift that is required of clients of this generation is illustrated in Mrs Bone's story. She told me that increasingly over the years she'd watched her church change until now the majority of its members were Black. She felt like an outsider in her own church. On the advice of, and along with, some friends, she journeyed to Surrey to attend a church which had remained white. Between our third and fourth meetings she made one such outing. When I saw her at the fourth session, she described how tired she felt from her journey. She would no longer be going to Surrey, she said. She talked with surprise and gratitude of the Black church making a space for her. They had accepted her and she felt looked after by them. I think that she was also talking about our relationship and about the shift in her mind which could allow her to accept help from a 'stranger'.

It seems to me that race becomes part of the content of the therapy in much the same way as it might have done with younger clients. Perhaps, in some respects, its transference meaning is much easier to see because older clients are not as burdened with politically correct attitudes as their younger counterparts. The therapist thus has an opportunity to address its meanings in the ongoing therapy.

## Ageing and death

Jungian psychology proposes an inexorable inner process of change which can be considered to be analogous to the course of the sun. The sun rises naturally from a nocturnal sleep, climbs and widens in the skies until, at midday, it begins its descent towards the extinction of its light. The sun has no goal other than its course, and its descent is a reversal, a contraction into itself. So the course of life, its 'archetypal intentions', ends in death. This fact is not of itself pathological. For Jungians, death would be seen as the last step of the individuation process, a real *process* rather than an event. The psyche prepares for this phase, as for other phases, through archetypal tasks and pathways.

All societies have to grapple with and to incorporate into their cultures the existential fact of mortality. Whereas past generations often provided overt and readily recognisable rituals for the end of life, modern society has tended to approach it with shame, blame and taboos. Events such as the preparation of a will used to be one such ritual which the individual carried out in full consciousness of her impending end, and which was an act full of symbolism. Now, wills are more often seen as economic necessities. Sudden death is by far preferred to the knowledge of impending death or an opportunity to prepare for death. Medication very often overwhelms the end of a life ensuring that the individual loses her psychological life before her physical.

We might also consider that our modern society has produced theories instead of rituals in its attempt to get to grips with this difficult existential fact. Thus Freud's notion of Thanatos (which literally means 'death'). This holds that there is an underlying instinct of all living beings to move towards stasis.

Melanie Klein's extension of Freud's theory proposes an innate death instinct which shows itself in internal and external destructive tendencies such as hate, aggression and envy. Such emotions are seen as impeding the will to generativity. Generativity, an Eriksonian term, is synonymous with a generous spirit and is associated with the more positive aspects of the personality. In Kleinian theory, such a stage is also associated with emotional maturity.

It can sometimes be hard to avoid an impression that, within the Kleinian framework, completion of (or the imperative to complete) unresolved or missing stages of emotional development, as it is hypothesised in the model, is an end in itself. The practitioner may then be the one to carry the sense of urgency for the elderly client. Time is slipping by and there is emotional work to be done! For, moreover, our theories suggest that our unconscious mind carries no knowledge of our own deaths, although it may be peopled with those of others in fantasy or actuality.

By contrast, the implication of the Jungian framework is that individuals may never 'complete'. They may selectively forget, or may demonstrate a wish to pursue other courses, all with the ultimate aim of finding an archetypal link with the end of life. The nature of the therapeutic work is therefore more properly described as 'soul work' and not the same as the more standard analytic work.

A further issue may be raised here, namely the extent to which the conscious and unconscious mind coalesces in meeting this ending phase of the life cycle. There may be a merging of conscious and unconscious knowledge. If we consider that the 'good death' in earlier times was synonymous with an active and conscious preparation for one's own death, then this suggests an element of conscious awareness and an acceptance of it as a normal event. This further presupposes a coming to terms with the loss of one's own life. Such a state is not easily won. It requires a tremendous psychological effort. Searles notes that the impact upon us is one of 'terror, rage and sorrow' (Searles, 1965: 509). He maintains that the poignancy of this knowledge is far more complex than a 'two-sided conflictual matter' – life or death – and is hidden not only by our culture's language of blame in talking about this subject, but also by our own thinking which approaches it within a simplistic model: that is, in terms of a life or death struggle.

The approach to death may be neither an unconscious and powerful instinct pushing towards oblivion (Thanatos) nor a drive towards a nirvana-like peace. Some of this complexity is described by my client, Mrs Bone, who showed a mixture of laughter, tears and playfulness. Should the moment of death be at the height of pleasure? Someone that she knew had died in the middle of eating an ice-cream cone. Would she? And did she want to go like that?, she wondered, convulsed with laughter herself at the imagined spectacle of her friend. At other times, she looked at me with resentment; I would be able to do the things she would now never be able to do.

As both Searles and Zoja have noted, this is a life cycle stage which may require active help to be traversed. If old age is a natural preparation for a normal death, it becomes even more important that societies offer the kinds of archetypal pathways proposed by the Jungian theorists. These involve active and worthwhile roles for the elderly, and the provision of 'space' for the changing roles and personalities if this is desired.

## Summary

So, all perspectives concur in the premiss that there is psychological work to be done in old age. But its nature, impetus and the implications for ways of working can differ according to one's model of what is happening in old age.

For the post-Freudian, the reality of old age, in the sense of it becoming a conscious part of the self-concept, is invariably a time of crisis because this meeting with age is like a collision – we sustain a blow to our concept of ourselves as immortal. The ramifications of this blow can send us into a crisis such as a depression, and reveal the extent of our psychic underdevelopment even while offering another opportunity to redress it. So the task for the therapist is to help her client to work through the maturational areas which are not very different from earlier developmental tasks. There is, however, one addition: in the distance there is the spectre of Death and the client's task is to grasp it.

On the other hand there is the Jungian model, a non-pathological view of ageing. In old age an internal involutional process has begun whose natural end is death. Age is a preparation for death. The individual can and may naturally follow an archetypal path towards this end. For example, we may observe people who alter their lives drastically. The selectivity of memory in the old is a well-known phenomenon. It may be an example of the way the older person attempts to fuse his/her memories into a mythical pattern. This idea becomes tenable if we accept that the unconscious is not random. It is therefore possible that memory selectivity is also not random but follows an unconscious 'project'.

Because the whole 'project' of old age or the end of the life cycle is different, it is inappropriate to use standard forms of therapy to readjust older people to life, or to help them to recover the past, in ways similar to work with young adults. The task of therapy is to enable the person to traverse the final stage to a 'future', albeit an unknown one.

The Jungian view is much dependent on society, for societies need to create opportunities which allow older people natural archetypal paths to ageing. Such opportunities may be the flexibility to assume different roles, to carry out roles in spite of age, or to be venerated because of age – the respected elder or the emeritus parent. These opportunities enable older people to fulfil archetypal needs. Indeed, the role of the respected elder or 'wise one' allows the person to fulfil the need to give psychological gifts to others.

The important role of the supportive cultural environment is also a part of Erikson's epigenetic model. His notion of generativity particularly links with the idea of a role for older people which ties them into the new generation in a productive way. Society is important not only for sociological reasons but also because it fulfils a psychological function. It is the cultural context against which older adults can work on and through (in the Freudian sense) the internal demands of this period. For the reality of this age is that there are depletions and losses and often the cast of characters who might help the person to work through intrapsychic problems is physically absent. An appropriate cultural context may provide substitute areas for the work of individuation or working through. Hildebrand (1982) noted in his clinical work that there was a marked intrapersonal gender shift in old age which had implications for people's interaction with their environments. However, there is little indication that supportive environments are easily encountered. Ours is still a society which deifies youth and does, indeed, see young and old as chronological and not intrapersonal categories.

Paradoxically, were we to achieve the sort of ideal environment proposed above, we would also need to take on a new view of the elders in our midst. I think that we would need to accept them as representing both continuity and discontinuity, perhaps a disconcerting prospect when the presence of old age may well represent for us comforting continuity.

Finally, there is death. Death is known about at both a conscious and an unconscious level, and there is a coming-together of these levels towards the end of life. Even the post-Freudians, who have tended to see death in its symbolic usage only, acknowledge that our clients may be dealing with anxieties about death even if this is not mentioned overtly, and in such a case it is often the therapist who holds this knowledge for the client. It is interesting that the Jungian model does not suggest that the nearness of death or the knowledge of its certainty is anxiety-provoking. It is Freudian therapists who describe the grieving for the self that is intrinsic to this knowledge.

## Conclusion

Women have an additional and imperative task, which is to achieve separation from the mother with whom they are both attached and identified. As the case history of Mrs Turner illustrates, this can be difficult to achieve. More and more frequently today the identities of mothers and daughters can be widely disparate. Some older women appear to be unable to cope with what is, in essence, a classic generation gap. They appear to need to see a continuation of their common identities in quite concrete terms. Difference in the daughter, as in life styles and values, affronts the older woman and appears to threaten her sense of self. Mrs Turner illustrates an identity that could not move beyond that of 'caring mother'. The continuation of her 'self' necessitated her being physically in her daughter's house living a surrogate maternal role alongside her daughter's.

Where society does not provide avenues outside the maternal/ carer areas, women may become locked into these roles, their identities becoming synonymous with the maternal. We catch a glimpse of how all women can unwittingly take a part in building this cage, for there is an interesting scenario when depressed elderly women recover from their depression. Often when ill these women have been very regressed, requiring a great deal of physical care and emotional support from their close relatives. Often they have appeared to be cognitively damaged. As the depression lifts and, more specifically, when, with therapy, some of the issues have been worked through, intellectual powers return. These women then find themselves confronted with the accusation that they have been shamming all along, the implication being that their illness has been used to obtain favours from their close ones. While we can imagine the hurt that such accusations may cause the elderly person, it is also a salutary lesson for us all in our tendency to fix our 'mothers' into whatever roles they occupy for us in fantasy or reality – 'the good mother', 'the wicked witch', or 'the ever-present friend'.

The stage on which both men and women live their lives is still circumscribed by society and reflects the traditional dichotomy between nurtured and nurturer, with the latter being equated with female roles. The expression of self in old age appears still to be tied either to the way in which one has lived one's life or to the only available and often traditional avenues. Women who successfully weather this period may do so in traditional ways, for example by being matriarchs in their extended families or becoming carers. But against this we must put Jung's idea that older people may choose to pursue new paths in this stage of the individuation process.

Women may choose to be unpredictable and non-traditional. They may have to find new internal satisfactions, new object relationships, and these may prove to be unacceptable to family and community relationships with younger men/women. Certainly older women now have to work harder at their relationships both within and outside the family, for families do not necessarily expect their older relatives to live with them as in former times.

The community as a whole needs to accept changes. Changes cannot be maintained outside the web of the individual's social context.

**Bibliography**

Cohen, N. (1982) 'On loneliness and the aging process', *International Journal of Psycho-Analysis*, 63:149–55.

Erikson, E. (1950) *Childhood and Society*, Pelican, London.

—— (1959) *Identity and the Life Cycle: Psychological Issues*, Pelican, London.

Grotjahn, M. (1965) 'Analytic psychotherapy with the elderly', *Psycho-analysis*, 42:419–27.

Hess, N. (1987) 'King Lear and some of the anxieties of old age', *British Journal of Medical Psychology*, 60:209–15.

Hildebrand, H. (1982) 'Psychotherapy with older patients', *British Journal of Medical Psychology*, 55:19–28.

Jaques, E. (1965) 'Death and middle life crisis', *International Journal of Psycho-Analysis*, 46:502–14.

King, P. (1974) 'Notes on the psychoanalysis of older patients', *Journal of Analytic Psychology*, 19:22–37.

—— (1980) 'The life cycle as indicated by the nature of the transference in the psychoanalysis of the middle-aged and the elderly', *International Journal of Psycho-Analysis*, 61:153–9.

Searles, H. (1961) 'Schizophrenia and the inevitability of death', in *Collected Papers on Schizophrenia and Related Subjects*, Hogarth Press, London 1965.

Segal, H. (1958) 'Fear of death: notes on the analysis of an old man', *International Journal of Psycho-Analysis*, 39, 1:178–81.

Zoja, L. (1983) 'Working against Dorian Gray: analysis and the old', *The Society of Analytical Psychology*, 28:51–64.

# Chapter 11

## Managing anxiety and the practitioner role

*Tara Weeramanthri*

### Introduction

In this chapter I want to consider the feelings and anxieties that the practitioner encounters in relation to clients, colleagues, groups, networks and institutions, and how she deals with these anxieties. The feelings aroused in the practitioner can be understood as being, in part, a communication from the client (or another) about experiences that cannot be talked about or perhaps even thought about. The client is using early forms of communication like that of the newborn baby who has no words but communicates through the evocation of feeling in another. Also, the helping task may stir up anxieties in the worker that come from her own unresolved issues and her inner phantasy life. Hence, not only is the worker a receptacle for the feelings and anxieties of others (both clients and colleagues), but she also brings her own anxieties (consciously and unconsciously) into the work situation.

Certain clients are notable for the level of anxiety that they induce in those around them. Reflecting on the worker's experience may lead to valuable insights into what the client is feeling or how significant others (in the client's life) are responding to the client's communications and may further the work with the client. Central to this is an idea that we communicate and receive feelings and anxieties through processes of projective and introjective identification, so that the recipient has a taste of what it feels like to be the client or, alternatively, may be inducted into feeling and behaving like a significant figure in the client's inner world.

Though I refer throughout to the practitioner as 'she', many of the issues described apply to both male and female practitioners. However, women's own experiences of socialisation, and expectations of them as women, may result in demands on female practitioners (from within themselves and from others) to be more empathic, nurturing and receptive (than their male counterparts) and consequently may lead to a sense of disappointment and failure when they are unable to meet these demands. Underlying this may be an unconscious phantasy of an all-knowing, all-powerful, nurturing mother, shaping the dynamic between practitioner and client, and such phantasies may also influence the dynamics of women's groups and organisations (Ernst, 1989). Ernst postulates that such phantasies are the feminine equivalent of masculine phantasies of mastery; at the root of both kinds of phantasy is the need to feel in control and the denial of uncertainty and limitation.

Practitioners (and organisations) engaged in *nurturing* tasks may also be unconsciously dominated by such feminine phantasies, generating unrealistic expectations of themselves. The first nurturing relationship is the mother–baby one and hence the ('feminine') nature of caring and nurturing tasks may influence the interaction between practitioner and client (Shapiro & Carr, 1991). For instance, in a hospital, ill patients may regress and experience very dependent and infantile feelings towards the staff and the staff may experience maternal feelings towards patients. A certain degree of dependence is functional in this situation as patients do have to put their trust in the professional expertise of the staff, but if omnipotent phantasies of the kind described above are operating, this may lead to infantilisation and over-dependence.

## Example one: the worn-out mother

Martin displayed a variety of behavioural difficulties. He was constantly disruptive at school, putting himself and others at risk, and he was aggressive to his siblings. His mother felt unable to cope and unsupported by Martin's stepfather, who left the management of the children to her. She felt perplexed, exhausted and worn out by Martin's behaviour, and at times even contemplated putting him into care. The two of them attended their local child guidance clinic. Their workers, Sandra and Alan, worked hard, seeing them in different combinations – both of them together, the mother on her own and Martin on his own. Sandra was particularly preoccupied with them; their problems filled her thoughts. She felt warm and sympathetic towards Martin who showed his feelings of anger and insecurity so clearly in her sessions with him. But, despite Sandra's hard work and her explanations to Martin and his mother as to why he got so upset, Martin did not get better; at times his behaviour seemed worse and his mother even less able to cope. Sandra reached breaking point on the case. She consulted a colleague, saying that she had never felt like this before about a case; she felt that she was 'at the end of her tether', as if she wanted to give up.

Reviewing the case together it became apparent that Sandra's sense of frustration and failure was just like the feelings that Martin's mother had been experiencing, feelings of trying and trying and never getting anywhere, feeling that there was no point and wanting to give up. Unconsciously, Sandra had tuned in to a key dynamic between Martin and his mother. Realising this helped her to understand something important about this family and to go on working with them.

## Early communication, containing and reverie

In example one, the mother *projected* something of her own feelings into the worker, making the worker feel a bit like she did. As a female practitioner, Sandra may have been particularly vulnerable to these projections, through her ability to identify with the mother, her wish to be understanding and helpful, and her difficulties in recognising the limits of what could realistically be offered. With assistance Sandra was able to reflect on her feelings and understand the communication that had been so powerfully conveyed through an evocation of feeling (in her) rather than through words. This is an example of *projective identification* (Klein, 1946): a bolus of feeling is implanted in another, who takes in that feeling and experiences it. (The worker may have a propensity to pick up certain kinds of projections more readily than others.) This kind of exchange is an everyday phenomenon. We can all think of examples of being affected by an atmosphere, or the experience of the boss getting angry with a subordinate who then gets angry with someone else. The feeling is passed down the line so that an unpleasant inner state is discharged into someone else, and sometimes even along a chain of people. The process of this happening in a therapeutic group and within an institution is well described by Hinshelwood (1989).

Bion drew attention to a process of normal projective identification as being the earliest form of communication. The young baby communicates with the mother (or other carer) by evoking a feeling state in her. The mother has to have a capacity *to receive* the baby's communications and *to think* about the baby's experience as the baby is unable to think for itself The mother has to use her own impressions, her own sensitivity to sense and interpret the child's experience and *to act appropriately*. If the baby cries, this will hopefully initiate a process of feeling and thinking in the mother, what Bion (1959) termed 'reverie'. When the baby cries, the mother experiences distress and thinks to herself 'What is my baby crying about? Is she tired, hungry, wet, dirty?' She carries out a kind of differential diagnosis in her mind in relation to the baby's distress. 'There, there, you're hungry', says the mother and picks the baby up, offering containment and comfort through the sound and tone of her voice, the way she holds her, the contact of her skin and the actions she takes (for instance, feeding the baby). In this way, the mother communicates back to the distressed baby that she is safe and understood and that the upsetting situation can be managed. This process of receiving and modulating the baby's anxieties is termed 'containing' (Bion, 1962).

Through this experience, the baby will have a sense of the empathic, nurturing mother who can think about her and will absorb this, and other experiences like this, into her own mind over time – a process of internalisation – which is the basis of the baby developing her own capacity to think for herself. And so, it is through the initial experience of being contained by another that the individual gradually develops the capacity for self-containment (including management of anxiety) and independent thought.

Just as the mother needs to have a capacity for containing and reverie, so does the practitioner. However, containing is a complex notion, incorporating receiving, processing and giving back to the other something that is now transformed through being thought about. It is often misunderstood as being an emotional 'sponge', soaking up everything that comes in one's direction, as if just being there and taking it is necessarily always helpful to the client. Women practitioners (or practitioners in organisations associated with 'feminine' nurturing tasks, such as social services) may have more of a propensity to behave like this through wanting to be helpful or having difficulties in setting appropriate limits. As mentioned before, underlying such behaviour may be an omnipotent phantasy (for example, of being an 'earth-mother' figure who can cope with everything and is loved by all), or perhaps a sado-masochistic phantasy, or the practitioner may be over-identifying with the client. On the positive side, women may find it easier to learn to empathise and communicate with clients, as the development of these skills has often been part of their experience of socialisation. For many women, the experience of being reared as a girl involves an idea of being an emotional container for others, as well as the prospect of conceiving and containing a real baby inside and outside one's body. Women practitioners may come to this work in some sense 'pre-set' and this is both a strength and a vulnerability.

The situation described above is the interaction between a baby and a mother who are able to communicate with each other and who live in ordinary circumstances. Some of the clients we see may not have had such favourable early situations. They may not have had parents who could respond to them in this way, or they may have been exposed to levels of trauma and external stress that generated unmanageable states of anxiety. (For some, both these factors may have operated.) Such clients may severely tax the practitioner's ability to contain them, and appropriate support and supervision may be necessary (as in example one).

In his illuminating paper, Altman (1993) shows how helping institutions may be experienced by economically deprived clients as both providing and frustrating, and this may correspond closely to the client's inner world of exciting and rejecting objects (a schema elaborated by Fairbairn, 1952). This results in a powerful transference to the institution and the workers within it. He looks at common occurrences such as missed appointments and presentations in crisis. Through missed appointments, the client conveys something of her own experience of unreliable figures by making the worker feel rejected, despairing or angry (just as she did). Similarly, presentation in a crisis may be the client's attempt to make contact with a rejecting and unreliable object (as she perceives the worker and the institution) – she feels she has to amplify her cries to be heard. Workers are often left feeling irritated and frustrated by such behaviours and it may be tempting to retaliate or to give up on the case. However, if these experiences can be borne and thought about, they may provide a unique probe into the inner world of the client and a real point of engagement.

### Example two: the boy who was alone

An outside consultant was asked to see a 12-year-old boy on a residential unit. The staff felt unable to understand this boy's behaviour; they felt helpless and desperate for advice. They described him in a way that made him seem only half human, almost a monster. He was urinating and masturbating in public, swearing and smearing faeces on the walls. The consultant felt quite frightened initially, anxious about her competence to deal with the situation and somewhat left alone with the problem by the helplessness of the staff.

Peter had a history of offending, running away and substance abuse. His mother had died a few years earlier and he had little contact with his father. The staff had observed that he had difficulty relating to his peers. For instance, he would often pick on bigger, tough boys.

His key worker described an interesting incident where Peter had confided to him that he felt that no-one liked him and that he had no-one. When the key worker touched him on the shoulder to indicate sympathy, Peter broke wind. The worker wondered if this behaviour was defensive, as if Peter could not cope with an understanding contact with another person and had to fend it off. The consultant found herself wondering whether some of his other difficult and repellent behaviours were in part designed to keep other people at bay.

Peter found meeting the consultant quite difficult. He got upset when he was asked questions about his family, especially his mother. He indicated that he cared about his family but did not want to talk about them. At one point he grabbed a sheet on which the consultant had written something about his family, crumpled it and stuffed it down the front of his trousers so that she could not retrieve it. He was defensive and angry when asked about his offences. He was reluctant to make any kind of connection between his present behaviours and his past experiences, although his offending behaviour and substance abuse had started after his mother's death.

The consultant felt that it was likely that some of Peter's difficulties related to the trauma of his mother's death and the likelihood that there had been insufficient family support to help him to mourn her loss. His problems stemmed from this unresolved mourning and from the lack of parental care. On reflection, the consultant felt that Peter had projected his feelings of being alone, helpless and frightened into the staff, and that they had then projected these feelings into her in the way that they had made the request for help.

The pain, anger and bleakness of Peter's world and his fear of close meaningful contact with others was revealed by his behaviours and the feelings he evoked in those around him. Behind the angry, destructive and repellent behaviour was a lonely, frightened, vulnerable and very distressed boy who was unable to contain his distress (his bodily products were literally leaking from him) and was terrified of making close relationships again.

## Example three: the mother with a sick child

Mrs Smith was a single parent with four children. Her youngest daughter had had several serious illnesses and many periods of hospitalisation. Mrs Smith was worried about her children as she felt they were out of control and hard to manage and she wanted advice. In the sessions with a counsellor, Mrs Smith talked incessantly, giving many examples in great detail of her daughter suffering at the hands of professionals (as she perceived it). She experienced herself as someone trying very hard to help her daughter and felt angry with these useless professionals who were to blame. She spent a great deal of time going to different appointments but not feeling satisfied with the treatments her daughter received. Whenever the counsellor attempted to offer suggestions as to how she might manage the children, Mrs Smith appeared not to take it in, rendering the counsellor useless too. She seemed to have a pressing inner need to complain, and seemed uninterested in what the counsellor could offer.

The counsellor felt increasingly angry with Mrs Smith and experienced a deep sense of frustration and impotence. She even started to wonder if Mrs Smith was exaggerating about her daughter's illnesses and whether her behaviour was merely attention-seeking. When she discussed the case with some medical colleagues, it became clear that the child's illnesses were indeed serious. It then became possible to see that what Mrs Smith was conveying through the feelings engendered in the counsellor (and no doubt in other professionals as well) was her anger and helplessness in the face of her child's illness and uncertain prognosis. At some level she wanted them to know what it was like to feel so useless and impotent over the fate of a loved one. Also, perhaps it was easier to blame the professionals, because this preserved the possibility that someone could control and manage the child's illness, rather than face the uncertainty of the future. Perhaps she blamed herself and sought to deny this by projecting the feeling of blame onto others. Deep down she may have felt hugely anxious about whether any actions (or mistakes) on her part could have enormous consequences for her child, and again it is likely that something of this was projected onto the professionals who were seen as being so useless and incompetent.

In the light of this discussion, it seemed to be important for the counsellor to find a way of communicating to Mrs Smith that she understood how anxious and worried she must be, as a prelude to working with her on managing her children in a different way.

### Example four: the abused girl

In this example, I want to look at *anxiety as a danger signal*.

Jane was a 17-year-old girl living in a children's home. Her relationship with her parents had broken down, resulting in her being accommodated. Jane seemed distressed and out of control. She would hint that she had been sexually abused but would then retract, leaving the workers confused, anxious and impotent. They became even more concerned when she started to cut her arms and they called in the local psychiatrist. The psychiatrist tried to enquire about her worries and concerns but Jane was hostile and reluctant to talk to her. Jane indicated that she did not want any help. The psychiatrist said to her that she thought that Jane knew what she was doing, and that if she continued to hurt herself she would be indicating to those around her that she was not able to look after herself and needed others to take control. The situation seemed to settle briefly but a few days later the psychiatrist was called in again. The staff anxiety was even higher. Jane had started cutting herself again and this time she was teaching other girls in the home how to do it as well. Jane was admitted to a psychiatric unit. She settled quickly as if relieved that someone had taken charge. She was able to talk to the psychiatrist who visited her in hospital and subsequently, when she had moved to another residential unit, she asked to see the psychiatrist again.

In this example, Jane's self-destructive behaviour, and the anxiety it aroused in those around her, signalled danger. Jane's distress was threatening to overwhelm her and she needed others to take protective action on her behalf. Though Jane was 17 and legally a young adult, her behaviour suggested that she was a younger child needing care and control. The staff, the psychiatrist, their actions and the psychiatric unit seemed to represent a firm but understanding parental figure that could contain her distress in this crisis.

## Anxiety in institutions

In this section I want to look more closely at how feelings and anxieties are managed in institutions and, in particular, at the collective defences that are mobilised in such settings. In Isobel Menzies Lyth's seminal 1959 paper 'The functioning of social systems as a defence against anxiety', she describes the results of a study of the nursing service in a large hospital, particularly focusing on student nurses and their deployment. Her thesis is that the nursing task, which involves life and death issues, damage, suffering and intimate physical contact with patients, arouses strong and ambivalent feelings in the nursing staff of love and hate, anger, guilt, resentment, envy and reparative wishes. In her view, the external work situation of the nurse closely resembles the inner phantasy situations (that exist in everyone and arise from libidinal and aggressive impulses) and it is therefore particularly likely to evoke these phantasies and their associated anxieties. That is, not only are there anxieties inherent in the task, but the task activates pre-existing anxieties belonging to the practitioner. Primitive mechanisms of defence are mobilised to deal with the arousal of these anxieties, and within an institution this may, through unconscious collusion between individual members, result in the development of collective, socially structured defence mechanisms (Jaques, 1955), which then become incorporated into the structure, culture and functioning of the organisation.

Menzies goes on to describe some of the defence mechanisms that she identified in the nursing service which she saw as having developed in this way. The aim of these defences is to reduce the anxiety generated by the task and many do this by reducing the possibility of sustained contact with a whole person. Examples of such defences are, for instance, splitting up the nurse–patient relationship through assigning task lists ('do all the temperatures') which minimises contact with any one person, or denial of the significance of the whole person through referring to patients as body parts ('the heart in bed five'). Other examples include attempts to reduce the weight of responsibility about decision-making by procedures and checks or by responsibility being diffused across several people rather than being located in individuals. Though anxiety is evaded in this way, it is not worked through, and the satisfaction that comes from dealing with whole individuals and helping them is denied to the practitioner. Also, necessary change in institutions may be avoided as, unconsciously, groups may cling to existing patterns of behaviour 'because changes threaten existing social defences against deep and intense anxiety' (Jaques, 1955).

Menzies sees the function of the social defence system as helping individuals to avoid the experience of anxiety, guilt, doubts and uncertainty. She points out that there are costs to this defence system. In her study, the nursing staff seemed to be under constant threat of impending crisis. The system was rigid and they found it hard to respond to the inevitable unpredictability of need and changing demands. Decision-making was slow, students were moved around excessively, there was no team spirit, and a sense of detachment and demoralisation prevailed. She found that there was underemployment of staff in terms of their real capacities, and a lack of personal satisfaction and gratification. (For instance, they were denied the pleasure of seeing particular patients get better, through being moved frequently and not having sustained contact with their patients.)

Her paper illustrates how individual practitioners enter institutions with their own inner worlds of phantasies, thoughts, feelings and anxieties, how the task of the institution with its own inherent anxieties may stir up primitive anxieties in its members, and how, unconsciously, individuals collude to develop collective mechanisms of defence in order to reduce the level of anxiety. As mentioned earlier, gender may shape the kinds of phantasies and defences that are operating. At times defences may be necessary. (For instance, staff in an operating theatre need a certain level of detachment and denial of feelings.) However, sometimes these defences may inhibit the optimal performance of the task, and may also reduce the potential satisfactions inherent in the task (if ways can be found to contain the anxiety generated by it). I have described this study in some detail, as the processes illustrated are relevant to the functioning of many groups and institutions. The particular task of the institutions and the capacity of its members will influence the form that the social defence system takes.

## Example five: the neonatal unit

The staff of a neonatal unit had a weekly meeting at which psychological and social aspects of the babies and their parents could be discussed. Many of these tiny babies hovered between life and death and raised tremendous anxieties in the staff. Sometimes this generated conflict between members of staff and between different disciplines such as doctors and nurses with, for instance, doctors wanting to pursue treatment and nurses wanting to stop. For some of these premature babies the prognosis was uncertain and to some extent the splits in the staff group reflected the terrible dilemmas that some of the parents faced.

On one occasion, a young doctor talked about a mistake she had made and her anxiety about the possibility that this might cause permanent damage to the baby. She was very distressed. Following her disclosure, a senior colleague talked about how she had made a similar mistake many years previously, and how she had felt at the time, and what she had learnt from it. Other staff joined in the discussion with examples of their own. This group of people had a capacity to share their experiences and to own responsibility for their part in what happened. There was a recognition that sometimes difficult and upsetting things happen even when people are doing their best.

In this meeting the members of this staff group had been able to face up to the painful reality that sometimes mistakes are made and that these mistakes have consequences for their patients. The senior colleague, who spoke up in support, represented the possibility that one could grieve over such an occurrence, learn from it, and survive. The thoughtful process of the group had helped to contain the practitioner's anxiety and to support her in continuing to work in such a difficult and demanding setting. Above all, the group discussion enabled both the individual and other members to learn from her mistake and hopefully to reduce the chance of it recurring.

## Women's organisations and women in leadership roles

Processes of mutual projective identification may occur between men and women, with a tendency to locate aggressive feelings in men and caring and vulnerable feelings in women. This kind of emotional division leads to difficulties for men in empathising and relating to others, and for women in asserting themselves and in setting appropriate boundaries and limits. At an organisational level this can sometimes result in women's organisations having a culture of being over-helpful and of having difficulties in drawing boundaries around the work. Within such a culture, practitioners may find it hard to be clear about what the task is and to work within those parameters. In my view, these kinds of dynamics can also operate in organisations with 'feminine' nurturing tasks.

Such 'feminine' cultures may denigrate authority, both the authority of the practitioner role and the authority of other colleagues in different roles. There may be a wish to obliterate difference (and potential conflict), leading to blurring of roles between staff and between practitioner and client. This obscures the task and thereby constrains the work that can be done. In contrast, 'masculine' cultures may be over-hierarchical and may denigrate 'caring'. In a culture where difference and conflict are suppressed, women may find it hard to express any negative feelings towards each other and a culture of unacknowledged envy may operate, which is all the more destructive for being covert.

Not surprisingly, women in leadership roles face complex dilemmas. In her paper 'Is authority a dirty word? Some dilemmas in idealistic organisations' (1993), Zagier Roberts describes a woman leader in a changing organisational context, torn between her wish to nurture and be loved by her staff and her anger with them for undermining her authority and refusing to co-operate in new ways of working to meet changing demands. Both women leaders and those they manage may be ambivalent about the exercise of authority. Staff may hope for a nurturing 'mother' figure from a woman leader (unconscious phantasies may shape such expectations) and her attempts to exercise authority may provoke anger, disappointment and derision from the staff. In Zagier Roberts' example, the woman leader was experienced angrily by the staff as a 'man in skirts'.

Women in leadership roles are at a particular disadvantage as there are relatively few role models to draw on. For many women, they will be the first in their families to take up such roles in the outside world. Some may identify with traditional male models of leadership, basing their leadership style on a masculine identification. Such women may feel that they have to be as 'tough' as men and may denigrate 'caring' aspects in themselves and in others. Other women leaders may simply try to reverse male patterns of leadership by an overemphasis on caring and egalitarianism, by blurring role boundaries and by paying less attention to the task (or to necessary role differentiation in the service of the task).

Zagier Roberts refers to Turquet's (1985) formulation of the leader as being on the boundary of the group and having to maintain contact with both the internal workings of the group and the world external to the group. The leader has to be able to *contain* the projections of the group, including their negative projections. In order to lead effectively, both women and men in leadership roles need to possess and to be able to integrate empathy, sensitivity, reflectiveness and the exercise of authority in role. In the example of the neonatal unit, the senior woman colleague exercised such leadership when, by her contribution, she sanctioned and facilitated further discussion of a difficult and distressing issue. At this time of change and transition, women in leadership roles may have unique opportunities to develop 'integrated' and more effective forms of leadership.

## Conclusion

In this chapter, I have tried to demonstrate how clients may be communicating important aspects of their inner experience through the evocation of feelings and anxieties in the practitioner. Recognition of this allows the practitioner further insight into the client's experience of her world and opens up new possibilities for helpful dialogue. Within institutions individuals may unconsciously collude in developing social defence systems that serve to keep at bay the anxieties generated by the task of the institution. However, if these anxieties can be faced, possibilities for development and growth for both the individual and the group may emerge. The nature of the task and the gender of the practitioner may have some influence on the dynamic interactions between practitioners and clients and within institutions.

## Bibliography

Altman, N. (1993) 'Psychoanalysis and the urban poor', *Psychoanalytic Dialogues*, 3, 1:29–49.

Bion, W. (1959) 'Attacks on linking', *International Journal of Psycho-Analysis*, 40:308–15. Reprinted in *Second Thoughts: Selected Papers on Psychoanalysis*, Heinemann Medical (reprinted by Maresfield Reprints), London 1984.

—— (1962) 'A theory of thinking', *International Journal of Psycho-Analysis*, 43:306–10. Reprinted in *Second Thoughts: Selected Papers on Psychoanalysis*, op. cit.

Ernst, S. (1989) 'Gender and the phantasy of omnipotence: case study of an organisation', in B. Richards (ed.), *Crises of the Self: Further Essays on Psychoanalysis and Politics*, Free Association Books, London.

Fairbairn, W. R. D. (1952) 'Endopsychic structure considered in terms of object relationships', in *Psychoanalytic Studies of the Personality*, Routledge and Kegan Paul, London.

Hinshelwood, R. D. (1989) 'Social possession of identity', in Richards, op. cit.

Jaques, E. (1955) 'Social systems as a defence against persecutory and depressive anxiety', in M. Klein, P. Heimann & R. E. Money-Kyrle (eds), *New Directions in Psychoanalysis*, Tavistock, London.

Klein, M. (1946) 'Notes on some schizoid mechanisms', in *The Writings of Melanie Klein*, vol. 3: *Envy and Gratitude and Other Works*, Hogarth Press, London.

Menzies, I. E. P. (1959) 'The functioning of social systems as a defence against anxiety: a report on a study of the nursing service of a general hospital', in *Containing Anxiety in Institutions: Selected Essays*, vol. 1, Free Association Books, London 1988.

Obholzer, A. & Zagier Roberts, V. (eds) (1994) *The Unconscious at Work: Individual and Organisational Stress in the Human Services*, Routledge, London and New York.

Salzberger-Wittenburg, I. (1970) *Psycho-Analytic Insight and Relationships: A Kleinian Approach*, Library of Social Work, Routledge and Kegan Paul, London and New York.

Shapiro, E. R. & Carr, A. W. (1991) *Lost in Familiar Places: Creating New Connections Between the Individual and Society*, Yale University Press, New Haven and London.

Turquet, P. (1985) 'Leadership, the individual and the group', in A. D. Colman & M. H. Geller (eds), *Group Relations Reader 2*, A. K. Rice Institute, Washington DC.

Zagier Roberts, V. (1993) 'Is authority a dirty word? Some dilemmas in idealistic organisations', paper presented at the 7th Annual Conference, Psychoanalysis and the Public Sphere.

# Index

abortion, 65
Abraham, K., 89
adolescence, 63ff, 218, 220
ageing, 72, 192ff
Alexander, F., 106
Altman, N., 217

Benjamin, J., 2, 109
biological clock, 59
Bion, W., 165, 168, 216
Black women, 134–59
Bochner, S., 144, 146
Bollas, C., 13, 17, 23, 24
Breen, D., 2
Brenman Pick, E., 21, 138
Britton, R., 6
Butler, J., 96, 98

Carr, A. W., 214
Chasseguet-Smirgel, J., 2, 25
Chodorow, N., 2, 4
containment, 165–6, 213ff, 221, 223
counter-transference, 20–4
    in intercultural work, 30–3, 148ff
cultural dislocation, 142–4

Daniel, B., 4
Davanloo, H., 106, 116, 118, 125
Davids, M. F., 69, 137
death, 206–10
    instinct, 207
Dinnerstein, D., 52
disability, 173ff
    see also learning disability
Doan, L., 95
Dominelli, L., 139

Eichenbaum, L., 2, 29, 49, 50, 51
Engels, F., 55–6
envy , 74–94
    between women, 74–94
    defences against, 79ff

psychoanalytic views of, 88ff
    in psychotherapy, 82ff
    of the young, 204
    see also penis envy; womb envy

Erikson, E., 59, 194
Ernst, S., 2, 29, 214

Fairbairn, R., 41, 42, 217
fathers, 6, 47
feminism, 4, 7
    see also Women's Liberation
        Movement
Ferenczi, S., 164
fertility, 58–9, 70ff
Foucault, M., 96, 98
Freud, S., 3, 5
    and envy, 88
    paper 'On narcissism', 7
    and transference, 14–15, 16
Furnham, A., 144

gender, 45–8
    and psychotherapy, 22, 25ff
Graves, R., 55–6
Griffin, S., 55–6

Heimann, P., 23
Herman, N., 60
Hildebrand, P., 210
Hopper, E., 19
Horney, K., 74

incest, 6, 160–72
    generational displacement
        in, 170ff
    and Oedipal development, 169ff

Jaques, E., 221–2
Joffe, W.G., 89
Jones, E., 89
Jung, C., 2, 6, 194, 203, 206

227